Barry Fantoni, novelist, broadcaster, jazz musician, reviewer, illustrator, film and TV actor, *Private Eye* contributor, former *The Times* diary cartoonist, was born on February 28th, 1940.

Barry Fantoni's Complete Chinese Horoscopes

WARNER BOOKS

To my family of Roosters

A *Warner* Book

First published in Great Britain in 1985 by Sphere Books
Reprinted 1985
Second edition 1986, reprinted 1986
Third edition 1986, reprinted 1986, 1987, 1988
Fourth edition 1991
This edition published by Warner Books in 1992

ISBN 0 7474 1147 6

Tyepeset by Leaper & Gard Ltd, Bristol, England
Printed and bound in Great Britain by
Cox & Wyman Ltd, Reading, Berkshire

Warner Books
A Division of
Little, Brown and Company (UK) Limited
165 Great Dover Street
London SE1 4YA

CONTENTS

ACKNOWLEDGEMENTS

I should like to express my thanks to all those many friends, relatives and strangers who have both knowingly and otherwise helped with the compilation of this book. I should like to thank in particular Gillian Jason who researched the beautiful Chinese illustrations, The British Library for granting permission to reproduce them, and Dr Hin Hung Ho for the delightful calligraphy. But the bulk of my gratitude is reserved for my Rooster wife who ploughed on relentlessly with the list of celebrities whose names are scattered throughout, and without which this book could never have been written.

INTRODUCTION

How do you introduce yourself? Do you first give your name, or say what school you went to, or where you live, or what kind of job you do? Whatever you say, the chances are that you will be attempting in some small way to summarise who you imagine yourself to be, and hoping that the label you chose will do the *real* you justice.

In the East, however, introductions may take on a very different form. Because of a system that has evolved throughout Eastern civilisation, everyone has a birth sign named after one of the twelve animals that make up the Chinese Horoscope. Consequently, when two strangers meet, instead of giving their names, they might well refer to their animal sign. 'I am a Dragon,' one might say.

'Pleased to meet you,' might come the reply, 'I am a Snake.'

As a result of this simple greeting, a great deal of unspoken information will have changed hands. In that particular case, if they had met to discuss business, both Dragon and Snake will probably have parted on good terms. However, if the Dragon had been another Snake I suspect that the two Chinese businessmen would have given the meeting a miss. And for a very good reason. For the Peoples of the East, an individual's personal animal sign, dictated by the year of birth, plays a central role in the conduct of their daily lives. Since I was introduced to the system some ten years ago, it has revolutionised mine. Chinese horoscopes have shown me a completely fresh way of viewing human behaviour, one that can be of great practical use. It can, for example, guide us to the best business associate, help us in our choice of marriage partners and even suggest the ideal lover. Chinese horoscopes tell us why we dress like we do, why some of us save every penny while others spend without caring. We learn why some are content to sit at home while others travel to the four corners of the globe. It explains who we really are, not only to the world at large, but more importantly to ourselves.

No one is certain how the Chinese horoscope first came into being, but there is, as with all mysteries, a legend which I believe makes up in poetical charm what it lacks in scientific probability.

Five centuries before the birth of Christ, so the legend has it, the Buddha sent out an invitation to all the animals in his Kingdom, asking if they would join him in the New Year celebrations. For reasons that seem only known to the animals themselves, only twelve turned up. In order of arrival there came: the rat, the buffalo, the tiger, the cat, the dragon, the snake, the horse, the goat, the monkey, the rooster, the dog and last of all the pig. Cheered by their presence, the Buddha decided to show his gratitude by honouring each animal with a year, calling it by their name. Moreover, all people born in that year would inherit the animal's characteristics. Rats would be charming and opportunist, Dogs would be anxious and loyal. Unlike Western astrology which is based on the movement of the sun and the stars, the Chinese use the lunar cycle. There are twelve moons in a lunar cycle, plus an extra moon every thirteen (our Blue Moon), which is why the Chinese New Year never falls on the same day. So, with twelve moons and twelve animals there evolved a perfect pattern. Heaven alone knows what would have happened if a few camels and ducks had decided to show up for the Buddha's party!

Given such an explanation, the most obvious question for us Western sceptics to ask is how on earth can all those born in the same year inherit the same characteristics? The answer is of course that we are not all identical. There are modifying factors such as our hour of birth and agents as we shall see. But it was only when I had stopped asking that same question about the thousands of people I didn't know, asking instead if it were true of myself, that I discovered that the system of

Chinese horoscopes really worked. Testing the system first on my own sign, then on my family and friends, and finally on a large number of celebrities whose lives I am familiar with, I was left in no doubt that it was startlingly accurate. In other words, instead of generalising, I looked at specific cases. And once I had shed my scepticism I began to understand more clearly the Chinese view of the twelve animal signs, and the influence they exercise over our lives.

The sign of our parents, the sign of marriage and business partners and the signs of our children all create variations on the way our own animal sign influences us. The eager to please Dragon son will benefit enormously from his adoring Rooster mother, while the passionate Rat will find the anxious Dog impervious to her advances. Time of birth is another factor which determines a subtle difference in temperament. Goats born in the summer will be less capricious than those born in winter, whereas Snakes born during a sudden thunderstorm will be in danger all their lives.

This book gives an idea of the markedly different attitudes between the two cultures of East and West. To seek pleasure and enjoyment from life is an inherent part of Chinese philosophy. The West on the other hand, frowns on those who treat life like a game. The East recognises that the games we play, both as adults and children are a form of make-believe which not only enhances life but in some mysterious way offers us the key to true self-discovery. The West puts men on the Moon, the East puts men in touch with their real selves; or in other words, the animal within.

Clearly no one can foretell our destiny, and even if one could, so many conflicting factors would make escaping it an absolute impossibility. The Chinese horoscope has little or nothing to do with the Western signs of the Zodiac. What it teaches is not a plan for tomorrow, but a way to know yourself today and every day. To learn who we are through our influencing animal is to take part in a wonderful ancient game that will make our lives both richer and happier.

HOW TO USE THIS BOOK

In order to discover your personal animal sign, first find the animal year that corresponds with the year of your birth. (These are given below.) If your birthday falls between January 20 and February 20 you must also check with the detailed dates of the New Year listed at the beginning of each chapter. This is because the Chinese New Year never falls on the same day. Remember, if you are born a day before or a day after the New Year you take the sign of the preceding or following year.

RAT:	1900	1912	1924
BUFFALO:	1901	1913	1925
TIGER:	1902	1914	1926
CAT:	1903	1915	1927
DRAGON:	1904	1916	1928
SNAKE:	1905	1917	1929
HORSE:	1906	1918	1930
GOAT:	1907	1919	1931
MONKEY:	1908	1920	1932
ROOSTER:	1909	1921	1933
DOG:	1910	1922	1934
PIG:	1911	1923	1935

Once you have established your personal animal sign, you may go on to discover some of the main features that distinguish your particular animal year.

The heart of each animal chapter is devoted to a detailed account of the animal's characteristics and influences, closing with the highlights of the three phases of the animal's life.

There then follows descriptions of the animal's compatibility with the eleven others, showing the compatibility of parent and child, business, love and marriage.

Each animal chapter closes with a look at how our own animal signs will be influenced in the year of the animal in question, ending with a list of celebrities who were born under the particular animal sign.

1936	1948	1960	1972	1984
1937	1949	1961	1973	1985
1938	1950	1962	1974	1986
1939	1951	1963	1975	1987
1940	1952	1964	1976	1988
1941	1953	1965	1977	1989
1942	1954	1966	1978	1990
1943	1955	1967	1979	1991
1944	1956	1968	1980	1992
1945	1957	1969	1981	1993
1946	1958	1970	1982	1994
1947	1959	1971	1983	1995

A SPECIAL WORD ON COMPATIBILITY

Throughout this book I have done my best to translate the Chinese view of compatibility with that of our own. But there are distinct differences between our two cultures which need clarification.

For the Chinese, love is seldom seen as something separate from marriage, an experience to be enjoyed in isolation. It is seen as part of a natural progression. In other words, love and marriage are thought of as a whole, and in this context their system of grading the compatibility of animal signs makes a lot of sense. In the West, if we have a love affair, we do so aware that it might or might not work out. In China that is not the case; there a couple find love later, accepting marriage as a kind of business relationship which is impossible to dissolve, no matter what. In China, it is imperative, therefore, that a Dragon, say, should marry a Rat, Rooster or Monkey; a Horse should marry a Goat, and a Dog should marry a Tiger.

But whatever your choice, the compatibility charts should not be read like the Ten Commandments, and not taken as law. They are more akin to a 'Good Food Guide'. We often enjoy meals in places with no stars, and are disappointed by five-star restaurants. It is the same with compatibility. If your partner is zero rated, but you love them, that's fine.

What the charts do, however, is prepare you for the future. Few people know what to expect when they embark on a new relationship. The changes that take place when a relationship develops badly are those we have all experienced; a sense of surprise followed by a sense of frustration. 'If only I had known this or that about him, or her', is a more than familiar expression, one we have almost certainly used ourselves.

Quite simply, the job of the compatibility charts is to take the sting out of such a process. To be warned is to be prepared.

Above all, the compatibility charts provide a choice, saying if you want a relationship that is tailor made then here are the candidates. And if you want to put your money on an outsider, then it's up to you. But in any event, it must be emphasised that the compatibility charts are not carved in stone. At the same time, it is also worth remembering that they have been in existence for thousands of years. That they have stood the test of time, is, I believe, a tribute to their effectiveness.

AUTHOR'S NOTE

Once you have become familiar with the twelve animal signs of the Chinese horoscope, I should point out that there are five animals which are known by different names. To avoid confusion, it is well worth making a note of them. The Rooster is sometimes called the Cock; the Buffalo the Ox; the Goat the Sheep; the Pig the Boar; and, as I mention in the Cat chapter, the Chinese refer to the Cat as a Hare, or a Rabbit. In the last case the oldest records describe the fourth animal in the cycle as simply being a 'creature with soft fur and weak back'. Cat, Hare or Rabbit all fit the bill, and all keep strictly within the accepted traditions. More importantly, the influence of the animal is the same, whatever the name given to it. In making my selection of names, I was guided only by the principle that the sign I chose should bear the strongest possible resemblance to the actual animal's characteristics.

The author is grateful to the following reference sources for additional material:

Chinese Horoscopes by Paula Delsol, (Pan)
The Way to Chinese Astrology, the Four Pillars of Wisdom by Jean-Michel Huon de Kermadec, (Unwin)
The Handbook of Chinese Horoscopes by Theodora Lau, (Arrow).

1

THE RAT

1900	January 31st to February 18th	1901
1912	February 18th to February 5th	1913
1924	February 5th to January 24th	1925
1936	January 24th to February 10th	1937
1948	February 10th to January 28th	1949
1960	January 28th to February 14th	1961
1972	February 14th to February 2nd	1973
1984	February 2nd to February 19th	1985

'What a fellow you are for giving in,' said the Rat reproachfully. 'Why, only just now I saw a sardine opener on the kitchen dresser, quite distinctly; and everybody knows that means there are sardines about somewhere in the neighbourhood ...'

The Wind in the Willows

THE YEAR OF THE RAT

The Rat's year is one for endless opportunism, and for those with quick wits and some extra cash to invest this is an absolutely splendid year. Under the Rat's influence, anyone prepared to risk a large investment should do so now. There's a chance, of course, as with any gamble that you could end up losing your shirt. But if it pays off, prepare yourself for champagne breakfast on the yacht.

Money is not the only investment worth making: equally well rewarded are those who take a chance on love. The year of the Rat is particularly rich for anyone embarking on a romantic adventure. And what romantic opportunities there will be: in the canteen; in the supermarket; on the holiday beach and on the journey home from work; everywhere you look there will be a pair of enticing eyes and a certain smile. After all, passion is second nature to the Rat, so the best advice to follow is that given by the heart. In May 1960, Princess Margaret and Anthony Armstrong-Jones were married in Westminster Abbey.

But because the Rat is not, generally speaking, cut out for routine work, there may be one or two hiccoughs, especially to do with administration. And there could be a few embarrassing moments. In the year 1900, there was the Boxer Rebellion, and 1972 saw the expulsion of 40,000 Asians from Idi Amin's Uganda.

However, troubles will not cast too much of a blight over the Rat's year, which is first rate for anybody who loves the good life and isn't inclined to work their fingers to the bone to achieve it. It is a year in which speed records are halved, prize winning novels get written and the harvest will be the

4

best ever. The West End theatre will thrive as it hasn't done for years, with packed houses at every performance. And what performances! No dancer will have ever been lighter on her feet, no actor more in tune with his role, and no impresario will have made a fatter return for his investment. If you fancy your chances as a theatrical angel, do it in the year of the Rat. It's also a good year for businesses to go public, and opportunist politicians to go to the country. In 1972, Richard Nixon was elected for a further term of office, and Greece declared itself a republic.

Although dotted with the occasional anxious moment, the Rat's year will pass more or less peacefully. The seeds of war may well be planted, but few will bear fruit while the influence of the Rat hovers over the proceedings. The motto is simple: 'Eat, drink and be merry, for the next twelve months belong to the Buffalo'. His motto is even simpler: 'Get on with your work'!

THE RAT PERSONALITY

'Lock up your larder and meet the warm-hearted, quick-witted opportunist'

It is a great tragedy for those born under the sign of the Rat that throughout his long association with Mankind, the rat has been given a universally bad press. They have been accused of bringing plagues, deserting sinking ships, and when it comes to describing our own often dismal struggle to survive, the 'rat race' is the term that comes easiest to our lips. Yet all these charges are totally false. It was, remember, the flea to whom the unfortunate rat is host who was responsible for the Black Death. When ships sink, rats merely join the crew and passengers. As for the so-called rat race, is it not in reality one of our own making for which the rat gets the blame? The truth about rats, as anyone who is familiar with them will tell you, is that they are a far cry from the fraudulent picture of the 'Dirty Rat' that Man has painted. Rats are extremely clever, passionate in their dealings, and creative creatures who live every day to the full and every day as if it were their last. If you are born in the year of the Rat, you keep splendid company. Shakespeare was a Rat, as were Zola, Tolstoy, Marlon Brando and the Aga Khan.

Above all, the Rat is the supreme opportunist. But this trait, coupled with his inability to deny himself anything, tends to produce a pronounced gluttonous streak. The Rat is born greedy for life and wants to experience it to the full. Ask a Rat to sample some new exotic cocktail, attend the opening of the latest West End show, or join you in a last minute weekend break in the Algarve and you will not find a refusal in sight. Another bottle of wine at the supper table? The Rat is there with the corkscrew. 'Enough' is the last word on a Rat's tongue. And no-one makes love with more energy, or expects so much in return.

The Rat has a rootless, nervous temperament which is better understood when we consider the difficulty he has surviving the often hostile world around him. The Rat is no farmer and not given to hours of routine toil. It is in the night club that you will find the Rat, not at home tending his vegetable patch. Unlike the agriculturally-minded Rooster, or the imaginative and hard-working Pig, the profiteering Rat has only his charm and wits to aid him. Since he is constantly on the move, he can never lay up stores for the future, and such mobility makes for less than prudent housekeeping. And should the Rat fill his cupboard, the chances are he will empty it in one sitting. The Rat's golden rule must be to strike whenever the opportunity arises – when the grain harvests are gathered in and the sacks of wheat, rice and barley overflow. It is during this season that the Rat thrives, when his instinct for the main chance is abundantly rewarded. Clever Rat with the sweet tooth, who will only eat refined, white rice – as rice growers have discovered to their cost. A Chinese chef once told me, 'Brown rice good for you, but white rice taste nice.' The Rat smiles in agreement.

But the Rat in winter is another story. It is here that the Rat is most at risk. The barns are empty and there is little to sustain him. At times like these, or when plans go badly, the Rat is the first to find fault and grumble. A sudden reversal will often highlight his rather shallow outlook, his gambler's disregard for reason, and his frequently callous attitude towards romantic encounters. But however bleak the future might seem, the Rat always has an ace up his sleeve. His trump card is charm. The sign under which the Rat is himself born simply oozes out, and few if any are capable of resisting it. No wonder a generation swooned every time Clark Gable strolled onto the screen.

The Rat's endless well of charm will turn loss into profit, failure into success, and should he desire it, night into day. And do not, under any circumstances, underestimate the Rat. There is much more to him than just a charming smile. Once he has set his heart on something he will use every trick in the book to attain it, pursuing the object of his desire to the bitter end. But this trait can often work against the Rat's best interest as Richard Nixon found when trying to talk his way out of Watergate!

Charm, opportunism, tenacity, these are the hallmarks of the Rat's considerable personality; ideal qualifications one might imagine – for a spy. The most accomplished, the most brilliant espionage agent of all time was a Rat – the exotic Mata Hari.

Given the Rat's need to make hay while the sun shines, it is not surprising that in living so much for the moment, he has precious little sense of time. If a Rat promises to come to

7

supper at eight, you might as well get stuck into a good book rather than sit idly waiting for him to show up. Indeed, he might not even arrive at all, especially if there is a party with more promise on the other side of town. A more possible outcome is the Rat will go to both – early for the sherry at one and late for the pudding at the other. As always, though, the Rat will be forgiven. He will uncap the lid of his tube of charm and spread over you like toothpaste on a brush.

I can give you a first class personal account of the way a Rat works. A few years back I was asked by a Rat colleague to assist in dramatically re-writing a musical he'd been commissioned to write. The show was due to open in seven weeks, and by working more or less round the clock, we delivered the final script just about on time. My Rat partner was delighted and showered me with thanks and praise. But when the posters and programmes were printed, my name was nowhere in sight. My bemusement was met by enough apologies to fill a book as fat as the Bible, and in the end I settled for a credit somewhere between the suppliers of cigarettes and the firm who did the laundry. I didn't, however, make a fuss and I was right to remain calm. Shortly after, the Rat and I spent nearly two years on a project of mine that came to nothing. He passed off the experience without so much as a shrug.

The Rat is naturally gregarious and adores company, above all if it is select and fashionable. Rugger clubs, ex-service gatherings, popular pubs and in-restaurants are where you will find the Rat, pursuing some scheme or another no doubt. But left alone for too long against his wishes, the Rat quickly declines. He grows anxious and his clear judgement becomes clouded. It is then that a Rat is at his most vulnerable and might easily embark on a self-destructive trail of excesses. Little can save a Rat thus stricken, except the love of another Rat, or the intervention of the powerful and influential Dragon.

But for all his poor timekeeping and living for the moment, the Rat has another, slightly more sinister, side to his nature. Should he seek a cushy number, say in the armed forces or Civil Service, places where punctuality is a form of religious observance, the Rat undergoes an astonishing character reversal. His habit of turning up late is replaced by an obsession to arrive at exactly the moment arranged. Instead of ignoring details, he becomes a stickler for them. The once easy-going Rat is now seen as a creature whose life is dominated by rosters, agendas, wall charts, desk planners, stop-watches and reams of written reports. The Rat's ever present undercurrent of nervous aggression finds an outlet in worrying about life's most trivial matters, and his hitherto warm and sentimental nature is taken over by an unpleasant stubbornness. In some cases, the nit-picking Rat in uniform can become positively dangerous. Hitler's Gestapo head, Heinrich Himmler, a mild-mannered schoolteacher until he put on his jack boots, was a Rat.

A lady Rat makes a wonderful hostess, and she'll preside over her supper parties dispensing a never ending flow of drink, food and gossip. But don't bother turning up on time: her soirées will always start late and go on 'til the small hours. And the last guest will leave only when the final bottle of wine has been emptied, and the remaining morsel of Camembert consumed.

Rat mothers are often career conscious to the point of aggression, but they devote a lot of what's left of their time to their frequently large families. Her child will be given the broadest possible education; after all, a Rat knows full well the importance of grasping every opportunity. To be prepared is the motto of boy scouts and mother Rats, and children who have a Rat as a mother will not grow up short of skills.

In spite of their love of fashionable places, most male Rats dress to be comfortable rather than to be in style. They generally put on what they took off the night before, picking up their outfit from where they had last dumped it. (Usually on the floor.) Lady Rats are quite different. If you see a chic-looking woman wearing the latest mode right out of

Vogue, the chances are that she was born under the sign of the Rat. And even if her clothes are not the very latest thing, the lady Rat has a way of dressing that makes them *look* as if they are. Should she wear Yves St Laurent, clothes or perfume, she'll be keeping in the club. M. St Laurent is a Rat.

It is a curious fact, but as a rule Rat men have terrible handwriting. It is as if they can't wait to get to the end of the sentence, which is true up to a point. The Rat loves speed, and if they could drive the car of their choice, it wouldn't be a one-litre family hatchback. Not only does speed cut down the gap between one exciting activity and the next, it emphasises the Rat's thrill of living for the moment – and dangerously. Rats everywhere would drive Lamborghinis if they could afford them. The satirical cartoonist Gerald Scarfe was driving a Lamborghini the last time I saw him. He's another Rat and he began his career at *Private Eye*.

When choosing a profession, the Rat must avoid routine work – routine loafing is okay – or dealing with long term investments. Both will irritate him and lead to bad decisions. Conversely, it is perfectly safe for the Rat to gamble with his own money, and will more often than not do well, as Andrew Lloyd Webber's over-publicised fortune amply illustrates. Apart from the MI5, the Rat is amply suited for a job in which he needs to do little more than wander around and be charming. The job of Prince of Wales is ideal, and Prince Charles is, indeed, a Rat. The job of critic is, of course, the Rat's best refuge. Uncluttered by grudges and lofty morals, he brings to the art of criticism an unclouded objectivity that has few rivals. Other posts for the Rat to fill are: journalist, author, travel-writer, politician, impresario, gun-runner, linguist, colonel, soldier of fortune, fortune hunter, car dealer, actor, and alas, pimp.

The three phases of a Rat's life are marked by an easy-going childhood; a more difficult middle period in which there will often be problems concerning romance and finance; and an easy old age. In the middle stage the Chinese warn that a Rat can be imprisoned or meet a sudden and violent end. Though few would grieve to hear it, Heinrich Himmler met with both. There was a sudden death, too, for the Rat who sought a life in the desert, Lawrence of Arabia.

As for the Rat's home, he will be contented with what's to hand. He will spend no fortune decorating it – there would be no point. At the drop of a hat he could be off somewhere new, in search of another experience. The Rat, therefore, tends to prefer rented accommodation and, unlike the Cat who fills the home with beautiful objects, cares for nothing more than an easy chair and a comfortable bed. As for his possessions, they can be packed in no time at all. If the Rat has a favourite home, it might well be yours.

RAT AS PARENT

It is not every Rat who makes the best of parenthood, and an additional Rat in the shape of a scheming child under the same roof could pose a bit of a problem. But the Rat knows all about his child's ploys and gambits, and will correct any bad habits before they get out of hand. And there will be a great deal of understanding. Whatever they run short of the Rat parent will make certain there is never a lack of love.

The infant Dragon will thrive on so much overt affection, and so will the young Monkey. Both children will be given every opportunity to develop, and in some cases pushed along with much determination.

The Piglet will certainly be applauded for his amiable honesty, but he must remember to eat his share and no one else's.

The baby Rooster will alienate her Rat parent. She has a direct tongue and will reproach the Rat father for his opportunism. And if he's caught double-dealing in any way, poor old Rat dad!

COMPATIBILITY OF RAT PARENT AND CHILD

Young Goats are at odds with all kinds of parental authority. Their ideas differ from everyone, including ma and pa Rat. As soon as she is able, the Goat daughter will find herself a new home.

The Cat is a careful creature, and as a child is self-contained. Cats pose too many threats for the Rat parent's comfort. Rat fathers are often frightened by their Cat daughters. But should they survive the early uncertain years, Cat daughter and father Rat will become good friends.

The tiny Tiger's ability to shine quickly will please the Rat parent, but what happens when the Tiger fades? Eager to prove himself, the Tiger will pack his bags along with the

Goat. On the way to the gate they will meet the young Horse.

Independent and very able, even from an early age, the Horse will find the low horizons of his or her Rat parent wanting. At least they'll be low by the Horse's high standards.

The Buffalo child is a stickler for work, and studies day and night. He will benefit from the Rat's vitality and wide range of interests, finding that his rather rigid views are constantly questioned, even laughed at. But it is up to the Buffalo to content himself with the Rat's great affection and worry less about his disorganised life-style.

The Snake daughter will bewitch her Rat father who might tend to be over-generous. When she is older the Snake daughter will be able to offer useful advice – so long as she isn't spoilt in the process of growing up.

Good news for the Dog. All a puppy really wants it to be loved without complications, and while he is still a child, the Dog has not yet learned to manufacture them.

RAT IN BUSINESS

A business partnership of two opportunists can only mean more work for the bailiff. Rats should avoid each other like the plague, and the spendthrift Rooster is no great alternative. The Dragon, with all his innate power is the Rat's best bet, so long as the Rat sits still long enough to listen to the Dragon's good sense, and lets the Dragon sign the cheques. The hardworking Horse will object to the Rat's long lunches and coming back to the office a little worse for wear.

The honest Pig will bring his own brand of industry to any enterprise he joins, putting in all the hours God sends. But the Rat is such a charmer and the Pig so easily duped. He'll be well advised to keep his share of the cake in a safe place. The ever-inventive Tiger will give the Rat plenty of scope to

COMPATIBILITY OF RAT IN BUSINESS
RELATIONSHIPS

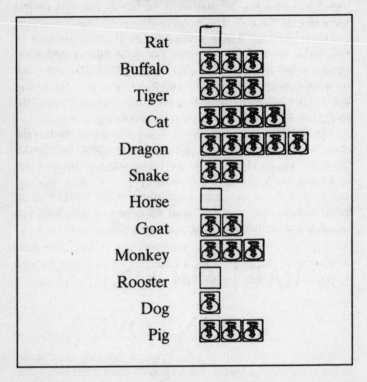

expand, but the Rat must play it straight. The Tiger won't hesitate to kick him out should he discover the Rat has been selling off his brilliant schemes elsewhere. Rats and Tigers have about a fifty-fifty chance of success. The artful Monkey has marginally more. But it won't be anything too grand: a company selling goods imported from Taiwan to King's Road boutiques is about their limit. In any event, the Monkey must curb his tendency to alter the truth to suit his own ends; bank managers like facts, not fiction. The Cat has an eye for bargains which the Rat finds useful. What's more, the Cat will bring a system to the Rat's chaotic business methods. But the

Cat must not fuss over details, or moralise.

The Buffalo, so long as he is allowed to make the major decisions will serve the Rat well, but must remember a Rat favours easy money. The volatile Tiger can find plenty of work for the Rat, and like the Buffalo, will do himself no favours by demanding too much too soon. The wise Snake is careful when investing her money and will not throw it away on just any madcap enterprise the Rat chases after, and there will be serious meetings after hours. The Goat, not unlike the Rat, lives by her charm when reason fails. Two charmers in the same office could either be a disaster or a success. But the Goat needs to be tethered to work, and where is the Rat when he's wanted? The Dog, loyal and trusting, will come in early and go home late and wonder why he only has the scraps.

A footnote to a pair of Rats. Should they stick together through the rough times, and not bite into too many sacks of corn at once, they can make millions. The trouble with Rats is not getting the green stuff, it's hanging on to it long enough to pay the tax. Sobering thought.

RAT IN LOVE

When it comes to passion alone, two Rats are the perfect match. As lovers they have few rivals, but the seducing Dragon and the playful Monkey are no strangers to the Rat's passion-filled world. The uncertain Dog can also benefit from the Rat's ardour on a short term basis, but the Rat will grow tired of the Dog's pessimism and the affair will not go the distance. And it's a short-term romance for the sexually complicated Buffalo. The jovial Pig is a great one for romantic interludes and will quickly fall into the Rat's charming arms, but the Pig is so full of himself at times, he

COMPATIBILITY OF RAT IN LOVE

might get a little out of his depth. The Tiger is ever eager for novelty, especially when love is in the air. He'll make hay with the Rat, at least until a new flame promises something better elsewhere. As in every other walk of life, the refined and cautious Cat presents trouble to the amorous Rat, who is open and demanding when in love. The Cat so loves to snooze in peace.

The Goat should make the Rat a good lover as they have so much in common. But that's the trouble, they are too much alike; and the Goat is such a moody creature, she asks for so much time and attention. As for the prim and proper Rooster, she won't listen to the Rat's shallow advances, and the vain, self-sufficient Horse can, as usual, take the Rat or leave him. Snakes advance their love slowly and surely, seldom choosing a partner who will be capable of rejecting them. Enter the romancer, Mr Rat who might well find he becomes a victim. Poor old Ratty.

RAT IN MARRIAGE

Not surprisingly, two Rats with the same objective will seldom choose the same path to achieve it. Promising each other the moon and the stars on their first meeting, they will be torn apart by their inability to turn down the main chance somewhere else. As lovers, two Rats are perfect. Anything else is doomed unless total discretion is the order of the day – and night!

The Dragon, who is adored by so many, will protect his friend the Rat, and use his power to curb the Rat's worst excesses. In turn, the Dragon will be flattered by the Rat's endless gratitude, so charmingly worded. The ambitious and similarly materialistic Pig will make a fine companion. The Pig is a homemaker, and where is the Rat who would turn down the offer of a well-stocked larder? The wayward Goat has a lot in common with the Rat, and shares his love of the good things in life, but the Goat will always have her own ideas about the best places. The Monkey lady will make the Rat a good wife. She is careful with money and understands the Rat's need to live off his wits. But both face hardships without much fortitude, so they should make sure they don't buy too much on credit. A healthy bank balance might be one way of seeing them through. Although Tigers can add a touch of idealism to the self-indulgent Rat, the Rat is not really interested in ideals, except as a conversation piece.

The Cat will bring cultured living to the Rat's home.

17

COMPATIBILITY WITH RAT IN MARRIAGE

Beautiful paintings will hang on his walls. Lucky Rat. But he will pay the price – his freedom. The Rat should also avoid the pessimistic Dog. He is easily unsettled by the Rat's social ease, and he'll grumble and make himself miserable, and it will be the Rat who will suffer in the end. But the wise Snake will tire of the Rat. She has no time for his shallow outlook, however much she admires his passion. The Horse, independent and a touch vain at times, will also grow bored by the Rat's one-paced life, even if the pace is at breakneck speed. The Rat, stimulated by argument, need look no further than the talkative and sensible Rooster. The Rat might not like the Rooster's moral scolding, but it will do him no harm once in a while. There is no harm either in a wedding of Rat and Buffalo. Mr Buffalo will work hard and his Rat wife won't object. But they don't have a great deal in common, and the Buffalo, dour, dutiful and stubborn can be a demanding partner. Listening to a record of the *St Matthew Passion* might move the Buffalo, but the Rat's idea of passion is quite different.

HOW YOU WILL BE INFLUENCED IN THE YEAR OF THE RAT

[A YEAR FOR OPPORTUNISTS]

This is the best of years for the Rat who will make every new opportunity count as never before. It will not be a poor year either, for anyone who is not adverse to using their wits and charm and chance their luck.

The Dragon will enjoy romance after romance and there won't be a day that passes without some new project landing in his lap. Both Rats and Dragons can start counting their pile any time they like.

The clever and artful Monkey won't be slow to realise that the rainbow's end has landed in his garden, and he will more than capitalise on the pot of gold.

The jovial Pig will find all the charm and good times right up his street and, never one to say no to an evening of wine, women and song, will find his list of invitations endless. He might well have the love affair of his life in the year of the Rat. The Buffalo won't find love, but he'll find plenty to occupy his mind. There'll be no shortage of work in the fields

A YEAR FOR OPPORTUNISTS

Rat	🂠🂠🂠🂠🂠
Buffalo	🂠🂠🂠🂠
Tiger	☐
Cat	🂠🂠
Dragon	🂠🂠🂠🂠🂠
Snake	🂠🂠🂠
Horse	🂠
Goat	🂠
Monkey	🂠🂠🂠🂠🂠
Rooster	🂠🂠
Dog	🂠🂠
Pig	🂠🂠🂠🂠🂠

and for once he won't find himself so remote from his fellow man. A warm glow will fill him when he meets an old friend.

The unpredictable Tiger will not have a good year. His ideas and energy are based in the concept of the 'best for all', and the Rat's is the 'best for me'. The industrious and individualistic Horse will also find himself at odds with the general mood of *laisser faire*, and will only work with half a heart. The capricious Goat has her own ways of having fun and they seldom coincide with the Rat's, but then again they might.

One splendid side to the Rat is that he doesn't care if you toil or slumber, it's all the same to him. The Snake only works

20

when she has to, and her year will have its ups and downs. The placid and refined Cat does not enjoy the Rat's disordered life and will have a miserable time trying to keep his world in order. The loyal Dog fares no better. His problem in the Rat year is that the Rat is simply not interested in faithful friends, just productive ones. As for the honest Rooster, with her head so high in the air, she misses all the scraps that the Rat has left scattered around the barnyard. But she won't starve.

FAMOUS RATS

Arts
Robert Bolt
Charlotte Brontë
Pablo Casals
Raymond Chandler
Gerald Durrell
Lawrence Durrell
Manuel de Falla
Haydn
Ian Hislop
Toulouse Lautrec
T E Lawrence
Lotte Lenya
Rodin
Dante Gabriel Rossetti
Gerald Scarfe
Ralph Steadman
Tchaikovsky
Tolstoy
Kurt Weil
Emile Zola

Sports
Bob Champion
Steve Cram
Barry Hearne
Brian Johnston
Ivan Lendl
Gary Lineker
Maradona
Gary Sobers
Dennis Taylor

Industry/Politics
George Bush
James Callaghan
Jimmy Carter
John De Lorean
Clement Freud
Richard Nixon
Enoch Powell
Yves St Laurent

Royals
Princess Alexandra
Duke of York
Prince Charles
The Queen Mother
Mark Phillips

Show Biz
Dave Allen
Charles Aznavour
Lauren Bacall
Marlon Brando
Noel Edmonds
Albert Finney
Clark Gable
Benny Hill
Roy Hudd
Glenda Jackson
Gene Kelly
Nastassja Kinski
Lee Marvin
John le Mesurier

Andrew Lloyd Webber
John Wells
Sandy Wilson
Vanessa Redgrave

Pop
Irving Berlin
Bobby Darin
Doris Day
Don Everly
Buddy Holly
Lulu
Lynsey de Paul
Olivia Newton-John
Roy Orbison
Wayne Sleep
Tommy Steele
Sarah Vaughn
Dinah Washington
Kim Wilde
Bill Wyman

THE BUFFALO

牛

1901	February 19th to February 7th	1902
1913	February 6th to January 25th	1914
1925	January 24th to February 12th	1926
1937	February 11th to January 30th	1938
1949	January 29th to February 16th	1950
1961	February 15th to February 4th	1962
1973	February 3rd to January 22nd	1974
1985	February 20th to February 8th	1986

'This beast is but simple, though his aspect seems to be very grave.'

Topsell

25

THE YEAR OF THE BUFFALO

There's no question about it, this is not the year for dead-beats and trendies. It's not much fun, either, for the work-shy. The year of the Buffalo is good only for the man of toil. As long as you put your shoulder to the yoke, put your nose to the grindstone and make sure it's your best foot that's forward, you will be rewarded. Do not, however, expect the reward to be too generous. This is the year for thinking profoundly about the future, planting seeds and laying foundation stones. If you intend to fund a museum or publish a book on Great Historical Events, do it now.

The Buffalo year will be constantly marked by major changes in world leadership. In the first month of the first Buffalo year this century, Queen Victoria died. 1973 saw the deaths of President Lyndon B Johnson, King Gustav of Sweden and the father of modern Israel, David Ben-Gurion. And there will be struggles at the top on the political platform, with only those capable of commanding real authority surviving. And in most cases, those politicians who finally win the right to govern, either by force or the ballot box, will do so with a rod of iron. In March 1973, the Gaullists won an absolute majority in the French General Election. In August George Papadopoulos became Greece's first president. October saw the start of the Arab–Israeli war. In November, the Greek army deposed George Papadopoulos. In 1961, John F Kennedy became the thirty-fifth president of the United States.

But apart from the bloodshed on the political stage, the

Buffalo year will pass relatively calmly, with no great floods or famines. The Buffalo, remember, spends most of his time in the fields. The harvests will again be bountiful and the promise of an honest day's pay for an honest day's work will mean that there will be many willing hands to gather in the goodies. However, those in love might find a day ploughing a field more fun than a night on the tiles.

Have children in a Buffalo year, join the church, walk over the Niagara Falls on a tightrope, but don't, whatever you do, make eyes at your secretary. And if you find you have the seven-year-itch and want to scratch it – don't.

THE BUFFALO PERSONALITY

'Put on a sober tie, wear a sensible skirt and meet the hard working, authoritative Buffalo'.

No one who has ever watched a herd of buffaloes moving calmly across an open plain can have failed to be impressed by their great natural majesty. When harnessed to the yoke, no other animal pulls a heavier load, and does so for such long hours.

With his ability to plough on against all opposition, and to arouse confidence in those around him, seemingly by his very presence, the Buffalo has not surprisingly occupied more than a fair share of the world stage. Those born under his sign are destined for greatness and to make their mark as

27

leaders of men. Napoleon was an outstanding example of a
Buffalo, and there are many others; Nehru, Emperor Hirohito, Archbishop Makarios, Castro, Geronimo, the Duke of
Wellington, and so the list goes on. But although the Buffalo
responds naturally to leadership, his facility to bring a
carefully thought out and often highly original solution to any
problem he faces makes him a splendid candidate for the
arts.

Musical composition, that most demanding and complex
of all artistic endeavours is well suited to the Buffalo's
temperament. The list of musical Buffaloes is impressive: J.S.
Bach, Handel and Scarlatti – all born, by the way, in 1685 –
Benjamin Britten, Dvorak and Sibelius.

The visual arts have also been enhanced by the Buffalo's
highly personal mind: Van Gogh, Walt Disney and William
Blake left us powerful, vivid visual legacies, achieved with
much hard work and carried out with strong reliable hands.

A conservative with big and small C's, the Buffalo despises
novelties and gimmicks. The modern world is not for him.
When a Buffalo buys a car, it will be a Morris Minor, and if
he collects records, they will be old 78s. If a Buffalo smokes,
don't expect him to be taken in by the latest brand advertised
on the television; a smelly old pipe will be more his style. But
look out when you meet a Buffalo wearing a gold medallion
round his neck, or asking you to join him in a Marxist
revolution. As we soon discover, the grass roots of Buffaloes
like Tony Benn are the most conservative of all. Neither will
you find Buffaloes drooling over abstract art, jogging round
the park with headphones, or taking lunch in a vegetarian
restaurant.

To try and understand the Buffalo is to set oneself a
thankless and unproductive task. Any attempt to get really
close to this most private of all creatures will only succeed in
getting him to clam up. And the harder you try, the further he
retreats. But because he is a born leader, any fears or
uncertainties he encounters can never be admitted, either to
himself or to others. No one will be trusted with a Buffalo's

innermost secrets, and unless an obvious outlet can be found, the walls he has built to prevent us from peering in will act as a prison. He will, in short, become repressed and eventually extremely dangerous. In such cases, a Buffalo undergoes a startling transformation. His energy directs itself inwards, back into the dark and terrifying corners that harbour hate and self-delusion.

It is interesting to note that the most original comic of the 20th century, Charlie Chaplin, was a Buffalo, born in the same year as a man who has, with some justification, been called one of the most evil the world has ever known – Adolf Hitler.

When a Buffalo suffers a bad reversal it will hit him hard, and he will not find it easy moving on to the next fence. Unless a Buffalo can quickly tap a new source to provide him with the resilience he relies on to survive, he will slide rapidly into a state of physical and moral decline. In particular, a Buffalo who has come out the wrong side of a broken marriage will almost certainly turn to drink, or even drugs in a pathetic attempt to revive his spent strength.

And what of the man who for many remains the world's greatest snooker player, the People's Champion, Alex 'Hurricane' Higgins? He may not only have his Buffalo sign to thank for his prowess, some say genius, on the green baize, but also for the discord that has seemed to dog his often less than private life.

Only Buffaloes experience such dramatic extremes, and this is best understood as merely being two sides of the same coin. When your local priest, say a Buffalo, tells you he has thrown his hat in with the Atheist Society, he will see nothing contradictory in his move. For the Buffalo, it is not *what* he believes in that is important, but the belief itself. What matters to him is to have a conviction, it can be in anything, but it must be firm. Conviction is what produces the Buffalo's sense of purpose, his great powers of oratory, in fact his very being.

As one might expect, the high-minded and ambitious

Buffalo cannot bear to be thwarted, least of all by another Buffalo. The general election of 1983 was a wonderful example of what happens when two Buffaloes are after the same top job. Who can forget the pounding of hooves and snarling nostrils whenever Margaret Thatcher and Michael Foot came face to face?

Mrs Thatcher is in every way a classic Buffalo, and her reputation as the Iron Lady is well justified. A woman in what is very much a man's world, Margaret Thatcher displays all the Buffalo's undoubted strengths and alas, for those who do not share her concept of an authoritarian society, all the weaknesses. On her credit side, Mrs T is hard working (up at six and in bed by midnight), resolute, and tireless in the pursuit of her ideals. And she loves her home and family. But she cannot compromise and becomes stubborn over issues that require flexibility. This, more than anything, caused her downfall. And the least attractive side of her personality is the fault of Buffaloes everywhere; the tendency to blame others for their own mistakes. Michael Foot mirrors this fault to a quite extraordinary degree. In his book on the last general election, Michael Foot blames the newspapers, TV advertising agents and his own party for the fact that he lost. Not once does he suggest it was his policies that were wrong.

I have considerable personal experience of the Buffalo as a builder of empires, that is if you can call the satirical magazine, *Private Eye*, an empire. Started by Oxbridge undergraduates and sold on street corners, it is now read by well over a million people. Yet of all those responsible for its success, no one has done more than the current editor, Richard Ingrams. Taking the editor's chair twenty-two years ago, he has guided *Private Eye* through its precarious youth, filled with countless libel cases.

Ingrams is a Buffalo, born in 1937, as indeed was just about everyone concerned with *Private Eye*'s origins. Now better known as writers and performers outside of *Private Eye*'s close circle, Paul Foot, Peter Cook, William Rushton, Christopher Booker and even peripheral figures like Peter

Jay, all played important roles in shaping the magazine we now read. And all are Buffaloes, like Ingrams, born in the same year. Whenever I am asked if those born under the same sign have the same or similar traits, I tell them the remarkable *Private Eye* story.

And if 1937 looks as if it has been something special for Buffaloes with a satirical turn of mind, it's also worth pointing out that Hollywood produced one or two names we won't forget in a hurry: Jane Fonda, Warren Beatty and Robert Redford, all of the class '37.

The Buffalo hates large modern cities and will always live close to nature given the choice. He will diligently farm any land he owns, whether it is a small garden or a hundred acres. His home will be extremely comfortable and his study full of clutter: his desk and shelves piled up with old postcards, old prints and photographs, school memorabilia, knick-knacks and junk. If he has a filing system, only he will know how it works.

What a Buffalo likes is a sense of continuity. If you meet an old Buffalo school friend after a gap of twenty-one years, the chances are high he'll still be wearing the same grey flannels. Because the Buffalo is a conviction man, he is usually religious, but always middle of the road; a catholic with a very small c. A Buffalo pays his bills promptly, and those who work for him a fair though not excessive wage. Although he demands great loyalty, he loathes toadying. And a Buffalo who has been betrayed will neither forget nor forgive.

The Buffalo is a mainly masculine sign, but the ladies differ only very slightly. They dominate any home and, although not artistic like the Goat, lady Buffaloes are domestically gifted. They love baking cakes and sewing, and often make beautiful clothes for their several children. Although male Buffaloes are virtually incapable of infidelity, female Buffaloes are less inhibited and display a less sexually phlegmatic heart. And if the Buffalo lady allows herself to be seduced from her home and family, the affair will seldom be tempestuous.

31

All Buffaloes are very punctual; it makes for a well-ordered and regulated life. Love, of course, is the great destroyer of routines and is perhaps why the Buffalo is so reluctant to let himself fall. Apart from the odd Buffalo in a thousand, who goes right over the top when in the grips of love, most Buffaloes find opening their hearts up impossible. On the rare occasion he lets you know his feelings, don't expect too much. If you want bunches of red roses and sonnets you'll be disappointed. What you'll get is a chance to darn his socks. Jilly Cooper and Princess Diana are both Buffaloes.

Buffaloes, generally speaking, do not enjoy travelling more than they have to, and seldom voyage to strange parts alone. They move in herds. But bearing in mind that the Buffalo is capable of any extreme, we should not raise our eyebrows to learn that the first man to sail single-handedly round the world, Sir Francis Chichester, was one.

As for choosing a profession, the Buffalo needn't bother. One will almost certainly choose him, and his adaptability to routine and placid dependability will be valued in whatever field he ends up.

There are three distinct phases to a Buffalo's life. Childhood will be prone to isolation and have no close friendships. He will read a great deal, build toy battleships and collect butterflies. Middle life is not easy, having financial and marital setbacks. There will usually be a second wife and a second family. Peaceful and placid on the surface, you won't need to scratch the Buffalo's skin too deeply to discover a profoundly neurotic vein. As a result, the final phase may be spent alone, giving the Buffalo time to reflect on those friends he might have done more to keep. He'll walk his dog, potter in the garden and when he isn't writing his memoirs, he'll read the books of his childhood.

BUFFALO AS PARENT

Since the Buffalo is an authoritarian, he will only make a good parent for those children who like being told what to do. Either that, or they must pretend to obey and make such a good show of pretence that they can carry on living their own lives without interference. In this respect, the Monkey daughter will find no problems coping with her down-to-earth father. On the contrary, she'll let no opportunity pass to get him out of his comfortable chair for a spot of disco dancing.

Another child to benefit from a Buffalo parent is the baby Rooster. Her conservative view of the world will be praised and her pronounced sense of morality encouraged. No encouragement for the young Dragon. None at all. The Buffalo father will not waste his time admiring the Dragon son's golden scales, especially when they're covered with the mud of the fields. And that is where the Dragon child will be forced to spend much of his day – until he learns how to use his wings.

Young Tigers, with their forceful idealism will get no praise either in the Buffalo's strictly traditional home. And the radically-minded puppy Dog will just face criticism. The Goat daughter fares little better. Her Buffalo parent has nothing but contempt for her idle whims and fancies. Not much love for the young Horse either. Although his Buffalo father will applaud his son's hard work, he won't go much for his child's self-awareness. No vanity, however deserved, is welcome under a Buffalo's roof. The Snake daughter will win over a Buffalo father. She has great beauty, and uses her charms wisely. The Pig infant will work hard to please his Buffalo parent, but the Piglet's obvious self-satisfaction might lessen the bond between father and son. But the Rat son,

COMPATIBILITY OF BUFFALO PARENT AND CHILD

Rat	😊😊😊😊
Buffalo	😊
Tiger	☐
Cat	😊😊😊
Dragon	☐
Snake	😊😊😊
Horse	☐
Goat	☐
Monkey	😊😊😊😊
Rooster	😊😊😊😊
Dog	☐
Pig	😊😊

with his lively personality and sharp wit will amuse his Buffalo father, and will be forgiven more than might at first be expected. The child Buffalo will make no such impression on a Buffalo parent and there will be a struggle for authority from the very start. Life with the Buffalo father and Buffalo son will be intolerable, but a Buffalo mum might prove more understanding. The home-loving Cat will do nothing to disturb the peace and quiet of a Buffalo's home, and will make a great show of keeping the log fire burning in the hearth. Sensible little Kitten.

BUFFALO IN BUSINESS

The problem confronting the Buffalo as a businessman is that whereas he has an overpowering sense of his own destiny, he doesn't often intend sharing it with anyone else. If the Buffalo moves into the City, it will have to be as the Governor of the Bank of England, and if there is to be a portrait in the boardroom, it will be of him and no one else.

As might be expected, the hard-working Horse will do everything the Buffalo asks of him. Their most profitable step together would be to open a dental practice, or share driving a taxi

The Pig is never work-shy and will get on terribly well in partnership with the toiling, original Buffalo. The Pig's at his best when he's forced against the clock; it concentrates his mind wonderfully. But the Buffalo knows this. Together Pig and Buffalo can do great things. Disaster for the Tiger, though. His endless stream of ideas puts the methodical Buffalo completely off his stroke. And it's no joy for the equally bright and original Dragon, which is a great pity since both Buffalo and Dragon command such respect. The truth is, however, that the Dragon's own ability to command power will work against their mutual interest.

The opportunist Rat will faintly offend the straight-dealing Buffalo, although he'll have enough sense to utilise it when necessary. But there will be too many arguments for the Rat and Buffalo to make a long-term partnership work. The Goat, wayward and artistic, will not, I'm afraid, get a crack at even short-term success. Goats and Buffaloes are non-starters in business.

The Dog has nothing to bring to a business partnership but loyalty, and is the very minimum required by a Buffalo. The Rooster, though a spendthrift to the bone, can profit under

COMPATIBILITY OF BUFFALO IN BUSINESS RELATIONSHIPS

Rat	💰💰
Buffalo	💰
Tiger	☐
Cat	💰💰💰
Dragon	☐
Snake	☐
Horse	💰💰💰💰
Goat	☐
Monkey	☐
Rooster	💰💰💰
Dog	☐
Pig	💰💰💰💰

the steadying influence of the Buffalo, learning how to invest money rather than throwing it away. The Cat, like the Buffalo, deliberates long and hard before deciding how to invest his money. The trouble is that business often requires swift decisions, but having made the right one Cat and Buffalo will prosper modestly, although they may have to work the occasional weekend to pay the Christmas bonus. The same, alas, is true for a company formed by two Buffaloes, should such an outfit ever happen. The clever Snake, though generous to a fault with his time, shares the

Monkey's tight fist when it comes to parting with cash, and a business needs more than wits and beauty to keep the shareholders happy.

BUFFALO IN LOVE

Love is something most Buffaloes wish had never been invented, and will settle whenever possible for something less dangerous. It conflicts with their idea of a well-ordered universe, so even when a Buffalo falls heavily in love, there are unlikely to be any displays of passionate abandon. The female Buffalo, though, is less inhibited than the male. They make a good match with the easy-going comfort-seeking Cat, and Buffalo ladies will admire the thoughtfulness that accompanies the passion of a Dog. A male Buffalo will not be threatened by the good intentions of a lady Pig, and the full-blooded excitement generated by the Rat in love will act as a spur for him to reciprocate.

The capricious Goat will seldom, if ever, waste her time trying to warm the Buffalo's timid heart. And the Horse is far too vain to bother, although a lady Buffalo and a male Horse might enjoy each other for a short period (about one night).

The Buffalo will be sexually attracted by the lively and positive Rooster; again it will not last. The Rooster is far more interested in spending her hard-earned pennies than playing second fiddle to a repressed Romeo. Miss Monkey will captivate the Buffalo, as she does everyone, and the Snake's sensuousness will also entice him, but he'll flee the moment she begins to coil her body around him.

The Tiger in love is thrilling and her passion will arouse the Buffalo to act, but the Tiger highlights his emotional uncertainty, and the affair will end in bitter tears. A pair of loving Buffaloes might work out, but one of them has to make the first move. Chances are they'll never get beyond

COMPATIBILITY OF BUFFALO IN LOVE

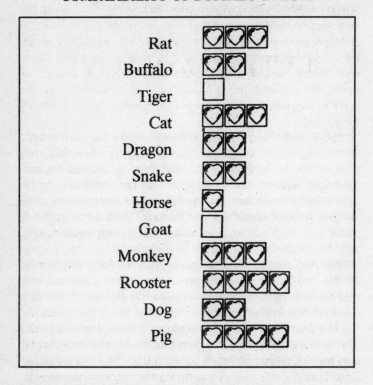

Rat	♡♡♡
Buffalo	♡♡
Tiger	☐
Cat	♡♡♡
Dragon	♡♡
Snake	♡♡
Horse	♡
Goat	☐
Monkey	♡♡♡
Rooster	♡♡♡♡
Dog	♡♡
Pig	♡♡♡♡

shaking hands. As for the sexually inexhaustible Dragon, a lady Buffalo might provide a little fun, but more for her than him.

BUFFALO IN MARRIAGE

Buffaloes, male or female, are not the easiest people in the world to live with. But whoever the Buffalo male marries, under no circumstances should it be a Tiger. They have absolutely nothing in common, and however great the attraction of opposites will be at the beginning – and it will be very great – they must not walk down the aisle. The Buffalo is deeply conservative in everything he does, and the Tiger is the world's greatest revolutionary. In such a home as a Tiger and Buffalo would create, every single decision would be made with the shedding of blood. My own observations, I am sorry to say, merely endorse what the Chinese have observed for so long.

The Rooster and Buffalo are tailor-made for each other, and can spend hours in the garden, digging up weeds and mowing the lawn. But the Rooster must guard against her forthright tongue, and reserve it for the Buffalo's many critics, and not the Buffalo. The impeccably-mannered Cat is another good prospect for the Buffalo. She'll be a splendid social aid; the Buffalo is not at his best in large gatherings, and the Cat is the very essence of diplomacy.

The Pig keeps a beautiful home – usually – and will always ensure that Buffalo hubby's meals are served on time, and that the kids have done their homework. But she won't like the Buffalo's stay at home life-style. Pigs like a bit of fun. A Snake might easily win the Buffalo's affection, but that is all. The Snake is too demanding sexually. Lack of warmth might also prove a stumbling block between a Buffalo and a Rat. A large family is one way of improving the union's chances – at least it will keep the Rat at home. As for the Dog, the Buffalo will always tend to misinterpret his or her loyalty as being spinelessness. This is a great pity since Dogs want nothing more than to love and be loved, to find someone in whom they can place their abundant trust.

Like the Cat, the Goat is wonderfully skilled at putting people at their ease socially, but he has such a wayward streak it's difficult to envisage how they would spend their evenings together. Would the Goat sit polishing her nails while he sat filling in the crossword? No prizes for the answer. A large family is the only solution.

After a seemingly promising start to married life, the

COMPATIBILITY WITH BUFFALO IN MARRIAGE

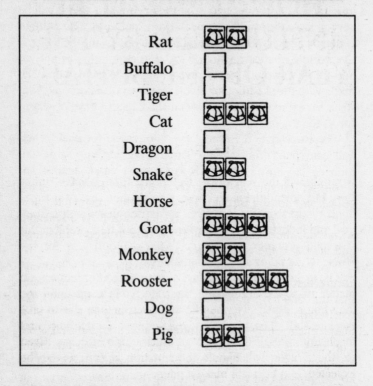

Horse and Buffalo will drift apart. The lady Horse is frequently vain, even egotistical at times and will soon be searching for compliments. In spite of their great differences a female Buffalo might marry a Dragon. And it might work so long as she doesn't expect the Dragon to help wash the nappies too often. The delightful lady Monkey will get along fine with a Buffalo as her husband, who will be enchanted by her wit and wisdom, but she must remember to play her little tricks a long way from home.

Almost as bad as a Tiger–Buffalo wedding is the marriage of two Buffaloes. They'll fight for who wears the trousers and there'll be no winner apart from the divorce lawyer. Be warned.

40

HOW YOU WILL BE INFLUENCED BY THE YEAR OF THE BUFFALO

A YEAR FOR THE WORKER

Not only will the year of the Buffalo be first-class for Buffaloes, but splendid for all those who do not shy away from honest hard work. It is a particularly rich year for the practical and industrious Horse. Money will not be a problem this year and promotion is on the cards. A good year for the Horse to get married or start a family.

The skilful Monkey is always able to look after himself, no matter what the influencing sign. He won't even mind the long hours, especially when he can get someone else to take the late shift. The brash Dragon unsettles the Buffalo, and might find himself the subject of much unfair criticism. Even so, the Dragon will handle the situation as well as can be expected, and he'll still make a pile.

The conservative Rooster has had a mean year under the previous year of the Rat, but things are looking up, and the Rooster will experience a delightful change of fortunes, above all in financial matters. For once, their scratching and pecking will pay off. A reversal for the Rat, though, who is thrown by the big emphasis on toil. He cannot meet the demands for steady results and will do himself no harm staying in the shadows for the duration. The obedient Pig will do all he is asked, and more. But he has a high opinion of himself and the Buffalo is not recognised for his largesse towards boastful characters. For the Pig, it might be that the plum job will have to wait until another year.

41

Rat	😊
Buffalo	😊 😊 😊 😊 😊
Tiger	☐
Cat	😊 😊
Dragon	😊 😊 😊
Snake	😊
Horse	😊 😊 😊 😊
Goat	☐
Monkey	😊 😊 😊 😊
Rooster	😊 😊 😊 😊
Dog	☐
Pig	😊 😊

The methodical Cat will get on with his tasks as usual – but the hours are *so* long, and it's nice to snooze in the shade. The Snake is not adverse to the odd nap under a stone when the sun gets hot, but if the Snake is to get anywhere, she must remember that this is the Year of the Elbow Grease. Intuitive wisdom comes some other time. The Dog's self doubts will be doubled by the Buffalo's strength of conviction, and the Tiger's spirit of adventure will be made terribly dull by all the heavy plodding. If the Tiger and Dog seek solace, they might well find it with the capricious Goat. Unhappy in the year of the Buffalo, her fickle pleasure seeking has no place in a field of dour workmen.

FAMOUS BUFFALOES

Arts
Martin Amis
Vladimir Ashkenazy
J S Bach
David Bailey
William Blake
Benjamin Britten
Peter Brook
Jean Cocteau
Jilly Cooper
Walt Disney
Dvorak
El Greco
Handel
David Hockney
Richard Ingrams
Oscar Peterson
Rubens
Sibelius
Tom Stoppard
Vincent Van Gogh

Sports
Gordon Banks
Frank Bruno
Geoff Capes
Harry Carpenter
Bobby Charlton
Francis Chichester
Joe Davis
Sunil Gavaskar

Alex Higgins
Niki Lauda
Dennis Lillee
Ian Rush
Bill Shankley
Peter Shilton
Fatima Whitbread

Industry/Politics
Laura Ashley
Menachem Begin
Tony Benn
Napoleon
Michael Foot
Adolf Hitler
Saddam Hussein
Arthur Scargill
Margaret Thatcher
Duke of Wellington

Royals
Princess Diana
King Juan Carlos
Emperor Hirohito

Show Biz
Warren Beatty
Pamela Bordes
Rory Bremner
Sarah Brightman
Richard Burton

Charlie Chaplin
George Cole
Jackie Collins
Peter Cook
Gary Cooper
Tony Curtis
Marlene Dietrich
Anita Dobson
Jane Fonda
Dustin Hoffman
Rock Hudson
Paul Newman
Meryl Streep

Twiggy
Alan Whicker

Pop
Shirley Bassey
Sammy Davis Jnr
Boy George
Robin and Maurice Gibb
Bill Haley
Alison Moyet
Bruce Springsteen
Rick Wakeman

THE TIGER

虎

1902	February 8th to January 28th	**1903**
1914	January 26th to February 13th	**1915**
1926	February 13th to February 1st	**1927**
1938	January 31st to February 18th	**1939**
1950	February 17th to February 5th	**1951**
1962	February 5th to January 24th	**1963**
1974	January 23rd to February 10th	**1975**
1986	February 9th to January 28th	**1987**

'Hold that Tiger, hold that Tiger, hold that Tiger . . .'
Tiger Rag

THE YEAR OF THE TIGER

No one can overlook the year of the Tiger. It is a year in which everything will be turned upside down, each day promising a terrific new scheme, each tomorrow another idea brighter than the one before. Change, energy, power and bravery are the keynotes for everyone in the year of the Tiger, and the mild and timid had better stay in bed for the duration. But if the Tiger's year begins with fireworks morning, noon and night, the final days will tell a very different story. A lot may have been altered (not always for the best), and when a Tiger does the altering, no matter what, it stays altered. Even so, there will have been plenty to celebrate, and nobody will moan for long when the party fizzles out.

There may be wars in the year of the Tiger, and governments overthrown. On the political stage, 1974 was particularly explosive. In the United States, President Richard Nixon was impeached following the biggest political scandal in American history. In Great Britain, meanwhile, Prime Minister Edward Heath's government introduced the three-day week, and was finally toppled. In 1926, Britain suffered the General Strike.

Nevertheless, in spite of the many ups and downs, the Tiger's year will smile on all those who aren't scared to step into the unknown, to spend their energy utterly, and to risk improvisation. If you are a jazz musician or an explorer, take heart. It's a year to find out just what you are made of, no matter what your job. Now is the time to begin the project which you think has the least chance of succeeding, and push it as hard as you can: it will be a tremendous hit. Visit distant places, and make sure they are well off the beaten track. The month of February 1962 saw America's first manned orbital space flight. So if you fancy a climb up Everest or rowing single-handed across the seven seas, do it. Live dangerously – it's the year of the Tiger.

THE TIGER PERSONALITY

'It's time for change, energy and action. Enter the brave and powerful Tiger.'

When the poet William Blake penned his immortal line, 'Tiger, Tiger, burning bright ...', he could not have chosen a more apt way of describing the Tiger as portrayed by the people of Asia and China. In particular, Asians have elevated the Tiger to a national symbol. Like a Third Party motor insurance policy, they believe that the Tiger will protect them from the Three Great Disasters: fire, theft and evil spirits. Similarly, we in the West have not been slow to recognise the Tiger's immense power. No wonder that a certain petrol company once urged us to put a tiger in our tank, and now call their lubricating oil, 'The Striped Protector'. And they are right, as anyone who has ever seen a tiger running at full speed will surely confirm. No beast on earth combines the same degree of beauty, strength and energy. Add bravery, and you complete the list of enviable attributes given to those born in the year of the Tiger. Physically and mentally, the Tiger is a powerhouse teeming with ideas. Lord Nelson was a Tiger, so was Oscar Wilde, David Steel, David Owen and Christina Onassis are typical Tigers.

But for all the Tiger's strength and determination, he is not without his opponents, and although he may win many a fight, the battle is a very different story.

Given any setting, the Tiger is not one to go unnoticed. He is a dynamic revolutionary who will not stand by while others are given a raw deal. And never try to push him around. The Tiger loves a scrap, and there are few better equipped to come out on top. The Tiger is both impetuous and idealistic, and is quick to find faults in others. He reacts outspokenly against authority of every kind, the more so when he sees it as corrupt. His attitude towards the Establishment is probably why the Tiger makes such a poor Chairman of the Board, yet such a splendid Head of Department. The truth is that the Tiger is a natural ringleader – just think of Karl Marx leading his band of brothers, and subsequently the whole Russian nation into the biggest revolution in history.

The Tiger will, in fact, take on any job which gives him a chance to show his courage and imagination. As head-waiter or chief-detective; director of publicity or captain of the team, the Tiger is free to play his two favourite roles. He can organise and inspire those under him while at the same time sit in on Board meetings and thump his not inconsiderably sized paws on the table for a better deal.

Viewed from a distance, the Tiger would seem to have everything in his favour. A smart and always elegant dresser, both male and female Tigers carry themselves with ease. In the Tiger's wardrobe you will find no sign of the Buffalo's sensible shoes. Nor will the dressing table be full of the Snake's pile of jewels and trinkets. The Tiger is a looker, and he knows it. And he knows, too, that the muscles aren't just for show. But the Tiger does have one flaw, and it's serious. You have only to watch him run a marathon to learn that the

Tiger is a sprinter. His powerful muscular limbs are not built for endurance, but for short spurts.

For all those born under the influence of the Tiger, the need to *be* somebody is paramount. This does not necessarily mean that a Tiger has to be someone famous, although no Tiger worth his stripes would turn down a chance to don a laurel crown. Whatever he becomes, it must be of his own making and he will go to any lengths to prove himself fit for his self-created role. One Tiger I know stepped from an extremely secure and well paid job in the Foreign Office to become a writer, not of just any old book, but a writer of serious fiction with a pretence to greatness (typical of a Tiger not to aim for the nearest star). To become an author he sold his beautiful home in Oxfordshire and lived off the profit. When that ran out he worked during the day and wrote at weekends and nights. Even his good lady wife, a Horse, helped win the bread. He wrote like a man possessed, first-rate stories pouring out one after the other. And he'd hardly begun one book before he'd ditch it and start a better one. No matter how many of his books become bestsellers, or end up on the remaindered shelf, the one certainty is that he's a Tiger that has truly become his real self.

Because of the Tiger's dynamic, and it must be said, somewhat impatient nature, they often act first and think later. But paradoxically, when faced with really important decisions a Tiger will often prevaricate. He'll get involved in details and miss the main point, ending up by making a hash of it. And when things go badly for a Tiger, he feels it right down to the bottom of his boots. A Tiger's depression can perhaps be explained by the kind of rules taught in a physics class – the amount of energy a Tiger puts into any one project will equal the amount of misery he'll suffer when the project turns sour. It is when a Tiger is cast down that he'll need his friends, and will accept all the consolation they can give. And when a Tiger licks his wounds, don't expect to find him much concerned about the wounds of others. Later, yes, when he's back in the hunt, the Tiger will be all ears, but not when he's low. The Tiger makes a poor nurse any time. Neither can he cope with sudden bouts of immobility. Stuck in the mud, he will listen to any advice given him, good or bad, and cling to any outstretched hand. Then, overnight, the Tiger will leap back into action. Shaved, tidied up and in a fresh set of clothes he will again begin pursuing his own destiny as if nothing had happened. And he'll do it with renewed hope and vigour, while at the same time showing little concern for those who had given him so much of their time. In his pursuit of tomorrow's goals, the Tiger has no time to consider yesterday's defeat.

The Tiger is the ideas man incarnate. No one else has a greater or more constant source, and Tigers are miles ahead of the field when it comes to summoning up the energy, and sometimes bravery, to realise them. In all history, one figure alone can lay claim to represent the Tiger's unique combination of courage and capacity to produce brilliant ideas. For many, Beethoven stands head and shoulders above his fellow composers, and I've met those who place him alongside the greatest men to have lived. As a child, musical composition came as easily to Beethoven as breathing. Ideas tumbled out faster than he could write them down, and as he grew into manhood, so his compositions grew more profound. As pianist, conductor and composer he was the toast of Vienna, but was never satisfied with his achievements. For his only opera, 'Fidelio', he wrote no fewer than four different overtures, discarding all but one. Then while at the summit of his career, fate struck the cruellest blow imaginable: Beethoven went deaf. The world's greatest musician was no longer able to hear his, or anyone else's music ever again. Little wonder, therefore, that he sank into a period of absolute desperation, even contemplating suicide. But led by his indomitable spirit, the brave Beethoven found a way to compose, and note by note his ideas began to flow once more. The fruits of his recovery rank with the most inspired music man has ever heard. Beethoven the Tiger had triumphed!

Although the Tiger is strictly a male sign, the female Tiger is every bit his equal. Lady Tigers are extremely good with children, both their own and other people's. They make exceptional teachers, winning the hearts of their pupils by the sheer weight of their personality. Never sticklers for homework, swatting up, or learning everything parrot-fashion, Tiger teachers achieve their success by striving to find the student's real interest, and exploiting it to the limit. And no one tells stories better than a Tiger. A Tiger's child will have his or her young imagination fired by endless spell-binding tales, told superbly.

But do not expect a lady Tiger to spend hours at the sink. And don't ask her to iron your shirt. Tiger ladies are liberated in every sense, and when a Tigress wants an affair she'll go ahead and have it. Starting like a whirlwind, an affair with a Tiger lady will leave both parties exhausted in no time at all. But that won't worry the Tiger. What's done is done and there will be no place for guilt. The consequences won't bother her in the slightest.

Lady Tigers dress with daring, and sometimes even with a touch of aggression. Their outfits will be instantly noticeable, often set off by a flamboyant dash of colour – a scarlet headscarf, perhaps, or a gaily striped neck-tie. Leather boots and leather belts are what lady Tigers like to wear, and they also go in for masculine fashions, making the most of a well-tailored suit.

Though he will often make money, sometimes more than he needs, the Tiger will also find he has to face lean times. But he will never go completely broke, because of the vast reserve of ideas he has. And because he takes so many risks, the Tiger's life is seldom peaceful. One thing is certain, a Tiger will never get stuck in a rut. Born under the sign of courage, Tigers will do any job that involves risk. Better still if the job carries the title Head, Chief, Boss or Captain. Tigers make great publicists, athletes (short distances only), film stars, models, jazz musicians and explorers. But as with all those who choose a life which entails risk there is a chance that the Tiger might not be around to collect his pension –

should he bother to have arranged one. Indeed, the Chinese say the Tiger might meet a sudden and violent death in the realisation of his great ambition to be himself. Tigers born around midday are particularly vulnerable. Sadly this is true of one of the most stunningly beautiful and desirable lady Tigers of all time, Marilyn Monroe.

Although Tiger ladies care a great deal about their homes, they do not over-furnish them, and the decorations are usually good quality and tasteful, but not lavish. Above all they will be comfortable homes. Male Tigers very often grow tired of their surroundings. They love where they are intensely, but only for a short while, and seldom become attached. Once their enthusiasm wanes for the place they live in, a Tiger quickly moves on.

In character, the Tiger often treats his friends much like he treats his houses. Extremely gregarious, the Tiger tends to put everything he has into the opening moments of a relationship. Thrilled by the intensity, he holds nothing back. In most cases, unfortunately, a Tiger's friendship does not last once the momentum dies. After a powerful and promising start, the Tiger frequently feels he has said it all, and before long you will begin to notice his calls become less regular, and his demand for attention less exacting. But however long a Tiger remains your friend – a week, a year, a lifetime – he'll never look you up without bringing a token of his warmth. And if it's a bottle of wine, it won't have come from the local supermarket. It will be the best he can afford. No one is more generous than the Tiger, either with his praise or money. And no one is less happy about being ignored.

All three phases of a Tiger's life will be unpredictable. During his childhood the young Tiger will be a constant source of worry to his parents, never being really sure of his whereabouts, or what their child is up to. But they will at last hear the familiar cry of, 'I'm home, I'm home, I'm ho-ome!' Indeed, that cry will accompany the Tiger's return, in one shape or another, throughout his life. The Tiger's middle period will be the most dangerous, but should he overcome the highs as well as the lows, the Tiger's old age will be as peaceful and contented as he wishes.

TIGER AS PARENT

Tigers can be counted on as making extremely good mothers once they overcome their often fiery youth, and tend to go in for larger than average sized families. Each child perhaps is seen as something of an exciting new project, a new challenge to be filled with the Tiger's ever expanding energy and vitality. But there may be setbacks for the Tiger infant, who just might not win enough of his parents' attention. After all, isn't junior Tiger so able and bursting with ideas? But the Tiger child may be asking for more than praise for his youthful idealism. On the other hand, the honest Dog's needs will be quickly attended to. They are instantly recognisable and the Tiger parent will spare him or herself nothing to make sure the Dog child is given every encouragement. In fact his open heart and moving loyalty will touch a Tiger mother like no other child. The young Dragon too, will flourish under the Tiger's parental eye. The Dragon's ability to shine at whatever he chooses can only bring out the best in Tiger mum or dad.

The baby Rat, even at an early age, is quick to spot the best seat and the biggest helping. His, alas, is an attitude that Tigers are not greatly enamoured by. The Rat can also see the wood for the trees, something his Tiger parent cannot. So it's an early departure from home for the rodent. There's always lots going on under the Tiger's roof – plenty of excitement and fun. But the Goat daughter prefers to make her own, thank you very much, and like the Rat will tie her spotted handkerchief round her possessions and hit the road while still in her teens. As for the Rooster and Buffalo babes, they want much more from a home than just the promise of jam today, even if they get it.

COMPATIBILITY OF TIGER PARENT AND CHILD

	Compatibility
Rat	(none)
Buffalo	(none)
Tiger	(none)
Cat	☺
Dragon	☺☺☺☺☺
Snake	☺
Horse	☺☺
Goat	☺
Monkey	☺☺
Rooster	(none)
Dog	☺☺☺☺☺
Pig	☺☺☺

The young Horse can swiftly adapt to his Tiger parent's constantly changing life, and will often be stimulated. The Snake daughter might find life a trifle hectic, and will probably need more space to breathe. Piglets are happy in any home that provides them with lots to occupy their eager minds. And the Tiger will give them more than enough to do. The young Monkey will adore all the comings and goings, but he won't be crazy about dad squandering his precious pocket money on some new hare-brained scheme. And that goes for the Kitten too; all that money down the drain, and it could have bought so much cream.

THE TIGER IN BUSINESS

When it comes to running a business a Tiger needs a steadying hand at his side. The Dragon, although sharing much of the Tiger's impulsiveness, has a better head for heights. Should the company make a fat profit, the Dragon will make sure there's a numbered account tucked away safely somewhere. The Horse, ever willing to take on his fair share of the load, will find the Tiger's lack of attention to details infuriating. But providing they don't have too many bust-ups early on, Tiger and Horse will make a solid enough partnership, particularly as manufacturers of speedboats, hang gliders or formula one racing cars.

Two Tigers must avoid each other in commerce, even though the odds against them trying are very remote. The chances of them ever agreeing are about the same as two fruit machines next to each other both coming up with the jackpot at the same time.

The sensitive and intuitive Snake works at her best in quiet and tranquil surroundings. The last thing she'll want in her beautiful art gallery is a Tiger bouncing up and down. He'll be forever rehanging the pictures and changing exhibitions in midstream. Snake and Tiger are best left to run their own shop. The Dog is an idealist and makes the Tiger a fine confederate when there's revolution in the air. But they should keep a million miles apart from each other when it comes to filling in the VAT returns.

The Rooster should just simply stay away from the Tiger altogether in business. His sharp tongue will be quick to criticise the Tiger's unpredictability, and their methods have nothing in common.

COMPATIBILITY OF TIGER IN BUSINESS RELATIONSHIPS

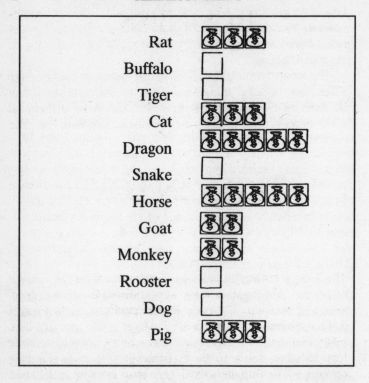

The capricious Goat will be happy enough to go along with the Tiger, so long as the future looks rosy, but when the creditors come banging on the door, don't expect the Goat to stay and face them. Rats on the other hand, complement a Tiger in business, and 'Ideas Man' and 'Mr Opportunist' can do well for themselves so long as someone else keeps the books.

Although Cats can always spot a bargain from the other side of the street, they take too long making up their minds to be of any assistance to the all-action Tiger. Monkeys, with their long memories, are useful partners to anyone, but the

Tiger has sharp teeth and the Monkey plays too many risky tricks. Better watch out, Monkey. The Pig, however, is as honest as the day is long, and will provide a firm if slightly ordinary foundation for the Tiger to build on. But the Tiger is easily bored and might ask for more sparkle than the Pig is capable of giving.

The worst partnership of all is that between Buffalo and Tiger, not because they would fail to make money, but because their opposing temperaments would have them at each other's throats long before their signature on the contract had a chance to dry.

TIGER IN LOVE

The Tiger and the Rat have much in common on the subject of passion, but together they do not always produce a deep loving partnership. The male Rat in particular might appear just a trifle insincere for the female Tiger at the moment that really matters. Two Tigers are too restless and volatile, and love so often needs to be a partnership of understanding opposites. The Buffalo is the Tiger's most extreme match, but both parties lack even the slightest awareness of each other's romantic needs. They live at the two poles of the emotional scale and should never attempt to meet. The male Tiger might easily find himself excited by the Cat's refined sexuality. But Cats don't make a lot of effort to keep their love partners, and the Tiger will quickly lose interest. The self-adoring Snake, so clever and sensual, will not be content to take the Tiger's love-making in sudden outbursts. But the sexually inspired Dragon will make an excellent partner. Both creatures loathe prisons of any kind and express their love of freedom through deep passionate relationships.

COMPATIBILITY OF TIGER IN LOVE

Rat ♡
Buffalo ☐
Tiger ☐
Cat ♡
Dragon ♡♡♡♡♡
Snake ☐
Horse ♡♡♡♡
Goat ♡♡♡
Monkey ♡♡
Rooster ♡
Dog ♡♡
Pig ♡♡♡

The elegant and often beautiful lady Horse can discover much pleasure with the energetic Tiger, and a male Horse will be patient with a Tiger lady during her periods of uncertainty. All Pigs enjoy a fling now and then, and the generous Tiger is happy to foot the bill. The anxious Dog may find himself surprisingly at ease with a lady Tiger, but must not allow himself to be over-awed by her brilliance. The fun-loving Goat gets on well with the Tiger providing they can sit still long enough to get the show started. But the affair will be strictly short term, and no hearts will be broken at the last goodbye. Tepid but very real love exists between lady Tiger and the Rooster, who for all his swagger is basically unsure of himself. He'll be secretly flattered by the dazzling attention his lover pays him. The lady Monkey might easily entice the Tiger, but she must again watch her tricks or she'll end up getting her tail bitten off.

TIGER IN MARRIAGE

The Tigers, although not richly endowed with a choice of marriage partners do have two options open to them. The irrepressible Dragon, so full of life, will be the last to wilt under the Tiger's explosive pace. He'll actually encourage it. At the other extreme, the faithful and trusting Dog will endear himself forever to the Tiger's strong sense of justice. Each will fight to the bitter end to protect the other. But Tigers walking up the aisle should make sure they never do it with a Buffalo; temperamentally they are chalk and cheese. The Snake, ever one to cling to what she wants, will not manage to keep the Tiger, who will see the trap and bounce far away. Hot-headed though he may be, the Tiger knows a prison when he sees one.

Both the Cat and the Goat are fond of Society and make excellent hostesses. Although the Tiger adores big parties, he is mostly a man of action. Perhaps too many planned evenings might prove an ordeal for him. Lady Pigs are among the best cooks in the world, and even the fast living Tiger will be happy to swop a few nights out with the boys for an extra helping of that divine chocolate mousse. What's more, the Pig is no mean nurse, and will find ample words of comfort when the Tiger hits one of his lows. The agreeable Horse, slow to anger and quick to please, also makes the Tiger a useful wife or husband. But there will be misunderstandings along the way, and both may seek time alone.

The Rooster is faithful, in spite of his boasting, and will

COMPATIBILITY WITH TIGER IN MARRIAGE

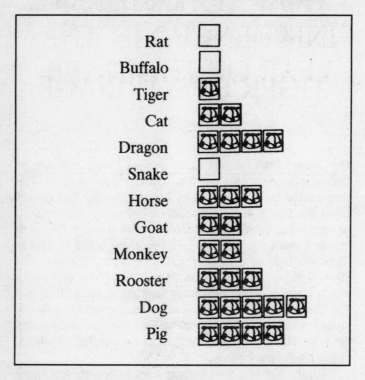

Rat

Buffalo

Tiger

Cat

Dragon

Snake

Horse

Goat

Monkey

Rooster

Dog

Pig

adore his Tiger wife. The problem here is that marriages are not only made from love, they also need financing. Both Tiger and Rooster can spend without thought, so they will probably end up poor but happy – or happy-ish. The Monkey and Tiger in wedlock can only work if both spend plenty of time away from home. That way they can enjoy themselves without treading on each other's very sensitive toes. Generally speaking, two Tigers under the same roof are bad news and not recommended. But as is often the case, when all the cards are on the table life gets simpler, and a pair of Tigers might just make it work. Many children will increase their chances. But not so for Rats, another partnership to avoid.

HOW YOU WILL BE INFLUENCED IN THE YEAR OF THE TIGER

A YEAR FOR ACTION

After two long and lean years the Tiger's pent up vitality is finally free to express itself – and how! Never one to sit with his feet up, in the year of the Tiger, Tigers everywhere will be on their toes and firing on all cylinders. But Tiger beware. The sudden rush of blood to the head might mean you will miss your golden opportunity through an excess of self-confidence, and your five-star rating will be gradually reduced to nothing. The honest Dog, whose life has also been, well, a bit of a dog's life during the Rat and Buffalo years, will find his loyalty and concern for the world's lost causes greatly appreciated under the influence of the Tiger. By contrast, the conservative Rooster will be thrown into a complete muddle by all the comings and goings. The Tiger's delight at cocking a snook at the Establishment is not for the Rooster, and she'll take refuge in spending sprees.

The Rat's charm is totally lost on the Tiger, who has no time to sit and get himself buttered-up by anyone. The placid and hard-working Buffalo also slips behind badly in the wake of the active, impulsive Tiger, although the even-tempered Pig will make his way comfortably forward without too many distractions. Snakes are sufficiently wise to discern which of the Tiger's instant band-wagons will be worth jumping on, and the adaptable Horse is not slow to recognise a good thing when it comes along.

The Goat has her own very special ideas about what needs changing, but it only seldom coincides with the Tiger's plans. Cats always weigh up the pros and cons before taking action, which is not the way a Tiger likes it. But a Cat might do well if he risks one of his nine lives on a madcap Tiger scheme – they so often pay off. The artful Monkey can always find someone to help play his tricks, and the Tiger loves games. The Dragon, resourceful as ever, is not in the least frightened by the vivacious Tiger, and will welcome him with open arms.

FAMOUS TIGERS

Arts
David Attenborough
Beethoven
Alan Coren
Alec Guinness
Laurie Lee
Rudolph Nureyev
Diana Rigg
Joan Sutherland
Dylan Thomas
Oscar Wilde

Sports
John Arlott
Jack Brabbam
Joe Bugner
David Coleman
Barry Sheene
Harvey Smith
Mark Spitz
Jimmy White

Industry/Politics
Dwight D Eisenhower
Richard Branson
General Galtieri
Geoffrey Howe
Ramsay Macdonald
Karl Marx
Lord Nelson

David Owen
Jonathon Porritt
David Steel

Royals
The Queen
The Princess Royal

Show Biz
Katie Boyle
Paul Daniels
Susan George
Hugh Heffner
David Jacobs
Ian Macaskill
George Melly
Marilyn Monroe
Pamela Stephenson
Julie Walters
Terry Wogan

Pop
Karen Carpenter
Eddie Cochrane
Phil Collins
Phil Everley
David Hamilton
Jimmy Saville
Tina Turner
Stevie Wonder

THE CAT

貓

1903	January 29th to February 15th	1904
1915	February 14th to February 2nd	1916
1927	February 2nd to January 22nd	1928
1939	February 19th to February 7th	1940
1951	February 6th to January 26th	1952
1963	January 25th to February 12th	1964
1975	February 11th to January 30th	1976
1987	January 29th to February 16th	1988

Before the Cat will condescend
To treat you as a friend,
Some little token of esteem
Is needed, like a dish of cream.

T.S. Eliot

THE YEAR OF THE CAT

No year shows a more marked contrast with its predecessor than the Year of the Cat, following as it does the turbulent Year of the Tiger. As the dust begins to settle, a strange but welcome calm will begin to make its presence felt. Gone are the daily calls to arms and the frantic pursuits of seemingly impossible goals, and in their place we discover a quieter and more easily paced world. Any calls made to us will probably be no more alarming than a gentle purr. The Year of the Cat will not be one in which great feats of endurance get entered into the record books: no Everests will be climbed, no one will run a three minute mile. But don't be fooled into thinking that nothing will be done. On the contrary, there will be considerable amounts of energy used up in all sorts of places – mostly on the Cat's own comfort.

It is a year for fine wines, art exhibitions and Paris will produce her finest collections. In May 1951, King George VI opened the Festival of Britain from the steps of St Paul's Cathedral. It was the most remarkable exhibition of British skills, crafts and technology ever. The French clarets of 1975 were truly outstanding, and considered by all to be every bit the equal of the great vintages. And although 1963 saw the vineyards of France produce a rather indifferent year, port of that vintage is viewed as the best in almost a quarter of a century.

The most that is likely to change in the Year of the Cat is the length of a dress hem or the colour we paint our bathroom, but for all the apparent tranquillity, it must be remembered that the Cat cannot cope with major disasters and global adversity. This means that should violence break out the Cat can do little to prevent it spreading. In 1939 Hitler declared war on Britain, and attempts to avert the conflict that was to engulf us all proved useless. President Kennedy was assassinated in 1963 while the world stood helplessly looking on. Yet the Cat has had his moments of peace-making, and in 1975 the dreadful war in Vietnam came to an end. Excluding wars, however, the Year of the Cat will pass in total harmony, and leave us greeting the New Year having had more than just a taste of the Good Life.

THE CAT PERSONALITY

'Put your feet up, sip wine by the fire, and meet the social, sensuous Cat.'

The most memorable cat of my childhood was not the 'Cat that sat on the mat', or 'Puss in Boots', but the cat Alice met on her trip through the looking-glass. The Cheshire cat is almost certainly best remembered for his extraordinary smile. Indeed, so extraordinary is it, that when Alice finally takes her leave of Lewis Carroll's unforgettable feline creation, the smile is all that remains. And what does this signify? Is it satisfaction or pleasure? Is he sizing you up for his supper, thinking of you the way cartoon cats dream of the caged canary as a fat sizzling bird fresh from the oven? Or is he simply smiling at the remembrance of meals passed? The truth is that the Cheshire cat's smile is the smile of cats everywhere, from Bombay to Bermuda; from Texas to Tokyo. And to understand why a cat smiles is to find the key to the most secret and subtle animal of all.

Born under the sign of virtue, the Cat is essentially feminine. Yet with the odd scruffy back-alley Tom as the exception proving the rule, male Cats share almost all the female characteristics. Exceptionally well dressed, refined and super diplomatic, Cats have a natural elegance. Cats decorate their homes with both taste and distinction, and fewer animals pay greater attention to their family's material needs. And in the business, no animal has a better nose for a bargain, or is better equipped to strike it.

If you were born under the influence of the Cat, your birth year will be shared with Prince Albert, Queen Victoria, Cary Grant, Frank Sinatra, Ingrid Bergman and the late Lord Clark (of *Civilisation* fame).

Blessed with an inner mystery that many find both frightening and bewitching, Cats have produced great men of thought: Trotsky, George Orwell, the baby expert Dr Spock, and perhaps the greatest physicist of all time, Albert Einstein.

Sensitive and circumspect in his dealings with everyone he meets, plus an overpowering need to be surrounded by a passive and agreeable environment, gives the Cat the best possible credentials for any office that requires diplomacy. The Cat listens carefully when spoken to, and can remember in detail any conversation or polite argument. With his open ear and readiness to sit quietly, the Cat makes a superb diplomat, and his objective judgement can be a great asset should he choose to take up the legal profession. As a barrister he can listen without necessarily being asked for advice; Cats are actually better equipped to give you a passive ear than active verbal aid. If you are about to get divorced, it is no use going to a Cat expecting him to tell you how to handle it emotionally: your talk of separation will only frighten him, reminding him of his own vulnerability. And any advice he ventures, like so much to do with the Cat, will be largely superficial. It is style and not content that counts. But if it's gossip you want, you will find no one better able to join in. However, if you must tell a Cat about your impending divorce, ask him about the settlement. Stick to advice on money, and the Cat's your man.

Floods, famines, wars, sudden death and disasters of every kind send a Cat shinning up the nearest tree. Confronted on any subject outside his home and family, if it's at all serious, he will almost certainly cave in. If your boss is a Cat and refuses your demand for an extra week off, push him hard enough and you'll get two weeks and a rise. An angry and upsetting scene is the last thing your boss Cat wants. But remember that a Cat's claws are razor sharp and his teeth can chew through the toughest old bones you can throw him: although a fight is the last thing on a Cat's mind, forced to defend himself, he can become lethal. The trick is to know how much he can take, but we seldom learn that important piece of information until the damage has been done.

In general, however, Cats do not favour emotional excesses and find it difficult coping with them. One male Cat I know becomes utterly squashed by any kind of raised voice, especially those raised in argument. And prolonged argument has a catatonic affect on him. I remember once having a heated discussion with his Buffalo wife in a restaurant. The subject was terribly trivial, but as our slightly drunken voices reached a climax, my Cat friend rushed from the restaurant and was almost sick in the street. Pale and shaking he returned to his seat and spoke not one word for the rest of the meal. A typical Cat, any emotional crisis will topple him like a paper house in a tornado. Listening to a very dramatic concert at the Festival Hall once, he actually passed out through the emotion generated by the music. Perhaps all those people one sees being attended to outside concert halls with glasses of water are Cats. It's a thought!

The Cat is not, generally speaking, a profound creature. Indeed, he is totally uninterested in what goes on in the big ugly world outside, and has an aversion to suffering that makes him behave in a quite uncharacteristic and sometimes unbelievably cruel manner when faced with it. The Cat places his home and its comforts above all else, and the need to

71

have them just as he pleases is fundamental to his existence. But should he be threatened in any way, or even appear to be, the Cat undergoes a Jekyll and Hyde style transformation. From his preferred position as a man of peace and refinement, the Cat will strike out with open claws to protect his home and family, and he will be completely indifferent to the suffering he himself may engender. It is not surprising, in view of this, to learn that some of the world's greatest despots have been born in the year of the Cat: Stalin and the late South African Prime Minister, Johannes Vorster, were both born Cats. It is my view that a Cat should never be given absolute power, for he will not be able to make the important distinction between what is right for him and right for others. In the end, both will suffer. My own picture of a Cat's 'other side' is when I see one of my cats clawing dispassionately at the body of a half-dead bird before either discarding it, or devouring every last bone.

But given the Cat's desire for a quiet life, unthreatened and free from talk of the world's endless disasters, he will make long strides in his chosen profession. So long as the work is not too physical, or the hours too long (the cat so loves those little naps) he will make a lot of himself. Clearly a Cat should avoid jobs which employ risk or conflict, and if possible he should choose a line in which he can be self-employed. In particular, he should go for a career that gives him an opportunity to combine his exceptional talents to weigh up financial pros and cons, and deal with people with his instinct for good taste. Cats should run art galleries, antique shops, bistros or hair-dressing salons. If a Cat lady has any ambition beyond her home, it will have to be fulfilled from beside the hearth, like short story writer or freelance illustrator.

Women often look their best when in the company of a male Cat, gay or otherwise. And it's appreciated. Male Cats know how women should dress, and to some extent know how they feel. The photographer, Patrick Lichfield, is a Cat. Both male and female Cats will always be fastidious in their dress. Whether the male Cat puts on faded old jeans or white tie and tails, his clothes will always have the look of just having been pressed. And there will be a flamboyant stitch or two, like a fancy waistcoat or bright green socks. For Cat man forced into the dowdy three-piece suit, he'll be instantly recognised by his risky, but never loud, neck-tie. Tom Cats rarely grow beards or moustaches, and if they do, they don't keep them a lifetime.

Methodical and cautious, Cats are not ones for making sudden changes – just reflect on the way that your pet cat ventures into new territory; one tentative paw at a time, as slow as a snail. What Cats enjoy is the familiarity with what they already possess. Consequently Cats tend to respond badly to new ideas, which are often interpreted as a threat to their established way of doing things. Cats live by routine, and their deliberate, methodical attitude can sometimes develop into an almost fastidious obsession. That chap in the accounts department who always brings his mackintosh to work in case it rains is sure to be a Cat. He'll be the same fellow who has his files stacked in neat racks, whose jacket always hangs on the same peg, whose felt tip is never without its cap and whose whole life is run with the detached precision of a Swiss watchmaker and the homogenised neatness of an operating theatre. His is a well-balanced, well-organised life with a time and place for everything.

Cats are blessed with a sharp though sometimes gossipy sense of humour – catty, some would say. They adore bright and lively company, more so if there is an element of high society to mingle with. Given a crowded room the Cat will, as if by some divine sense, drift towards the most glamorous and socially 'in'. Though not generally a snob, when he is, he does it in style. He will even get his own television series to meet the world's rich and famous, and in the end, will become just as rich and famous himself. David Frost is a Cat, so was Malcolm Muggeridge.

Cat ladies spend a lot of time on their often extremely beautiful hair. Most grow it long, especially if it's dark. But

73

even should they flirt with a tight bubble perm, or get it cropped short, a Cat lady will always favour the long, sleek look in the end. Unless it is a perfectly cut suit, Cat women prefer frilly, flowing dresses to trousers, and they are very keen on lace and printed fabrics. Victorian modes will always look well.

Cat ladies usually have neat, often artistic, handwriting, whereas male Cats must work hard to produce anything more than a scribble. The journalist and author, Auberon Waugh's writing looks like a row of dislocated miniature noodles, and is so illegible that he has to train secretaries to decipher it. Considering his weekly output, his secretarial bills must be crippling.

One important point to remember when doing business with a Cat is that he is not one to change his mind. A deal is a deal and he'll hold you to the very last letter. But by the same token, a Cat who owes you money will pay you back to the last penny. He will remember every favour you do for him and pay you back in kind. And when a Cat comes to your home he'll only come empty handed if that is the way you enter his. Reject a Cat, and he'll disappear from your life for good.

Many Cat ladies prefer to live alone than marry for the sake of it, but without a man to fuss over she may become a little melancholic, spending more time than she needs at the Women's Institute or helping with the bring and buy stall at her local church. Lonely Cat women, indeed Cat women of all varieties, tend to cry easily, often at small, rather childish, things.

In spite of the charge that Tom cats are insatiable Romeos, the truth is that most male Cats are extremely faithful. Although we all know the Tom who kicks up such a din in the middle of the night, wandering from one garden to the next, most Cats are happiest getting in a good night's sleep.

The three phases of a Cat's life will not be very distinct, each marked only by the love of a comfortable, well-appointed home, agreeable conversation and a well-ordered, sometimes fastidious, routine.

The people of China refer to the Cat as a Rabbit, or Hare, believing it to bring long life. In *The Handbook of Chinese Horoscopes* Theodora Lau reminds us that at the Chinese mid autumn festival children carry paper lanterns decorated with the image of a hare to the hilltops. There they can see more clearly the shape that we call the 'Man in the Moon', but what they know as the 'Moon Hare'. In the West we talk of cats having nine lives, and it is not so different from the Eastern idea of cats being associated with longevity. My oldest cat is a fine example of a long-lived animal. She's nearly twenty and has hardly a grey whisker. Sir Robert Mayer once famous for his children's concerts, I noticed, was 105 when he died in 1985. And didn't Queen Victoria's life span practically an entire century? But Cats must earn their longevity. Unhappily they are the universal victims of prejudice and superstition, and for centuries the West has considered the cat as a powerful ingredient in the practice of witchcraft. Even today black cats are thought by many to bring bad luck. And allergies caused by cats are quite common. So the Cat should be warned and take care whom he walks with. For unless he chooses his companion well, like the cat in the famous Rudyard Kipling story, he would be better to walk alone.

CAT AS PARENT

Cats of both sexes make excellent parents. For a Cat, the welfare of his family comes before anything and so no child will suffer indifference or over-indulgence. Remember, the Cat's is a balanced world at best with neither too much nor too little. Both love and discipline will be given in moderation, and comfort offered in family-sized packs. Not given to

COMPATIBILITY OF CAT PARENT AND CHILD

Rat

Buffalo

Tiger

Cat

Dragon

Snake

Horse

Goat

Monkey

Rooster

Dog

Pig

much self-sacrifice, the parent Cats will nevertheless do everything to make certain that their Cat offspring are seen in the best clothes they can afford, and their children will be given every chance in life. The young Dog in particular will grow up less anxious with a Cat at the head of the family, leading him away from his tendency to dwell on his inadequacies – nearly always imagined or self-imposed. Cat fathers will be seduced by the beauty of their Snake daughter (as is the Dragon father). But realising this, she'll tend to be a rather clinging child. Poor dad.

Baby Pigs always demand praise for their earnest toil, and the Cat will not deny it. The praise, when it comes, will just be a little reserved. Goats and Cats are both social creatures to the tips of their respective hooves and claws, and mother Cat will do everything she can to make certain her daughter Goat knows the right places to be seen in – and the right people to be seen with. Conversely, the tiny Rat, so ambitious and hungry for experience will irritate the Cat parent. The child Buffalo poses an even greater threat to the Cat's love of stability. He will, extraordinary child that he is, actually scare his Cat mother or father, highlighting their timidity. Tiny Tigers make almost as much noise as fully grown Tigers. They also terrify Cat parents, but to mum and dad's relief quickly become their own masters and move out.

The child Horse, so graceful and erect, might well prove a threat to his father's own vanity. The young stallion, too, will probably leave home early. The headstrong Rooster needs a far less refined atmosphere to develop, and when she throws one of her tantrums, she is looking for the kind of positive response a Cat simply is unable to produce. Child Dragons spend their time planning and dreaming of great achievements. But Cats are not great achievers as a rule, and only artistic, gentle Dragon children will have a harmonious relationship with their Cat parent. Young Monkeys can get along with anyone, anytime, anywhere. But they must not forget that the Cat is short on levity around the home and stands for no nonsense. Peace is the motto, Chez-Cat, take it or leave it.

CAT IN BUSINESS

The cat has a natural flair for business and will make a name for himself so long as he avoids too much competition. His social ease and good manners make him an ideal partner, and are invaluable assets when dealing with people at any level.

COMPATIBILITY OF CAT IN BUSINESS
RELATIONSHIPS

Rat	💰💰💰💰
Buffalo	💰💰💰
Tiger	☐
Cat	💰💰💰💰💰
Dragon	💰💰💰💰
Snake	💰💰💰💰
Horse	💰💰💰💰
Goat	💰💰💰💰
Monkey	☐
Rooster	💰💰
Dog	💰💰💰
Pig	💰💰💰💰

But the Cat, for all his great skill in sniffing out a bargain, has not got an original mind. Neither has the Monkey, who relies heavily on his strong memory. Alas, businesses need investment and new ideas.

The Tiger is the perfect man for thinking up new schemes but he will quickly tire of the Cat's dithering and a business union between them is a bad idea. However, a good idea is a business formed by the chance-taking Rat and the Cat. Both will profit, so long as the Rat isn't expected to spend too long behind his desk.

The big-hearted Pig will press on happily with any task

that is placed before him, but although the Pig and Cat might make a fortune, their company will never hit the headlines. The equally hard-working Buffalo will make money with the Cat. But he will be too critical of the Cat's inability to solve problems in an original manner – the Buffalo's stock in trade. The Dog, so full of doubts, will become a moderate business-man with a Cat at his side. The Cat values the Dog's honest integrity, but they should give the high-risk City a miss and stick to manufacturing pine furniture.

The Rooster, if she is the type to save rather than squander her money, will do well in the company of a Cat. Both keep a clean set of books, but again, the business will not expand greatly and there is a chance one will blame the other. Goats adore hustle and bustle and will make the cat a perfect partner in a boutique or small intimate restaurant. Recommended, too, are partnerships between Snakes and Cats and Dragons and Cats. The imaginative Dragon and the wise Snake will both subtly lead the Cat away from his cautious stance, replacing it with a sense of urgency.

The industrious Horse will make good use of the Cat's methodical ways, and although the Horse will want to be boss, the Cat is too much of a diplomat to make an issue of it. Played right, the Cat and Horse team can sit back and watch their share prices zoom.

But for the most successful combination of all, a pair of Cats has few rivals. Although their business might start modestly, and their profits grow slowly, it will be rock solid and stay that way.

CAT IN LOVE

On the surface, a love affair between two Cats would seem to contain all the ingredients of a wonderful romance. But it is not in the Cat's nature to go overboard – he's such a poor swimmer. And for all the talk of randy Toms, most Cats prefer a night filled with fine wines and congenial company to crazed passion on a hot tin roof. If two Cats must fall madly in love, then it's probably better that they are gay cats.

The extrovert Rooster is actually a conservative romancer. She needs a great deal of attention to win her favours, and it is unlikely that the Cat will have the energy. The lady Cat might attract the Buffalo, who in turn will be fascinated by her soft warmth. She will delight in his complex heart, believing that she might awaken something deep within him. What she'll probably awaken is not a tough and sensuous lover, but someone who wants his socks washed. Poor Pussy. The lively Tiger will soon tire of the Cat's detached swoon-ings, and the passionate Rat will demand a far deeper response to his amorous advances. Both should steer well clear of feline flattery. The Dog, ever one to please, will always be a welcome visitor to a Cat's boudoir. He poses no threats and asks little of her. The chivalrous Pig can make a good romantic match for the Cat, as can the humorous Monkey. But all three have high opinions of themselves and there might well be a few squabbles over who was best at what.

The Horse, proud and vain, complements the Cat, as does the captivating Snake. But both are competitive lovers and the affair will not flourish. The flirtatious Goat sees the Cat as her soul mate, and so long as there are plenty of good times in the offing, she'll put up with his placid pace. However, it is the sexually out-going Dragon that makes the

COMPATIBILITY OF CAT IN LOVE

Rat	♥
Buffalo	♥ ♥ ♥
Tiger	♥
Cat	♥ ♥ ♥ ♥
Dragon	♥ ♥ ♥ ♥ ♥
Snake	♥ ♥ ♥
Horse	♥ ♥ ♥
Goat	♥ ♥ ♥ ♥
Monkey	♥ ♥ ♥
Rooster	
Dog	♥ ♥ ♥
Pig	♥ ♥ ♥

ideal match for a Cat. He'll tolerate any mood she creates in order to be near so much feline sensuousness. Well, almost any mood.

CAT IN MARRIAGE

A Cat greatly values marriage and devotes a lot of his or her time in making sure it works – the smoother the better. But Cats are almost always the passive partner, and are at their best when playing second fiddle. Their senses are refined and a Cat will make a perfect marriage with anyone sensitive enough to realise just how much refinement can be put to use. In this respect, the emotionally confident Dragon will be quick to take advantage of a wife who displays sensitive and artistic qualities. The eloquent Snake will also make a match for the Cat, bringing an air of mystery to the relationship.

The graceful Horse loves company, and to be seen in it with an equally graceful partner will create great harmony between them. As for two Cats, no marriage could be arranged better, either in earth or heaven. The Goat is a splendid social companion, and like the horse, shines alongside the Cat. But Goats, unlike Horses, are very prone to moods. The volatile Tiger will be happy enough sharing a home with a Cat, but he will find the long evenings listening to tasteful music and talking about art a trifle, shall we say, bland? The Monkey, ever one to keep his eye open for the next Big Thing, might, like the Tiger, grow impatient with the Cat's stop-at-home attitude and look elsewhere to open his bag of tricks.

The ambitious Rat will upset the Cat's methodical life – she'll never know what time to get his dinner ready, and the often tactless Rooster will only criticise the Cat's good manners. She'll find them dull. On the other side of the coin, the plain speaking Dog will find refuge in the Cat's refinement, although even he might grow weary of her sudden collapse in the face of hardship. Whereas the love affair of a Cat and Buffalo has only a marginal chance, a marriage

COMPATIBILITY OF CAT IN MARRIAGE

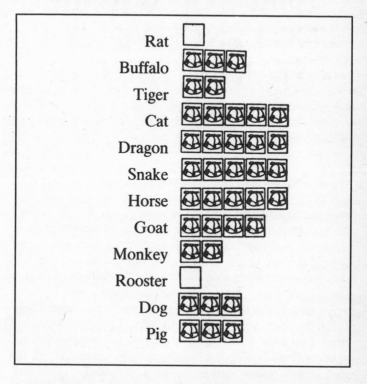

between them holds greater expectations. The lady Buffalo is a splendid mother, and Mr Cat adores his children. A lot depends on the ambitions of the Buffalo wife. The Pig, charitable and popular, tends to indulge himself a little too often and a little too much for the sensitive Cat. Here, the Padre's blessing might be the only one.

HOW YOU WILL BE INFLUENCED IN THE YEAR OF THE CAT

A YEAR FOR REFINEMENT

Unlike the Cat, who is in his glory, the opportunist Rat has a lean time in a year when so much emphasis is placed on a well-ordered, refined view of the world. Even though they are distant cousins, the ever volatile Tiger will be hampered by all the attention to tiny details. The Buffalo wants nothing more from life than to get on with his work, and the Cat will certainly do nothing to prevent him. Nor will the Cat give him much help. The dutiful Rooster knows how to work when necessity calls, but needs more push from behind than the Cat will ever be prepared to offer. Only the capricious Goat equals the Cat for enjoying a year full of opportunities at every level. Having been sitting on the sidelines for far too long, the Goat can start living life as she wants. You'll find her once again at all the most fashionable spots, full of gossip and flattering everyone who comes near her.

In the year of his so-called rival, the honest Dog has a better year than might be expected. The over-riding air of good manners will help him forget his personal problems and bring him out of himself. The Cat will soothe, not anger, an anxious Dog. The jovial Pig and popular Horse will both find their lives enriched under the Cat's influence, perhaps by the addition of a member to the family or in moving to a more desirable house. But Cats do not, as a rule, work as hard as either the Pig or the Horse, so there might well be problems at the office.

84

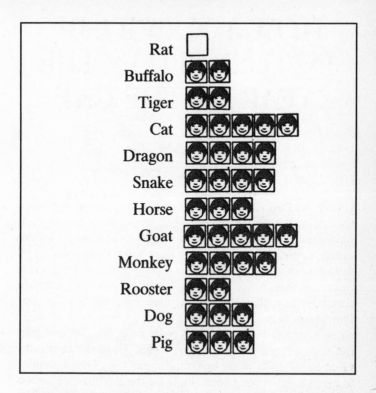

The adaptable Dragon shines in any company, and along with the artful Monkey will use the tranquillity as a backdrop for their fireworks and tricks. It's a good year for Monkey and Dragon to force their ideas forward. The serene Snake will also make the most of any peace and quiet that's going around, and will emerge from beneath her stone to assert her charm. She has had bad years under the Tiger and Buffalo and will make the most of the Cat's sensitivity. For financial and romantic rewards, few will be better off than the Snake in the Year of the Cat.

FAMOUS CATS

Arts

Fra Angelico
Alan Ayckbourn
Cecil Beaton
Ingrid Bergman
Lord Clark
Johnny Dankworth
Margaret Drabble
Bob Fosse
James Galway
Michael Gambon
Stan Getz
Germaine Greer
Barbara Hepworth
Billy Holiday
Hugh Johnson
Paul Klee
Patrick Lichfield
Arthur Miller
George Orwell
John Piper
Joshua Reynolds
Ken Russell
Elizabeth Schwarzkopf
Kenneth Tynan
Auberon Waugh
Julian Lloyd Webber

Sports

John Barnes
John Conteh
Kenny Dalglish
Eddie 'The Eagle' Edwards
Rachael Hayhoe Flint
Evel Knievel
Stanley Matthews
Alan Minter
Jack Nicklaus
Sheila Scott
Jackie Stewart

Industry/Politics

Nancy Astor
Stanley Baldwin
Lord Beaverbrook
Leon Brittan
Fidel Castro
John Cole
Marie Curie
Moshe Dayan
Albert Einstein
John Profumo
Rommel
Stalin
Terry Waite
Trotsky

Royals

Prince Albert
Queen Victoria
Henry III
Henry V

Show Biz

Pamela Armstrong

Melvyn Bragg
John Cleese
Ken Dodd
Paul Eddington
W C Fields
David Frost
Sandy Gaul
Bob Hope
John Hurt
Penelope Keith
Nanette Newman
Selina Scott

Lena Zavaroni

Pop
Ginger Baker
Tony Hatch
John Peel
Edith Piaf
Neil Sedaka
Frank Sinatra
Dusty Springfield
Sting

THE DRAGON

龍

1904	February 16th to February 3rd	1905
1916	February 3rd to January 22nd	1917
1928	January 23rd to February 9th	1929
1940	February 8th to January 26th	1941
1952	January 27th to February 13th	1953
1964	February 13th to February 1st	1965
1976	January 31st to February 17th	1977
1988	February 17th to February 5th	1989

'The Dragon's eyes are precious stones, and bright as fire, in which there is affirmed to be much virtue against many diseases.'

Topsell

THE YEAR OF THE DRAGON

From the first spectacular day, the year of the Dragon announces itself as being one of dazzling exuberance. In China, New Year is marked by an exotic paper and tinsel replica of the Dragon being paraded through the streets. To symbolise the passing of one year and the birth of a new, the Dragon is ritualistically burnt.

The new year will often begin with news of a major or extraordinary event: in the early days of 1928, Corinth was destroyed by an earthquake; in February 1952, King George VI died and in January 1976, the world's first supersonic passenger aircraft went into service. Perhaps *Dragon* would have been a better name than *Concorde*? However, in the Year of the Dragon, one thing is absolutely certain; any event will be larger than life and as colourful and noisy as a firework display.

The Chinese value the Dragon above all others because he brings good fortune in matters of money. In 1964 the Beatles were the first artists in history to sell 1,000,000 copies of a record before it was released. But the Dragon brings luck to everyone. Batsmen will score centuries, politicians will win elections with huge majorities, and as for the Big Love Affair, Cupid will be rushed off his tiny winged feet. It is a time to throw caution to the wind, lose our scepticism, and to trust the golden leader of the carnival parade. But whether you choose to join in, or watch from the sidelines, the year will be a non-stop carousel. Opportunities will unfold with the ease of a summer rose; every door will be wide open. But don't delay, the year is only twelve months, and comes but once in twelve. Like the streets in the tale of Dick Whittington, the ground beneath our feet is paved with gold. All we have to do is pick it up, and remember that the shining metal in our grasp just has to be gold, and not a brilliant but worthless imitation. The end of the year will be a repeat of the beginning. In October 1976 the biggest coalfield in the world was opened in Selby, Yorks. On December 29th, 1940, London was ablaze from Hitler's incendiary bombs. Guildhall and no less than eight of Wren's Churches were razed to the ground. There will be sparks and flames in the final hours of the Dragon's year. But as the flames die and the ashes cool there is the promise that the Dragon will once again return to lead life's carnival parade.

THE DRAGAON PERSONALITY

'Stop what you are doing – at once! The Dragon is about to grace you with his divine presence.'

For the People of China, and her immediate neighbours, the Dragon is a national emblem, a symbol of power and strength. He is the splendid and magnificent leader of the carnival who brings with him the Four Great Blessings of the

91

East; long life, virtue, harmony and wealth. If there is a Dragon in your home, then one, if not all of these benedictions will be yours.

There is no doubt when you meet a Dragon that you are in the company of the world's supreme showman. He is a larger than life character, boastful, arrogant and precocious in the extreme. And he is as stimulating and exciting as the Dragon conjured up from the brightly coloured paper, tinsel and gold paint that the Chinese parade through the streets each New Year.

Gifted beyond measure, the Chinese are in a sense in awe of their own creation, and they are right to be. What gifts the Dragon has! From oracle to overlord, from pop star to millionaire, the Dragon can turn his dexterous hand to whatever he chooses. And by dint of his amazing self-reliance and resourcefulness, turn the object of his choice, and himself, into a resounding success. It is as if the Dragon says to himself not, 'I think, therefore I am', but, 'I am, therefore anything I think I'll do – so don't stand in my way'.

If you were born in the year of the Dragon you share it with Jesus Christ (assuming he was born when the records say), Yehudi Menuhin, Shirley Temple, Sigmund Freud, George Bernard Shaw, Florence Nightingale, Geoffrey Boycott, Marlene Dietrich, Barbara Cartland, Paul Getty, Bing Crosby, Pele and Cliff Richard. But whether the Dragon becomes a globe trotting mega-star or stay-at-home mega-mum, the Dragon will inspire in us all that most valuable and rare of gifts – the power to believe in ourselves.

The ace up the Dragon's sleeve is nothing more or less than an absolute self-belief, which by virtue of his extraordinary willpower, he manages to pass on to others. Put another way, the intensity of his belief in *himself* helps us to believe in *ourselves*. Some Dragons, like Yehudi Menuhin, may do it with the sweet and tender playing of a violin. Others, as in the case of Sigmund Freud, may choose the complex path of psychoanalysis. But whatever his method, in the end it is the sheer weight of purpose that the Dragon brings to his every action that finally wins our admiration, and adulation. But it is not all plain sailing living close, or working next to a Dragon of either sex. The Dragon has an almost fanatical desire for perfection which makes him utterly intolerant of anyone who does not give 101%, twenty-five hours a day. *He* gives it, why can't you? I have a story which illustrates to a tee the Dragon's insistence for absolute commitment:

Not long ago my favourite aunt, an elderly woman, was taken to hospital, suffering as many old people do from a need for a little extra care and attention. The day I went to pay her my first visit was no different from usual. I had drawn my cartoon for *The Times*, and since the subject was not controversial, I expected no last minute problems (if events change suddenly, a topical cartoonist must be prepared to re-do his cartoon). I arrived at the hospital for the afternoon visit and was helping Aunt Mary get through a box of chocolates when a young nurse tapped me on the shoulder. 'There's a phone call for you,' she said. 'Sounds urgent.' I rushed to the phone and discovered that my house had not burned down, been broken into, or my wife held hostage by some crazed terrorist. It was, in fact, a colleague from *The Times*, who had tracked me down to my aunt's bedside, only to tell me that he'd very much like me to make a few minor alterations to my drawing – just to make it absolutely right. Exasperated, I explained that I had only just arrived, but he would have none of it. Bidding my bemused aunt farewell, I drove like a loony through the rush hour, the ice and rain – it was Christmas time – and did a second drawing which reached *The Times* just before the presses began to roll. As a Dragon, I understood his demands, I only hope my Aunt Mary did.

There is an even more extreme example of the Dragon's obsessive need for perfection to be found in the case of the bestselling author, Jeffrey Archer. His first novel, published almost a decade ago, earned Archer well over a million pounds. Following *Not a Penny More, Not a Penny Less*,

Archer has gone on to write books that have netted him ten times that sum. Most authors in Archer's position would simply retire to a tax-free haven and forget about books. They certainly would not give much thought to a novel that they wrote ten years previously. But not Archer. He actually *re-wrote* chunks of *Not a Penny More* ... and forced the publishers to bring it out again in a new edition. As a stylist, Archer might not be a Tolstoy or a Proust, but he is, as his American publishers might say, 'one hell of a perfectionist'.

In the West our understanding of the Dragon has been clouded by the fact that in our myths we represent him as an evil force. Dragons are slain, usually by characters with names like Perseus, Cadmus and Marduk – heroes every one of them. They enter the Dragon's cave, chop off his head and rescue the lovely maiden whom the Dragon was about to either seduce or eat for supper, or both. The most famous Dragon slayer is the maiden's friend and saviour, Saint George. Throughout the Middle Ages no one had a good word to say for the Dragon, but there was one objective critic. Bartholomew, writing in the 13th century observed, 'Dragons dwell sometime in the sea and lurk sometime in caves and dens and sleep but seldom, but wake all night.' No mention of maiden snatching there.

However, it must be admitted that there is more than a grain of truth in the charge that the Dragon is a seductive creature. No one has more admirers than the Dragon, and those who fall in love with him will do so completely and helplessly. And yet the Dragon will rarely love deeply himself. When he does, though, you will know it as clearly as you know the touch of burning coals. As his lover, you will be the single object of his passionate vitality, and his genius for self-expression will centre on you and you alone. When declaring his love, the Dragon has no peers. If you run from the Dragon, he will not chase you – he's not like the Snake. And if you should cool towards him he won't care – that's why he is so hard to walk out on. If it is the Dragon's ardour that cools, he won't suddenly desert you. He is, for all his brashness and swagger, a sentimental soul who cherishes his friendships forever. Nevertheless, sexuality lies at the very heart of a Dragon, and expressing himself sexually is fundamental to his love of freedom. In the Dragon's soul, the sexual act is the key which unlocks the door of his scale-covered skin, releasing him to float freely wherever he chooses. For the most part, his lovers are no more than instruments to bring about his great escape.

The Dragon is a poor gossip monger and will always get his facts wrong. He hates to be a prisoner – trap a Dragon, or put him in jail, and you will condemn him to madness. And he is no hypocrite; wound his pride and he'll never forgive you. No one is more venomous when his pride has been injured, or his good intentions sneered at. The Dragon's pride is by far his most recognisable feature, and seems to pervade his every action. In a game of chess it is the Dragon who always insists that his move is the right one, doing a crossword, his word is the one that fits – and it so often is. But try to go one better and you'll have a fight on your hands. Ridicule his errors, and in a matter of a second you will have made an enemy for life. The bigger the dent you make in his pride, the longer he will harbour a grudge. And the raging Dragon knows about revenge, so lock up your daughters, keep tabs on your wife and hide the silver. But don't confuse the Dragon's innate bad temper and irritability with vengeance. They are quite different. And if the Dragon is most irritable with those he loves, behaving like an enraged bull over trivial, silly little incidents, he has the patience of Job when dealing with a loved one's problems – however small. You can treat a Dragon as cruelly as you like, and providing he genuinely loves you, he'll take it all. And he'll forgive you.

The Dragon has one particular disadvantage, unlike the Buffalo – that he cannot cope with even the slightest routine. A rut is another prison sentence, and high office often calls for much routine work. What is more, the Dragon is no diplomat. He says what he thinks, often without considering either the truth of what he says, or the hurt it may cause.

Sir Harold Wilson is a Dragon, and by all accounts was a better public speaker and debater than administrator. He was fortunate to have the perfect partner at his side, not his wife, but the Monkey, Lady Falkender. In her book, *Inside No 10*, Wilson's personal and private secretary paints a picture of her boss doing little more than making the odd, often contradictory speech, while she drew up the resignation honours list on lavender paper. But whatever the truth, as Monkey and Dragon, they made a powerful partnership regardless of what their opponents (and there were many) did or said.

Another of the Dragon's bad traits is his impulsiveness. Dragons simply cannot bear to wait, viewing hanging about as another form of imprisonment. As a result they rush at everything full tilt, very often without judging the worth of what they're doing.

Although the Dragon is a predominantly male sign, the female of the species shares a great many characteristics. She dresses simply and for ease of movement rather than for effect. Dragon ladies seldom disguise themselves with too much make-up and fancy hair styles. Again, it's their self-belief that they are selling the world, not a face-pack or a bottle of hair dye. And clothes are another way in which Dragons of both sexes express their need for freedom. Dragon men favour casual shoes and soft jumpers instead of three-piece suits. (Don't be surprised if a Dragon turns up to a swanky dinner party dressed in a T-shirt and training shoes.) Dragon ladies wear neat but simple outfits, and both male and female tend to decide on a style and stick to it. Uncertainty is yet another form of restriction, so you won't find a Dragon spending hours in front of the mirror. And a Dragon will avoid following fashion at all costs. The Dragon creates fashions, others follow him.

Dragon ladies do not as a rule make the ideal mother or wife. They often marry too young and outgrow their spouse; marry late and remain childless; or they simply don't bother to get married at all. What one often finds is a Dragon lady with two children living on her own, an entourage of ardent admirers and an ex-husband with a drink problem who is behind with his alimony.

Dragons have huge appetites, and unless they are on some cranky diet, will eat anything that's put in front of them. Despite this, Dragons frequently suffer ill health. Perhaps because of the nights spent alone in dank, dark caves in olden times, Dragons do not sleep well and experience minor problems with their respiratory system – catarrh, sinusitis, asthma and so on. Because of this tendency, Dragons take a great deal of care when looking after themselves, almost to a point of obsession. But when a Dragon is really sick, they recover quickly and with no after effects. However, a Dragon without a sense of purpose, or one who has lost his self-belief, will rapidly become fat, lazy and bitter. Such Dragons are to be avoided!

Dragons, for all their impetuosity and arrogance, give their time and money generously, and their advice is always worth taking. He gives without cost or expectation of reward or repayment, whether it's his passion or his life's savings. It is as if the Dragon forgets his gift. After all, isn't hoping for a favour returned, yet another form of life behind bars?

The Dragon's three phases of life will be varied. He will have a difficult childhood; misunderstood by parents, teachers and schoolfriends alike. His need for perfection will daunt those around him and alienate them. His middle life will be mixed, and though he will make a lot of money, he will make as many enemies as friends. But from his late forties through to his old, old age, the Dragon will be King. The Chinese sign for the Dragon is luck. But with the Dragon's gifts, luck is just about the last thing he needs.

DRAGON AS PARENT

Dragon men do not generally make ideal fathers. A more detached and less ebullient figure is required at the head of a family. However, when a Dragon parent gives his all to a child, there will be no one more caring.

Rooster children, with their strong moral sense and fierce independence will draw the very best from a Dragon parent,

COMPATIBILITY OF DRAGON PARENT AND CHILD

Rat	😊😊😊😊
Buffalo	😊
Tiger	😊😊😊😊
Cat	😊😊
Dragon	😊😊😊😊😊
Snake	😊😊😊😊😊
Horse	😊😊😊
Goat	😊😊😊
Monkey	😊😊😊😊
Rooster	😊😊😊😊😊
Dog	☐
Pig	😊😊😊

and the Snake child's beauty and wisdom will win her every attention. The Dragon child, so often completely self-assured, will demand nothing but food and shelter. Seeing himself mirrored will fire the Dragon's pride. And he will be so pleased his son or daughter lets him get on with his own tightly packed life. The Rat will ask much, as in all things, but the Dragon is such a sucker for charm; and the baby Monkey, all big eyes and cuddly will certainly get her own way. The elegant and witty Horse daughter will make the Dragon father proud fit to burst, but in the end, Horses are only interested in themselves and quick to sever family ties. Poor Daddy Dragon.

The Goat is very often an artistic child, which pleases the Dragon, but she is a child of so many moods, and if she must use her charm, she must use it sparingly. The Cat displays its fastidious nature from an early age, but it is not the same as the perfection that the Dragon seeks. And with the little Kitten there are always so many tears. But the young Tiger's lively mind will win over her Dragon parent, who will do everything to ensure their child's ideas are put into practice.

The hard-working, honest child Pig might find his efforts overlooked unless he speaks up for himself – and he might well. The Dragon will always give encouragement when asked. But the solitary Buffalo child will be left to fend for himself – which is perhaps the best thing. As for the Dog – such an anxious Puppy – his self-doubts will send Ma and Pa Dragon clean through the roof.

DRAGON IN BUSINESS

The Dragon's ace up his sleeve is nothing more or less than his ability to believe utterly in himself. In the world of commerce, as in every other, it is a most valuable asset.

COMPATIBILITY OF DRAGON IN BUSINESS RELATIONSHIPS

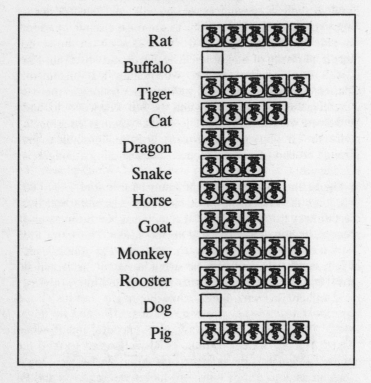

Rat	🐉🐉🐉🐉🐉
Buffalo	☐
Tiger	🐉🐉🐉🐉🐉
Cat	🐉🐉🐉🐉
Dragon	🐉🐉
Snake	🐉🐉🐉
Horse	🐉🐉🐉🐉
Goat	🐉🐉🐉
Monkey	🐉🐉🐉🐉🐉
Rooster	🐉🐉🐉🐉🐉
Dog	☐
Pig	🐉🐉🐉🐉🐉

Although he makes his power freely available to all, it does not suit everyone. Honest creature that he is, the Dog will be overshadowed, and spend his time criticising the Dragon. The authoritative Buffalo likes to be his own boss, and shares the Dog's mistrust in the Dragon's razzle-dazzle approach to money-making. If the Goat can harness her artistry to the Dragon's strength they will go far; singer and songwriter perhaps? The intelligent and industrious Horse can also make a profitable partnership with the Dragon, but the Horse can only put up with so much professional competition. And the Dragon does make such a noise and is so overbearing.

In the case of two Dragons together everything is fine until one asks the other 'who's boss?' But for the Rooster, 'who's boss?' is the last question he or she will ask. The Rooster is happy to leave the big decisions to someone else, and just get on with the job in hand. And with a Dragon on the scene there'll be plenty of honest toil. The clever and observant Rat is well liked by the Dragon, who values his judgement. Chancer and magician can do well together so long as there is a creative angle. Both the Pig and the Monkey will help, and be helped by, the Dragon. The Monkey brings cunning to realise the Dragon's grandiose plans, and the Pig is able to get through no end of routine chores – the one thing a Dragon is hopeless at.

The Snake has just the right instinct for a good deal and will guide the Dragon towards making the right choice. But the partners had better be of the same sex, or business and pleasure might get mixed a little too often. The impulsive Tiger will be given his head by the Dragon, and praised even in failure. The Cat will also be swept along by the Dragon's gusto, but there is a danger that the Cat's less than original mind will conflict with one so adventurous.

DRAGON IN LOVE

The Dragon sees himself as a grand seducer, and both male and female Dragons imagine the world is their proverbial oyster. But not everyone has the same high opinion of the Dragon as he has of himself! Ms Dragon for one is more interested in herself and has her own scene to worry about. Two Dragons in love is rare, but can be a wonderful thing. And a Dragon's love is not highly recommended for the lady Dog, however amorous she might feel in the Dragon's company. She can easily see through the Dragon's smooth talk, and although she wants to show her devotion will only

COMPATIBILITY OF DRAGON IN LOVE

Rat	♥♥♥♥
Buffalo	♥♥
Tiger	♥♥♥♥
Cat	♥♥♥♥♥
Dragon	□
Snake	♥♥♥♥♥
Horse	♥♥♥♥♥
Goat	♥♥♥♥
Monkey	♥♥♥♥♥
Rooster	♥♥
Dog	□
Pig	♥♥

end up by criticising him. Nothing alienates a Dragon more quickly than criticism.

The Lady Buffalo presents a considerable challenge for the Dragon, and like the Dog, might easily fall for him against her better judgement. But when the Buffalo lady falls in love, she falls hard, and she must remember that her charm stock has its limits where the Dragon is concerned. The Goat, on the other hand, has charm by the yard, and it's the kind Dragons go for. But Dragons want a heck of a lot more than just a coy smile now and then, and lady Goats would do well to bear this in mind when packing their bags for that weekend in a quiet hotel.

It's not a big night out for the Rooster either. Yes, the Dragon can take another show-off like himself, but the Rooster has such a virtuous streak and is a total stranger to the Karma Sutra. Passion, however, is in no short supply when the Rat is around. But it's worth pointing out that the Rat is a sexual athlete, and the Dragon a sexual artist. The Tiger, like the Rat, is not scared off by raw emotion, and alongside the sensuous Cat makes a perfect love match with the Dragon. Big Cat or small Cat, how the Dragon likes to feel her purring with contentment by his side.

The Horse is born under the twin sign of elegance and ardour, and there isn't a male Dragon anywhere who can resist a lady Horse. An affair between them probably won't last, but the memories . . . ah!

The artful Monkey knows about love and is dextrous in her display. The Snake can also take the Dragon's heart. She is, after all, a reptile like the dragon, but without wings. The Pig is amorous enough in her own right, but the Dragon is in a different league. Nevertheless, she has a soft spot for the Dragon and will not be put off by his fiery style.

DRAGON IN MARRIAGE

Anyone thinking of putting money on a marriage lasting should think twice if there's a Dragon involved. The upright and candid Rooster, though, knows just how to handle the Dragon's Big Shot ways, and with some give and take on both sides should reach a harmonious resolution. The Monkey, with her artful and clever manner will act as a useful foil for the Dragon. Both are ambitious and will help each other.

The Dragon makes an excellent marriage partner with the tender-hearted Rat, who, in return for a full larder, will give all she is asked. The placid Cat will complement the Dragon

COMPATIBILITY OF DRAGON IN MARRIAGE

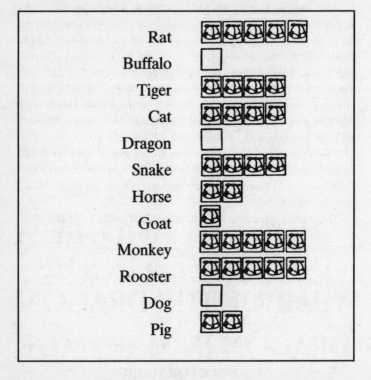

Rat

Buffalo

Tiger

Cat

Dragon

Snake

Horse

Goat

Monkey

Rooster

Dog

Pig

and not wish to share the glory she has helped to bring about. The Tiger, on the other hand, does not take over-kindly to being left in the shadows. But the Dragon will not mind if she is by his side when the Oscars are dished out.

But the same cannot be said for the innocent Pig. She has too high an opinion of her worth, merited for sure, but not always by the self-occupied Dragon.

The bewitching Snake, though wise and deeply sensual, has the habit of clinging in a crisis – something Dragons do not care for. But when she flashes her eyes ... ! Far from clinging, the capricious Goat actually needs tethering, and the Dragon is far too important to spend his time fastening bits of rope round the Goat's neck.

The female Horse, so witty, pert and beautiful will make too much fun of the Dragon's bragging. She will laugh in his face. And the lady Dog will do nothing but find faults, and repeat them endlessly. Foolish Dog. As for a pair of Dragons marrying, it will either be a raving success or more likely, the biggest disaster of all time. Safer not to try. The same is true for a Buffalo and Dragon. In the home, as in public life, Dragon and Buffalo vie for the centre of the stage. Both are natural leaders, and yet have no understanding of each other. No matter how favourable the circumstances, nothing will keep these two formidable animals from tearing each other apart.

HOW YOU WILL BE INFLUENCED IN THE YEAR OF THE DRAGON

A YEAR FOR MAGIC

Everything a Dragon touches becomes gold in his year, and there are few who do not benefit from the carnival leader's largesse. It's a bumper year for the Rooster, who can at last let her hair down and turn some of her daydreams into hard cash. The Snake, so wise and sensible will dart from her hiding place and make the most of her clever schemes. The Rat, ever the opportunist, along with the artful Monkey, will find the magic of the Dragon's year works equally well for them both. The Rat will discover the grain sacks bursting and the Monkey will swing from branches groaning with fat ripe fruit. If you invest with a Rat, this is the year for the big pay out.

105

Rat
Buffalo
Tiger
Cat
Dragon
Snake
Horse
Goat
Monkey
Rooster
Dog
Pig

The Tiger will for once have all his endless ideas turned into reality; a good year for a Tiger to write a book, compose a concerto or get married and start a family. The vain and independent Horse will take only what he wants before ducking out of the limelight – it's all a bit too frantic. As for the coquettish Goat, she certainly won't care for all that attention being paid to someone else, especially someone as large and so full of lustre as the Dragon. But she'll hang around long enough for some of the gold dust to rub off on her.

The timid Cat will find his methodical world in shreds, and the Dragon has no time to sit around listening to small talk. Not a good year for Buffaloes, either – stuck in their fields day after day, heads down, work ... work ... work ... Not for them the clashing of cymbals and dancing in the street. The Pig will find work to do, but there'll be no great attention paid to him for his efforts. No fun either for the anxious Dog, even though the Dragon wants so much to give him a helping hand.

FAMOUS DRAGONS

Arts
Count Basie
Sarah Bernhardt
Roald Dahl
Salvador Dali
Placido Domingo
John Gielgud
Giles
Graham Greene
Stanley Kubrick
Bernard Levin
Yehudi Menuhin
Glenn Miller
Stockhausen

Sports
Geoff Boycott
Marco Van Basten
Chris Brasher
David Broom
Jimmy Connors
Pat Eddery
Jimmy Greaves
Jimmy Hill
Len Hutton
Dennis Law
John Parrott

Pele
Nelson Piquet
Mary Rand
Sir Gordon Richards
Viv Richards
Alan Wells

Industry/Politics
Paul Getty
Che Guevera
Edward Heath
Martin Luther King
Clive Sinclair
Cyril Smith
Harold Wilson

Royals
Lady Sarah Armstrong Jones
Prince Edward
Ex-King Constantine of Greece
Lady Helen Windsor

Show Biz
Jeffrey Archer
Bugs Bunny
Sir Alistair Burnet
Barbara Cartland

Julie Christie
Kirk Douglas
Faye Dunaway
Bob Holness
Gloria Hunniford
David Icke
Bonnie Langford
Elaine Paige
Nicholas Parsons
Gregory Peck
Esther Rantzen
Zandra Rhodes
Alexei Sayle
Mel Smith
Patrick Swayze
Shirley Temple

Pop
Joan Baez
Bing Crosby
Chris Cross
Stewart Copeland
Val Doonican
Adam Faith
Tom Jones
John Lennon
Manfred Mann
Cliff Richard
The Righteous Brothers
Kevin Rowland
Phil Spector
Dave Stewart
Ringo Starr

THE SNAKE

蛇

1905	February 4th to January 24th	1906
1917	January 23rd to February 10th	1918
1929	February 10th to January 29th	1930
1941	January 27th to February 14th	1942
1953	February 14th to February 2nd	1954
1965	February 2nd to January 20th	1966
1977	February 18th to February 6th	1978
1989	February 6th to January 26th	1990

The earth doth like a Snake renew
Her winter weeds outworn:
Heaven smiles, and faiths and empires gleam,
Like wrecks of a dissolving dream.

Shelley

THE YEAR OF THE SNAKE

At the beginning at least, the year of the Snake will very largely depend on how the Dragon left the preceding year. If all the grandiose schemes hatched up by the Dragon end up as triumphs, then the Snake's year will automatically begin on a high note. If not, then the early months will be uncertain and possibly dangerous. In March 1917 the Russian revolution took place, and the same month, a day later in fact, 1941, USA declared war on Germany. But as the year of the Snake gathers momentum under its own very definite influence, it will swiftly become apparent that its characteristics are in marked contrast with the year it succeeded. Gone are the crackerjacks and displays of swagger, their places taken by a more subtle, sometimes even mysterious, mood.

The Snake's year, if allowed to follow its own lights, will progress much in the way the Snake itself moves – economically and deliberately. The Snake travels by feeling, using its senses. In 1953, Edmund Hillary and Sherpa Tenzing inched their way to reach the summit of Mount Everest, the first men in history to make the climb. But do not be deceived. Under the surface there is deep thought going on; intuition is the foundation stone on which great changes are being made. And because they result from such a profound source, whatever changes occur will remain so forever.

Although the Snake's year will see great steps taken towards world peace and reconciliation, they will be made cautiously. The hallmark of the Snake is wisdom, and all movements will be governed by much wise manoeuvring.

There will be no flash displays of courage and bravado. No one will be told to work day and night, and those who do will be left to slog on unhindered. In fact, the Snake's year can be a boom for all those who are ambitious, either to attain high office, or bank large sums of money. In 1965 Lyndon B Johnson was inaugurated the thirty-sixth president of the United States.

There will be much demand for the arts, and painters, poets and musicians. Pop singers with more in the way of good looks than good melodies will climb to the top of the charts. The Snake's year is definitely one for beautiful people, and if you fancy your chances as a model or Miss World, this is the time to get into your two-piece and find yourself a tan.

It is a splendid year for unearthing buried treasure, and it's possible that gold, oil and commodities of all shapes and sizes will go through the roof pricewise. Either that, or they will crash through the floor. The American slump and Wall Street's collapse happened in 1929. Too bad that there is no way of knowing. There will also be many scientific discoveries made in the year of the Snake, and major advances in the field of medicine.

Above all, it is a time to think about romance, though not marriage or starting a family. If you find that love comes your way in the Snake's year, grasp it with both hands; it will be an affair you will neither regret, nor forget. If you feel like a little discreet gossip, go ahead, but if you gamble, do it another year. This is not the time to throw your hard-earned savings on a property speculator's promises. Resist planning too far ahead, think for a moment before you act, and before you know it, love and lucre will just fall into your lap.

THE SNAKE PERSONALITY

'Tread silently, sit comfortably and listen carefully. The Snake is wise, and the world holds so many mysteries.'

Through the eyes of the western world, the Snake is seen as the infamous serpent who was the key figure in the fall of man. In the Garden of Eden, the wicked snake offered dear old Eve the forbidden fruit and got her and Adam cast out and damned. The Bible story goes on to tell us how God then cursed the serpent above all creatures, which was rough justice when you come to realise that it was God who made the fruit and not the serpent. And let's face it, where would we be today if Adam and Eve were still hanging around Paradise? Because of this interesting but mythical story, snakes are viewed by most Westerners as cunning and untrustworthy. Nothing, but nothing is further from the truth. Call someone a 'snake' in the West and it is taken as an out and out insult. 'You snake in the grass!' Utter damnation! But tell the Chinaman in the street, or Chinalady for that matter, that he or she is a snake, and watch as their eyes light up with a mixture of satisfaction, gratitude and pleasure. You can pay the people of the East no greater compliment.

Deeply feminine, the Snake herself is born under the sign of wisdom, and as such is respected throughout the Eastern world. She is believed to bring good fortune in matters of

114

love and wealth, and if there is a Snake in the family, the Chinese believe that their children will make good marriages and that the rice fields will grow rich and fertile. What is more, Snakes are extremely beautiful, the Snake woman particularly so. Both Princess Grace of Monaco and Greta Garbo were Snakes, as is Jackie Onassis. Male Snakes too, are not without their good looks as the late president of the United States, John F Kennedy testified. Liberace is also a fully paid up member of the serpentine community, and no one would argue about *his* good looks!

Because the Snake is endowed with both wisdom and beauty in equally large proportions, it is worth stating at the beginning just exactly what kind of wisdom and beauty we are talking about. As far as lady Snakes are concerned, their beauty is not necessarily the sort Hollywood treats us to. When examined inch by inch we may discover that the lady Snake is just a shade too thin, a trifle wide across the hips, or her nose could do with being just a fraction shorter. But make no mistake, whatever the 'blemish', the Snake lady's proportions will be absolutely perfect, and her appearance will be both stunning and bewitching. Whatever her shape, the Snake lady will have small and delicate hands, beautiful skin and beguiling eyes. Clear and bright, they will radiate her deep sensuality, peering deeply into the soul of everyone she meets. Whether she knows it or not – there is much innocence contained within the Snake's exotic skin – she is what can only be described as the *femme fatale*. She's the original sex-siren, the widow that goes into the witness box to tell of her late husband's death, dressed in black silk stockings and a veiled hat. Snake ladies go in for clothes that emphasise their store of hidden secrets. They wear skirts with slit sides and trousers that fit tighter than an extra layer of skin.

Above all, Snake ladies adore accessories of every shape and size. But you won't find her walking out with a cheap string of imitation pearls around her soft, silky neck; they'll be the real thing, and probably cost her a year's salary. Show me a woman wearing a forty-eight carat diamond on her

115

finger and real mother of pearl, and I'll show you a Snake. But if all these baubles, bangles and flashing thighs take your fancy, take a tip from the Chinese. They'll tell you, 'beware'. Once the Snake has made you the object of her passion she will never let you go; never, never, never. Like the famed boa constrictor, she will coil herself around you and squeeze until you feel as if the very last breath is about to leave your body. When we talk about being possessive, the Snake has no equal.

As an example of the Snake's tenacity to cling to the object of their desire come hell or high water, there is a morbid story about two pythons in an Australian zoo. Placed in the same cage before feeding time, both snakes remained in different corners sizing each other up, never having set eyes on each other before. Eventually they were fed, in this case a rabbit. Very cautiously, both pythons slithered towards their prey and one got his jaws round the rabbit's head, while the other attacked its rear. Slowly and deliberately both snakes began their grisly task of devouring the rabbit whole. Inch by inch they began swallowing until both pythons came nose to nose in the rabbit's middle. With grim determination they held fast to what they had already devoured, their hard black eyes no more than a few centimetres apart. As the keeper who put the snakes together stood helplessly looking on, the pythons simply held fast. Neither budged for what must have seemed an eternity. But who would relent? Who would finally back off and admit defeat? The story has a most terrible climax. The slightly larger of the two pythons continued to devour the rabbit and didn't stop when he came to the head of the other python. It took him an hour but he ate his cell mate and the rabbit. And his cell mate would rather be eaten than let go! In his report, the keeper noted that the surviving python was off-colour for over a month, and never fully recovered from his act of cannibalism.

While on the subject of the actual creature who influences all those born in her year, it is not irrelevant to note briefly that there are 25,000 species of snakes. They range from the tiny bootlace snake to the giant forty-foot anaconda, who is capable of devouring a horse whole. It is no wonder, therefore, that those born in the year of the Snake so often suffer from stomach complaints. Like her distant cousin, the Dragon, the Snake has extremely fragile health, and her nerve system is the most delicate in creation. It is, perhaps, why the Snake has such a powerful intuition. After all, the nerve system has its centre in the region of the stomach, and any shock immediately affects the stomach.

In addition to his power to bewitch and possess, it has to be said that the Snake has, to put it charitably, an individual interpretation of morality. And however staid and straight the Snake might become in his later years, there isn't a Snake anywhere who hasn't enjoyed a string of affairs both inside and out of marriage. But it would be pointless reprimanding a Snake for her shallow morals, she just doesn't see it your way. Like the Dragon, the Snake uses her sexuality as part of her life force, as an act of self-discovery. And it is frequently the case that the Snake's love-making is very selfish. It is imperative, therefore, that you never cross a Snake in love. If a Snake finds that she has been two-timed she will act instantly. Hide and she will seek you out. Lie and she will find you out. Play her for a fool and the Snake will become treacherous. And do not forget that the Snake's memory is long, and no one's vengeance runs deeper. The Snake is believed to have cold blood running through her delicate veins. If that's what you believe, forget it. Her blood steams through.

The Snake's wisdom is similar to her possessiveness, becoming apparent the moment she is tested. But because her sagacity comes from such a deep and mysterious centre, the Snake has very little control over it. Very often the Snake will say something without the slightest idea of why she has said it, or indeed know what she has meant. It is as if she is guided by some inner spirit. Whatever the source of the Snake's often uncanny insights, there can be no doubt that it plays an important role in her leanings towards spiritual and sometimes supernatural worlds. Snakes are capable of embracing a wide variety of philosophical and religious thought, adapting easily to the passive and meditative nature of religious life. Whether it is the latest craze in Zen Buddhism, or some cranky religion based on the sightings of UFOs, there'll be more than a few Snakes in the congregation. Bearing this in mind, it should come as no surprise to learn that the most inspired leader of modern times, a man who single-handedly changed the political and religious aspirations of an entire nation, Mahatma Gandhi, was born in the year of the Snake.

In addition to their contribution to religious thinking, Snakes have another string to their bow. Throughout history, they have enhanced both painting and music with an almost divine inspiration. Perhaps the most lyrical and prolific composer of all time, Franz Schubert, was a Snake. During his thirty-one years, Schubert composed over a thousand songs, nine symphonies and countless chamber works.

Pablo Picasso was also a Snake, and might easily be described as the most extraordinary painter the world has ever known. A child prodigy, Picasso created an endless stream of masterpieces, painting until the very day he died, aged ninety-two. Whatever one might think about his unique view, it cannot be denied that Picasso changed the face of modern art; it could even be said that he actually invented it. Nor is there any question that he died the richest painter who has ever lived, his vast fortune still in dispute a decade after his death. The mention of money, or more precisely, piles of money, brings us neatly to the Snake's third great gift – the power to amass wealth. J. Paul Getty was a Snake.

Yet the Snake's attitude to money is something of a paradox. Whereas they will give of themselves, advice, and time, the Snake can often be found wanting when hard cash is what's wanted. They will not lend money, invest it, or spend it on themselves. This is particularly the case of Snakes who have experienced a difficult or deprived childhood. In cases like these, the Snake may well turn into one of those miserly old folk living in a squalid bed-sit with a fortune stuffed in the mattress. The multi-millionaire Howard Hughes ended his life in conditions not far from those I have just mentioned; in a penthouse in a rather shabby apartment block in gaudy Las Vegas. He had darkened all the windows and sealed all the doors to keep out 'the germs' he thought would kill him. He ate nothing but pills and although over six feet tall, when they finally took him away he weighed under eight stone. He had hair down to his waist, fingernails two inches long, and the day he died (of kidney failure caused by malnutrition) Howard Hughes' fortune stood at 2.3 billion dollars.

Whatever she may become, either through extremes of wealth or beauty, or as a result of some romantic encounter, the Snake knows her own worth in this world. Moreover she values it. There is always something private, secret almost, about the Snake (the Chinese have one word for both private and secret). Yet she will always speak her mind when asked, and she will choose her words with care. She will never gabble, but articulate slowly and precisely with a clear, pleasant voice. As a result of their pure tone of voice, Snakes often become singers. Nat King Cole and Art Garfunkel were born in the Snake year.

Although Snakes listen carefully to good advice, and often take it, most prefer to trust their own instincts and rely on their own sensitive judgement. But whoever's advice she takes, a Snake cannot bear to be left in a state of indecision. In two minds, the Snake is in serious danger. Forced to decide quickly, without time for her in-built wisdom to guide her, the Snake will invariably make the wrong decision. And it will not help her to reason out the problem, it only makes matters worse. My father was a Snake, and waiting for him to choose from a menu in a restaurant would try the patience of Job. With those around him growing ever more hungry, he inevitably chose the dish he liked least and spent the evening grumbling. And logic doesn't help the Snake either; that's if they in fact possess it. Logic just kills off their intuition completely.

119

Snakes are also very often gifted with clairvoyant powers, which can be as startling as they can be useful. Both my wife's uncles are Snakes. Their eldest sister, my wife's mother, died quite suddenly, and without their knowledge. The day of her death, the youngest brother walked into his lounge and 'saw' his sister and mother, who had been dead for many years, sitting on the sofa talking. I shivered when he told me the story, but my wife's uncle seemed to think it perfectly natural.

All Snakes have an acute sense of humour, bringing any company to life with their often clever and observant remarks. What could be more witty than a Cole Porter song? What more whimsical than the world of Jeeves and Bertie Wooster, created by P.G. Wodehouse? Socially, a Snake's humour is used partly to win your admiration and partly to disarm you; the Snake knowing full well that when you laugh, you can pose few threats to their desire for a peaceful and meditative life. And should her jokes fall a little flat, the lady Snake can always undo another button of her blouse.

A common misunderstanding by those who have written books on the Chinese horoscope, is to describe the Snake as lazy. The confusion again comes from the Chinese word *hsien*, which has two meanings: idle and leisure. It might well be that when we see a snake coiled up under a rock, she is not being idle, but taking her leisure. And it must be said that snakes do not like rushing about. And they need to rest after eating, making love, after practically every event. And in the winter, of course, snakes hibernate. Far from lazy, Snakes work hard. Once having made a commitment to their family, business, even their lover, they will toil with an unparalleled tenacity to achieve their goal. Yet if the Snake seems slow to react, do not be deceived. It is when the Snake is motionless that she is at her most mentally active: thinking, plotting, planning the next move. In fact, the Snake's mind is seldom still. And when she acts she does so with great thoroughness. Snakes work very odd hours.

The Snake will take many different roles during his or her lifetime, shedding many different skins. But the professions that best suit a Snake are those where her fine voice, beauty and wisdom can be put to their best use. Snakes make wonderful singers, actresses and dancers. Male Snakes can succeed as politicians (so can lady Snakes, if Mrs Indira Gandhi is to be taken into account), gossip columnists and millionaires. I would add fortune-teller, but I hardly think it counts as a profession these days. But the Snake is most effective in society when allied to some form of peace-keeping activity. Snakes loathe violence, and will only resort to a violent act in extreme situations. After all, with charm and beauty as weapons, who needs fists to solve a dispute? (Which is another reason the Chinese value the Snake so highly.) The CND leader, Monsignor Bruce Kent, is a Snake.

Male Snakes are less ostentatious dressers than the female, although you might well find Mr Snake out in a Fedora and a sharp-looking suit. He goes in for leather jackets, striped shirts and silk ties. Snake men never appear dressed shabbily, and will probably put on their Sunday best to pop round to the corner shop.

What we in the West call destiny, Buddhists call karma. But there is a subtle difference in that karma means much more than just how your life will pan out. It means that each action we perform is influenced by the previous action, which in turn influences the action that follows. It's a bit like knitting a never ending sweater. Both the Snake and Dragon, as well as being reptiles, are karmic signs. This means that whatever they end up as will have been as a direct result of how the Snake and the Dragon lived their lives.

The three phases of a Snake's life will be marked by a solitary childhood in which the Snake child will frequently be misunderstood. Snake children develop painfully slowly and their parents often become frustrated that their great concern and love is hitting stony ground. The Snake in mid-life will suffer the sudden loss of a loved one, and the second period will not be without its setbacks. But the final phase will find the Snake surrounded by caskets brimming over with jewels. One word of caution, however. The Chinese say that a Snake

121

born in summer will find wealth and happiness, but a Snake born during a winter's storm will be threatened by danger throughout his life.

SNAKE AS PARENT

Because they are so close in their understanding, Snake parents face no problems bringing up a Dragon child. The Snake father will be captivated by his Dragon daughter and the Snake mother, wise and beautiful, will be stimulated by the brilliance of her Dragon son. As always, the Goat daughter demands much from her parents, wanting freedom on one hand and the comfort of home on the other. But she makes her pleas with such charm that the Snake parent will happily consent to anything the Goat wishes.

The Cat is a patient child and listens willingly to the good advice his Snake parent gives him, but there are times under a Snake's roof when the Kitten might feel a little out of his depth spiritually (Snakes are very strong on spiritual matters). The Dog will adore life with a Snake mother. She'll genuinely enter into every one of his childish plans as if it were the cleverest thing that had ever been. She'll cling to him as all Snakes cling to the object of their love, but the Puppy won't mind a bit. In fact he'll find it a real comfort in his many anxious moments.

No child can win a Snake father's love easier than the Monkey. The Monkey has only to open his mouth to have his or her Snake papa falling off his chair with laughter. A very good relationship, so long as the Monkey doesn't play his parent for a fool. The tiny Rat is adorable, and quickly wins the often intrusive love of a Snake parent. There'll be a big demand on resources when the Rat son is around, and there is a limit on just how often daddy Snake is prepared to dip

COMPATIBILITY OF SNAKE PARENT AND CHILD

into his pocket. The child Rooster loves dressing up and although mum Snake won't mind her borrowing her perfume and wearing her tights, she won't care overmuch for the Rooster infant's moralising.

The Buffalo son will not find inspiration in the Snake's home, and neither will the young Pig; perhaps the Snake is wise enough to know that neither child needs pushing. The young Horse will feel imprisoned by the Snake's often possessive parental love, and as he does so often, pack his tiny suitcase as soon as he can. The adolescent Tiger will likewise feel restricted in a Snake's home, and will almost certainly join the Horse in the march to the front door. But of all the

123

children, a Snake child fares least well. While still young, the Snake's intuition exists without a voice. A Snake takes time to develop and often only realises himself late in life. Try as he might, the young Snake will not be able to answer his father's questions, and his silence will only serve to intensify the questioning. In the end communication will break down completely, and with so much unspoken, their home will not be a happy one.

SNAKE IN BUSINESS

Snakes as a rule do not make good business partners. They operate best when listening to their own intelligent advice on matters of every kind, especially money. But if they do go into partnership, they should choose someone who will appreciate that the Snake's wisdom is deeply intuitive, and is not always easily explained. The thoughtful Cat is useful to a Snake. Cautious and good with money, the Cat complements the Snake's two strongest commercial talents, and Cat and Snake will do a great deal to protect each other from taking risks – should they ever dare to do so. A smart advertising agency or escort agency would suit Snake, Cat and Co. down to the ground.

The Dragon is also good value for the Snake. He'll bring his fire and showmanship to any clever scheme the Snake dreams up, and put him off the less clever ones. But a team of Lady Snake and Mr Dragon must avoid mixing the boardroom and the bedroom; there is such a powerful mutual attraction between the two serpents.

The industrious and intelligent Horse admires the Snake's witty and elegant business approach, but the Snake must not interfere too often when the Horse is putting the plans into practice. The opportunist Rat will only hinder the Snake, and

COMPATIBILITY OF SNAKE IN BUSINESS RELATIONSHIPS

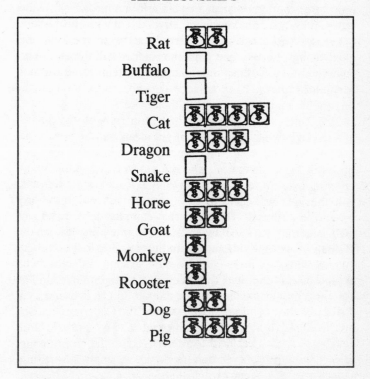

upset his powers of intuition, but the Rat's a good front man to have on your side, and his charm has many uses. The Dog only has his loyalty to offer the Snake, who will not be ungrateful, but Snakes need a lot of support when the firm hits lean times, and he will need more than devotion to help get the overdraft paid off. The Pig has a simple attitude to business – just keep on working. That's fine for the Snake, and the two of them will probably do very well. The only snag is that they won't form much of a friendship, and really successful businesses have partners who are both workmates and buddies.

The sharp Monkey can match the Snake's thrift and on the surface a partnership between them looks a commercial must. But they have such very different approaches to the same end – one calm and meditative, the other a little flashy. What the Snake needs is a darn good organiser, and he'll need to look no further than the methodical Rooster. The Rooster has two hats, one marked secretarial, the other spendthrift. A fat bank balance depends entirely on which one she wears in company with the Snake.

The Tiger would like to go into business with the Snake, he's so receptive to the Tiger's bright ideas, but the Snake will ponder, as is his wont, and the Tiger will heave a sigh and push off. Tigers can't wait. The Buffalo won't mind the Snake chewing over an idea before investing, it makes good sense. But the idea will have to be his or he will not show any interest in it himself. Oh dear, what complications. Even less well suited are two Snakes. In business, everyone has to take a gamble one time or another, and two Snakes will both take ages making up their minds before placing different bets. What's worse, both bets will lose.

SNAKE IN LOVE

There need be no shilly-shallying when it comes to naming the ideal playmate for the Snake. The Chinese are emphatic about it; 'the Dragon is in love with the Snake', they say. The otherwise arrogant, imperious Dragon will do anything the Snake lady demands. She has only to bat her eyelids and pass a few flattering remarks in her cool and elegant voice for the poor old Dragon to drop to his knees. The handsome Horse is easy in the company of both sexes, and his fondness for romance will find quick favour with the Snake. But as lovers, they must try to please each other once in a while. The

COMPATIBILITY OF SNAKE IN LOVE

Rat
Buffalo
Tiger
Cat
Dragon
Snake
Horse
Goat
Monkey
Rooster
Dog
Pig

sensuous Cat will enjoy being squeezed a little by the passionate Snake. But must he squeeze quite so hard? The Rat won't mind a passionate squeeze, however hard, but he likes his freedom, and he might find the bedroom door locked when he tip-toes off at the crack of dawn. The big-hearted Pig will also find himself feeling a little trapped at times, and might get the idea he is being fattened up for something. Mmmm ...? The Pig had better keep a closer check on his Snake lover's excuses.

The loyal Dog will also find his Snake lover's stories a little thin when gone into, but like the honest Pig, he'll stand for her indiscretions; she is, after all, so bewitching, so desirable.

Not so the Rooster. He's far too high-minded and full of himself to share his lover with some Tom, Dick or Harry. And even if Ms Snake has been on the level with the Rooster, he'll accuse her of two-timing him anyway. He's that sort of chap. But the Rooster lady will get on extremely well with the male Snake as a romantic companion; it'll be all delicious dinners and little gifts. The poor old Buffalo is not built for the mysteries of sex, and that puts him right out of the running as far as the sexually mysterious Snake is concerned.

The Goat enjoys nothing more than a night out flirting with danger, but the Snake is no flirt and the Goat is never the Snake's master. It's not hopeless, but each can have better times elsewhere. The lady Monkey intrigues the male Snake who might easily find himself led up the garden path. A happy start with an unhappy ending. The vigorous Tiger is at his amorous best when his partner can respond with the same vitality. But in love, the Snake mesmerises and the Tiger pounces. They might as well sleep in twin beds. Snakes in love only act to emphasise their worst excesses, clinging to each other long after the flames have become embers. And when Snakes are hungry, they will devour the first thing that moves – even, it has to be said, another Snake.

SNAKE IN MARRIAGE

The volatile Tiger must at all costs avoid marrying the gentle and peaceful Snake. Tigers of both sexes have minds that bubble with ideas, pouring out in an endless stream. The Snake is the philosopher, and his mind is still when he thinks. As a married couple, they couldn't have less in common. One will talk on and on, while the other sits with closed ears; dreamer and schemer, chalk and cheese.

Single-minded, and not in the least romantic, the Dog will

COMPATIBILITY OF SNAKE IN MARRIAGE

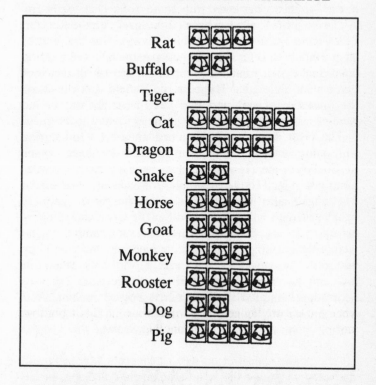

be captivated by the Snake's beauty. She, in turn, will reward his devotion by remaining at his side, even during the bad times. But she is a Snake, and has her own ideas about fidelity.

The Dragon has a lot to bring marriage, when he desires it. The Snake is serpentine, like the Dragon, and they have much to tell each other. They are well recommended to life together, with one proviso; the Snake must not cling or let her emotions run away with her. No Dragon can bear to feel beholden.

The sociable Cat provides the Snake with the best partner in marriage. He has all the domestic graces and is subtle and gentle in all his ways. He loves to gossip and enjoys life at a moderate pace. A splendid match! A good social life, too, for the artistic Goat when married to a Snake, especially if the Goat is the male partner. But both partners are prone to a little fun on the side, and who will pay the milk bill if there's no one at home on Saturday morning? The male Snake is less fickle than his female counterpart. This will suit the Snake who marries a female Rooster. She'll clear his head of any fancy ideas and produce a large noisy family to keep the Snake in his place. The same is true when the wedding bells chime for Ms Snake and Mr Pig. The only danger in this set-up is that the Pig will become so besotted with his wife's beauty he'll tend to her every whim. This is not good for the Pig or the Snake, who will begin to take the Pig for granted.

The Buffalo will fall for the Snake's bewitching charms, and he'll do everything he can to make her happy. But the only way a Buffalo knows is by working. What will the beautiful, bewitching Snake wife do all day while her husband toils in the fields? One dreads to think. The witty Horse shares the Snake's finely tuned sense of humour, which goes a long way to keep a marriage together, but both are terribly vain, and vanity has been known to be the downfall of many.

The Snake male will do well to choose a Monkey bride, and they will share the same amusements. So long as they don't involve too many extra-marital affairs it could go the distance marriagewise. The charming Rat will be happy enough with a Snake lady at his side. But she's the *femme fatale* and he's Mr Opportunity. Could work, could be a disaster. If Snakes must marry, they'll have to declare a truce – all little black address books must be thrown on the fire. That way they have an even chance of a few good years together.

HOW YOU WILL BE INFLUENCED IN THE YEAR OF THE SNAKE

A YEAR FOR MEDITATION

A perfect year for the Snake, at last she has peace. Even the impulsive Dragon will be calmed by the influence of the Snake, but will make a success of his enterprises as always. Even so, the Dragon will find he spends more time than usual sitting and reflecting.

This is an exceptional year for the Goat, whose love of a peaceful life is mirrored by the Snake. It is most certainly the best year for the capricious Goat to put on her favourite dress and plug into high society. There will be gossip in abundance, which will not go unnoticed by the chatty, social Cat. She'll find the year rewarding if only for the relative peace and quiet it brings following the Dragon's endless carnival.

The Monkey has much in common with the Snake in the wisdom stakes, but he uses his skills in such an acquisitive, material way. And he's a real show-off. The Snake's wisdom, however, is more mild. It might bring wealth, but it does so in a very low key, so the Monkey will be well advised to make his fortune quietly. The plain-talking Dog will not find support lacking for his strong ideals, and he'll end many a day on a bright and promising note. The popular Horse will find no shortage of admirers, but business will slow down to what he thinks is a virtual standstill. For the Horse it's a time to stay in bed and let someone else run the office. No green grass for the ardent Rat. He'll be stung hard by love in the Snake's year and he'll go to seed when it turns sour. Because there's no shortage of gossip, the Rooster's social life will take a big turn upwards. There's nothing she likes more than a chin-wag with the rest of

131

Rat
Buffalo
Tiger
Cat
Dragon
Snake
Horse
Goat
Monkey
Rooster
Dog
Pig

the hens. And her business won't do too badly either. Not so good for the resolute and tireless Buffalo. His long hours under the yoke bring few rewards in a year when such emphasis is placed on meditative thought. It's a year for thinkers and experiencing the senses. A Zen Buddhist Buffalo might make out OK.

The Pig is another glutton for toil, but like the Rat, love will grip him by the throat and not let go. Poor Piggy. He'll spend too much time staring into the eyes of his beloved and not enough at his sales figures to make money this year. As for the Tiger, he'll not be short of his customary flood of ideas, but he'll forget that the Snake glides so stealthfully, and that she bites with venom when startled. If only the Tiger could move without bouncing.

FAMOUS SNAKES

Arts
Bartok
Brahms
Brigid Brophy
Len Deighton
Elgar
Fauré
Miles Kington
Anita Loos
Matisse
John Osborne
Picasso
Dorothy Parker
Joan Plowright
Edgar Allen Poe
Andre Previn
Schubert
P G Wodehouse

Sports
Muhammed Ali
Roger Bannister
Pat Cash
Eddie Charlton
Stefan Edberg
Graham Gooch
Lucinda Green
Graham Hill
David Moorcroft
Stirling Moss
Arnold Palmer
Helena Sukova

Industry/Politics
Paddy Ashdown
Benazir Bhutto
Indira Gandhi
Mahatma Gandhi
J Paul Getty
Denis Healey
Howard Hughes
J F Kennedy
Bruce Kent
Lord Longford
Norma Major
Ferdinand Marcus
Baden-Powell
Jeremy Thorpe

Royals
Elizabeth I
Queen Anne
Princess Grace of Monaco

Show Biz
Ronnie Barker
Jim Davidson
Nigel Dempster
Christian Dior
Greta Garbo
Audrey Hepburn
Griff Rhys Jones
Howard Keel
Jan Leeming
Liberace

133

Magnus Magnusson
Cecil B de Mille
Jackie Onassis
David Puttnam
Brooke Shields
Mae West
Victoria Wood
Mike Yarwood

Pop
Paul Anka

Burt Bacharach
Eric Burden
Nat King Cole
Bob Dylan
Art Garfunkel
Julian Lennon
Hank Marvin
Mike Oldfield
James Taylor
Midge Ure

THE HORSE

馬

1906*	January 25th to February 12th	1907
1918	February 11th to January 31st	1919
1930	January 30th to February 16th	1931
1942	February 15th to February 4th	1943
1954	February 3rd to January 23rd	1955
1966*	January 21st to February 8th	1967
1978	February 7th to January 27th	1979
1990	January 27th to February 14th	1991

*FIRE HORSE

136

When I consider the most wonderful work of God in the creation of the Horse, endowing it with a singular body and a noble spirit, the principal whereof is a loving and dutiful inclination to the service of man.

Topsell

THE YEAR OF THE HORSE

A hectic year with work for everyone who wants it, with few strikes and the minimum industrial unrest. The year of the Horse shows a considerable change from its predecessor; gone are the hours spent in peaceful meditation, and gone too, is the benign wisdom. In the place of spiritualism, we find noble and industrious effort. The Horse year will begin as it means to continue (and end) with an all-pervading spirit of elegance and independence. And although the Horse is universally admired for his industry, he also knows how to enjoy his leisure. As a result, the Horse year will bring about many great sporting achievements with new sports stars setting records which will remain unbroken for decades at a time. In 1954, Roger Bannister set the most significant sporting record in history, by becoming the first man ever to run a mile in under four minutes.

The year of the Horse will also be noted for the many political changes taking place, mostly following the collapse or the overthrow of kings and presidents. The month of November 1918 witnessed the abdication of the Kaiser, and in 1978 Mrs. Gandhi was expelled from the Indian parliament. The Horse is seldom far from the political arena, but when in control he makes few dramatic changes. Those he does make will be slight, and always for the best.

Horse years tend to provide us with optimism for our many projects and there will be a general atmosphere of good humour. There will, of course, be the odd black moment, and even serious conflict, but it will not last. However bloody, confrontations will fizzle out, sometimes in a matter of weeks, sometimes days, or even in a matter of hours. Mrs Gandhi spent only six days in prison. However, wars, famines and pestilences are not so lenient in the year of the Fire Horse. Occurring every sixty years (1906 was a Fire Horse year, so was 1966), the Chinese believe that whatever happens in the year of the Fire Horse, both good and bad, will be intensified many times over. San Francisco was destroyed by an earthquake in 1906, and in 1666 London was burnt to the ground. In the first nine months of 1966 airline disasters accounted for a record number of 460 lives lost, and in July of the same year, England won the World Cup, beating Germany 4–2 with goals that are still disputed.

Love will hit hard in the year of the Horse, and hit quickly. And love should be allowed its freedom. Above all, the year will contain an air of expectancy throughout, and there will be a constant promise of life looking up. In 1954, the London gold market re-opened after a closure of fifteen years.

In the year of the Horse we will all adapt more easily to shifts in circumstances, and the way to proceed is not by sitting for hours in deep contemplation, but by chancing your arm. And don't be afraid of taking advice; remember that the best advice you can get is straight from the Horse's mouth.

THE HORSE PERSONALITY

'Time to be out and about, seeing new places, meeting new people; let the elegant Horse be your guide.'

Of all the animals on earth there can be no doubt that the graceful Horse, with his inner spirit of freedom, is by far the most popular. Certainly no creature has worked harder, or longer, for Mankind. Whether it's the majestic stallions from the Vienna riding stables, or the delightful shaggy-maned Shetland ponies that carry our children so obediently across the summer beaches, every one of us has our favourite. And there are so many horses from which we can make our choice; Arabian thoroughbreds, show jumpers, pit ponies, hunters, plough pullers, steeple-chasers, flat racers, mountain trekkers, cab horses, cart horses, dray horses, donkeys, mules, asses – all part of one enormous equine family. And the seemingly infinite variety of skills, shapes and sizes are also to be found in all those born under the Horse's powerful influence.

A strongly masculine sign, both male and female Horses brim over with personality. Easy-going, the Horse has a natural flair for leadership and will be found at the heart of any gathering. Horse women in particular are strikingly beautiful, and are frequently seen captivating an ever present band of admirers with their witty observations and brilliant chat. And should a Horse lady lack just a little in looks, she'll make up for it in sheer style, of that you may be absolutely certain. Her hair will have been cut in the very latest 'in' salon, her shoes will have Italian design written all over them, and her perfume will have cost her half a year's salary. No other creature is as beautiful and witty as Ms Horse in her best form. Sorry, gals, but that's how it is.

Male horses are conspicuous by the strength of their personality, as well as their good looks, and many have an instant sex appeal. Aware of his powers, the Horse does not brag, although it must be said right at the start that the Horse can be very vain. If you were born under the sign of the Horse, the following will be kindred spirits; Paul McCartney, Clint Eastwood, Barbra Streisand, Billy Connolly, Chopin, Lord Snowdon, Princess Margaret and Sean Connery.

Born under the sign of elegance and endurance, the Horse is noted for his highly original sense of humour. He is also extremely practical, and his industry knows few peers. What is more, the Horse's natural sense of public ease and his great inner reserves mark him for the very highest posts in public life. He can address crowds of thousands as if he were having a chat to a chum in the pub. The evangelist Billy Graham is a Horse, as is Shirley Williams.

One of the central reasons why a Horse is so successful is to be found in his great capacity to work round the clock when the occasion demands it. Indeed, it must be said that Horses do work very odd hours, and you'll often find them packing up just as you start, and turning up just as you are about to go home. But however many hours a Horse works, he'll still approach every problem put before him with a clear head, and solve it with a sharp decisive mind. And to add another string to the Horse's already overloaded bow, he is capable of working methodically and speedily, seeing the job on hand through to the end. When there's work to be done, you'll not find the Horse hanging around in the canteen; that comes later.

I have a friend who is a Horse, and worked for many years as a journalist on *The Sunday Times.* He thought nothing of flying off at a minute's notice to one of the world's trouble spots with nothing more than an overnight bag and his wits to enable him to get his story. Each assignment would always present the same string of problems: first he would have to find accommodation (often in some godforsaken dot on the map), an interpreter, a telephone, transport to the scene of the action, contacts, informers, other journalists, and so on.. After getting his story, he'd write it, send it to the newspaper over the wire and, if he was lucky, get back to London in time to check the proofs before the paper was finally put to bed. As an important member of the *Insight* team, Peter Gillman was a key figure in compiling the special reports investigated by *Insight* and turning them into instant paperbacks. His record here is impressive, even by the high standards of the Horse. On the book about the Iranian Embassy siege, he wrote no less than 24,000 words in *four days*! And for *The Sunday Times*' book on the Falklands war, he wrote 30,000 words in fourteen days. But journalist Horses are not the only ones who can churn it out. Didn't that most brilliant and original of all British humorists, Spike Milligan, write one Goon Show script a week for over a decade? It's just as well that the Horse has been endowed with more than his fair share of stamina.

Because the Horse is capable of making a decision quickly, without fuss and, more often than not, without error, he makes a formidable opponent on the political rostrum. Lenin, Krushchev and Leonid Brezhnev were born in the Year of the Horse. So was Neil Kinnock.

One quite astonishing power that a Horse possesses is his ability to grasp the point you are about to make almost before you have even begun to make it. There are times when he will finish your sentence, and do so more eloquently than you would have done yourself. This is not necessarily a question of a sixth sense, or indeed, horse sense. It is, quite simply, a case of the Horse's logical mind. In other words, if what you are telling a Horse makes sense, he'll get the point without the frills. He might like embellishment, but the Horse doesn't really need it. And be warned. If you expect the Horse to take you seriously, do not jabber on. Nothing is guaranteed to irritate him more, and the Horse who is irritated by gibberish will show his feelings openly. Be prepared to be ridiculed. And it will fare even worse if you cross him in debate with some half thought-out nonsense. In such an instance you might actually send the Horse into a rage. Although he is not easily vexed, the Horse's anger is something to fear. And once you have been on the receiving end, you will never forget it. Even though he is quick to apologise for what are often rather child-like tantrums, you will never view the Horse in quite the same way again. You will certainly feel less easy in his company. I am sure that riders who have been thrown by a rearing Horse know the feeling.

As a rule, Horses are not jealous or possessive about those they love and do not impose double standards. They require their freedom, and realise that their partners expect the same. But the Horse likes to have his own way. And one sure way to get him riled is to cross him in public – which I suspect brings us back to Lenin and Co. Remarkably calm in a crisis, the Horse will seldom put his view forward unless he is absolutely certain of his facts. Whether discussing cricket averages, political history, or some off-beat pastime like bee-keeping, the Horse will never quote you a wrong statistic or give you a woolly-minded opinion. For all his high spirits, wit, and free and easy manner, the Horse is above all a practical creature. He deals in facts, not opinions. And should he make the occasional error, as we all do, the Horse's practical approach will be a useful tool to help talk his way out of trouble. He can sound convincing even when he's barking completely up the wrong tree.

The male Horse is a really tough guy to win over, and if that is your intention, steer well clear of topics that introduce an element of mysticism – Zen Buddhism, reincarnation and zodiacs. The way to win his interest is by a well-informed dissertation on mountaineering. French wines or how to plumb in your own solar energy system. If all else fails you can always hook a Horse with a little scurrilous gossip. Horses like to stick their long necks over the five bar gate, and far too many of them find that they are given secrets they cannot be trusted to keep. They also talk too much. But Horses are not generally speaking judgemental, and are most willing to accept faults in others, passing them off with a shrug. They are however, extremely competitive.

With a practical mind and ability to adapt his moods to suit the situation, the Horse can and does take on a number of professional roles. When one considers the huge variation of jobs that man has given the horse, it is easy to understand why no door is really closed to him. For reasons I am not clear about, I seem to know an extraordinary number of Horses, ranging from long and devoted friendships, to casual work acquaintances. One of my closest and best loved friends is an Anglican monk, who is responsible for novices in the home of the Mirfield Fathers, near Leeds. Another is the managing director of *Private Eye* who, by way of relaxation, runs a small farm in Sussex. I have Horse friends who bind books, edit film, teach the history of art, lay out *The Times* newspaper, write books on India, write about interior design, play trombones, edit gossip columns, edit *The Listener's* book pages, run art shops, antique shops and take fashion photographs. I don't, in fact, have any friends who are turf accountants, but it would provide any Horse with a chance to exploit his many gifts. It would combine his love of outdoor sport, ability to think quickly, and his pleasure in large, good-natured crowds.

No matter whether the gathering is large or small, the Horse loves company and is an inveterate party thrower. To put it to the test, my wife and I drew up a separate list of our favourite party throwers. Marks were given for interesting guests, food and wine and the general standard of hospitality. A Horse featured in the first three places, with a double Horse partnership passing the post by a short head. My feelings are that if you can spare five minutes to draw up your own top host and hostess list, you too will find a Horse with his or her head in the frame every time.

Although fiercely independent, one of the Horse's most endearing qualities is his way of asking for advice, even when it might well concern deeply personal aspects of his private life. Unlike the Monkey, say, who will trick advice from you, the Horse will take you quietly to one side and come straight out with it. He will listen carefully, weighing up in his own mind what you are saying. Whether he takes it or not, whether he acts on either your good or bad advice, the Horse will go to some considerable lengths to show his gratitude. But however he rewards you, he will never forget your concern.

If it appears on the surface that Horses have got everything going for them, it must be remembered that they often face troubled times when caught in the web of romance. Horses fall in love at the drop of the proverbial hat and can do very little to counter such blows to the heart. With his great sex appeal, good looks and personality, any advances he cares to make will, in almost all cases, meet with little resistance. In the case of a lady Horse, she will have an endless string of offers, and fortunately or unfortunately, depending on the circumstances, she will not find herself very often saying, 'no'. Although they don't get bitter and twisted when love doesn't work out in the way they had expected (Horses do have very high standards of love-making), they do nevertheless have a tough time coming to terms with love's sharper angles. Because the Horse is so practical, he'll attempt to reason love out. But love cannot be reasoned and the Horse will frequently become confused, and ultimately disillusioned. What is worse, in matters of the heart the Horse never learns from his or her mistakes. He thinks that every affair is the one that will last, and therefore throws himself at it hammer and tongs. Alas, for all of us, we can make many mistakes before choosing the partner who will suit us best, but the Horse has more trouble than most in making that choice. Consequently the Horse may often marry many times before finding Mr or Mrs Right. But when you have experienced a Horse's love – the female Horse is so stimulating – the chances are that you will never forget it. As one very worldwise Dragon friend once admitted to me about his Horse wife; 'She's the most *exciting* person I have ever known.'

Because the Lady Horse very often has the kind of looks that put her on the covers of the world's glossy fashion magazines, she very often knows how to dress in the latest thing, looking neither outrageously trendy, or as so many do, a little silly. Born under the sign of the Horse, Jean Shrimpton was the most talked-about fashion model for almost two decades, and her beauty and individuality created a set of ideals about the nature of young women's looks which apply even today. If the latest thing is a boiler suit and stiletto heels, the Horse will be wearing them before anyone else. And if tomorrow's in-thing looks ghastly, on a Horse it will look great. And if you want to know what the latest in hairstyles is, look up your Horse friend. Horses are very conscious about their manes and tails, and grooms spend no end of time fussing over them.

Male Horses display a different attitude to the way they dress, and their wardrobe will be full of straightforward clothes that hang easily. Although he might wear a bright neck-tie or buy expensive shoes, the Horse will never overdress. He likes to feel relaxed and comfortable. Unless his job demands it, the Horse is not likely to own a dinner jacket. As much as he loves social gatherings, he prefers the less formal kind. But he will always dress with distinction, allowing his great individuality full rein.

Because the Horse is so adaptable, he is also likely to change his life more than most; some might argue that the Horse is in fact a victim of change. And it is true that in addition to sometimes changing his wife (or her husband), the Horse does seem to be constantly jumping from one job, hobby, interest and pastime to another. It can be very confusing to learn that the chap you have known as a do-it-yourself winemaker has now started to learn Urdu, or the woman who worked as a fashion editor has become one of Mother Teresa's helpers. Much worse follows when you discover that whereas last week you were the most divine thing ever to have crossed the Horse's path, she can now hardly recall your name, let alone your telephone number. And for all their practicality, Horses do not plan for the long term. When they want something, they must have it at once. Do not try to prevent a Horse achieving his aim by standing idly in the way. He'll stampede over you as if you didn't exist.

The Horse's home will be a mixture of comfort and refined taste. The accent will always be on simplicity, but the practical side of the Horse will express itself in that he will buy quality, seeing no sense in spending money on sofas that will collapse in five minutes, or carpets that won't stand more than a week's wear. And there will be many touches of the Horse's individuality, perhaps in the choice of pictures that hang from uncluttered walls, or the colour of the furnishing fabrics. And there will always be plenty to eat in a Horse's home – the Horse can get his gnashers through a meadow in no time at all.

Because his love of freedom is paramount to a Horse, it will largely determine the three phases of his life. Horse children very often leave home at an early age, finding even the most well-meaning of parental control a restriction. The middle period will be mixed, with the Horse's constant changing about acting against his better interests. However, old age sits comfortably on a Horse's shoulders, and even though, as in the case of Neil Armstrong, he has been to the moon and back, the Horse will be quite content to roam around the lush pasture, dream of his many colts, mares and victories, and watch the world go by. The Chinese say that the Horse born in the summer has an easier life than a Horse born in the winter. If that is the case, no one is better able at reversing his lot than the Horse. Absolutely no one.

HORSE AS PARENT

The Horse automatically becomes the key figure of any family circle, yet he is sometimes more keen on life at the office than he is with his wife and kids. Perhaps it has something to do with the Horse's great need for independence. However, the Horse is great with his children once he actually decides to come home, but he isn't always over-amused by the young Rat. Horse fathers want to see their

COMPATIBILITY OF HORSE PARENT AND CHILD

Rat	(empty)
Buffalo	1
Tiger	4
Cat	3
Dragon	4
Snake	2
Horse	2
Goat	4
Monkey	4
Rooster	2
Dog	2
Pig	2

sons in a skilled trade, not raiding the tea caddy on the mantelpiece. The baby Buffalo fares marginally better in the Horse house, but here it's a case of too much study. Stamp collecting is OK in its place, but the Horse loves the sound of laughter now and again.

The infant Pig will please his mother Horse. He'll giggle and wiggle his toes, but his looks ... well, couldn't they be just a little more *attractive*? The puppy Dog is such an open-eyed little soul, and so serious. One day he will set the world to rights. Such worthiness, alas, is a bit of a lead balloon in the home of the Horse. The young Rooster son has plenty to say for himself and likes a lark. His trouble is he has too much to say, and usually in the wrong places. The Kitten will behave herself, though, and make the right kind of noises, but she'll have to do more than purr for her dish of cream.

The Horse father will not understand his Snake son. Why does the child sit around the house all day doing nothing? But the Snake needs his parent's attention and understanding, and will win it in the end, though at some considerable cost. The Dragon child is quite another matter. The Horse parent knows talent when he sees it, and will give the young Dragon all the encouragement he needs. But a Horse mum might tend to mock the Dragon son a little too often – he's so full of himself and she's so quick witted.

There will be no affection shortage in the life of a young Tiger if his parent is a Horse, and the Tiger daughter will be steadied by the firm hand of a Horse father. The Goat daughter makes her intentions clear from the very start; freedom to do her own thing is what she wants, and lots of it. That won't worry the Horse mother, who is herself a libertine at heart and no hypocrite. The baby Monkey is a quick learner and will be much admired under the Horse's roof. Her skills won't be overlooked and so long as she remembers that the Horse is boss in his own home, everything will turn out fine. But *will* she remember?

The business of head of the family will present the Horse child with a problem. The stallion will be in constant conflict with his father, and although the bond between Horses is very strong indeed, they sometimes find expressing family ties difficult. As is so very often the case, the young colt will make an early departure.

HORSE IN BUSINESS

Each animal in the Chinese horoscope has one polar opposite – creatures who can see eye to eye on absolutely nothing. In the case of the Horse, it is the opportunist Rat. The Horse demands a practical mind from those he works with, not sharp salesmanship. Two Horses on the board of directors have an equally poor chance of agreeing. Their problem is one of practicality, not when a deal should be struck, but how? The Pig is dependable, and puts the hours in. But he is ambitious beneath his cloak of joviality, and the Horse won't like too many fingers in his pie, not at management level. The Cat has the kind of slow and methodical approach to work that the Horse finds he can handle. But the Cat must make sure he doesn't fuss too much.

The Buffalo will make a splendid partner for the Horse. His ability to toil under pressure mirrors the Horse's own great capacity for endurance. The Horse will flatter the Buffalo to keep him happy, but is that always wise? The artistic Goat will work happily and faithfully under a Horse, and will benefit from the Horse's high-powered and positive approach. But the Goat must stick at it, and not talk too much about how well their rivals are doing. An even better partnership is that formed by the Horse and the well-organised Rooster, who can always be relied upon to deal with the tricky customer on the phone. A high-class estate agents is tailor made for the Horse and Rooster partnership, or possibly a betting shop.

COMPATIBILITY OF HORSE IN BUSINESS
RELATIONSHIPS

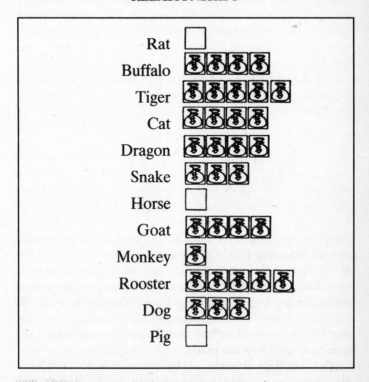

Tigers are people who just love ideas, and Horses love putting them into practice. No problems at all here, except that the Tiger might dry up before they bank their first million. Both Horses and Snakes can get on in a business relationship, but the Horse uses his personality to resolve difficult situations, the Snake uses her intuition. There could be conflict. The loyal Dog will do his share alongside the Horse. Both can lay claim to have worked the hardest for Man, so why not for each other? The only drawback is the Dog's inborn pessimism.

The clever Monkey can be practical when he wants, as

well as industrious. Under the hand of the honest Horse, he might even find he enjoys playing it straight. But the chances that the Monkey will change his ways are slim, and the Horse will not stand for too much double-dealing. The Horse is a great one for changing his plans, even when things are going well. The Dragon is adaptable, and will put up with change, so long as the changes are for the best. Dragons and Horses should go into the film business. As artisan and showman they have few equals.

HORSE IN LOVE

The Horse is not exactly a fickle romancer, it is just that he falls in love easily, and often. In fact, when a Horse is hit by one of those little arrows Cupid fires, he gets hit good and hard. But a Horse enjoys love, and generally speaking can handle it quite well, for all the heartache. The amorous Pig is also one to give his heart quickly. But Pigs look for security in love, which is something that the freedom loving Horse can never provide. The old-fashioned Rooster wants a total commitment from her lover, and once again the Horse will be found wanting. The Monkey in love with the Horse will fare even less well. The Monkey *is* a fickle creature whose lovemaking can very often be both transparently one-sided and insincere. This can only have a negative effect on the Horse. Pigs, Roosters and Monkeys will never enjoy the Horse's love, and for all concerned, perhaps it's better that way.

The lady Rat is an irrepressible flirt and does not understand the meaning of fidelity. A short, sharp affair is the most likely outcome with the Horse becoming more and more frustrated. The lady Horse might well become attracted to the male Buffalo, admiring his strong will and sense of

COMPATIBILITY OF HORSE IN LOVE

purpose, but she'll soon grow tired of his unromantic flannel pyjamas, and long, uncomfortable silences. Lady Dogs are not so much romantic as loving, and they adore Big Strong Creatures like the Horse. She'll be *so* anxious to please, she might even stop criticising his every little fault. In return, the Horse will protect the loving Dog.

Two Horses are made for each other. Stallion and Mare will simply sit gazing into their eyes, telling themselves just how lucky they are to have been born so wonderful. Vanity also plays a big part in the romance between a Snake and a Horse. Bewitched by the Snake's mysterious beauty – his is so up front – the Horse will do everything he can to please the ardent reptile. And she'll adore his wit and social ease. But the Horse will show his speed when the Snake begins to coil her body. The sensuous Cat will enjoy the Horse's good humour, as well as his more personal attentions. But she mustn't expect the Horse to fall in with her routine. The Goat has no sense of routine, but a great sense of humour. As lovers the Horse and the Goat will get on terribly well – real harmony. But the Goat must never take the Horse for granted.

The Tiger is always the extrovert in matters of the heart, and the Horse loves action. Again, a fast and furious affair with no regrets at the sudden end. Not one. And when the lady Horse falls for the seductive Dragon, the whole thing will be over even faster. He won't stand for her merciless teasing for more than a night, unless of course she is very beautiful, very witty, and very elegant. In that case the Dragon will be hooked, poor old thing.

HORSE IN MARRIAGE

The Horse is a family man at heart, whatever ideas about himself he might have to the contrary. Once married and settled down, the Horse takes on his responsibilities without fuss and gets on with the job with an admirable self-assurance. A marriage between two Horses is highly recommended. But Horses take note. Animals with *such* an independent nature must define their boundaries in advance. Otherwise you can kiss your five-star rating *adios*. The sensuous lady Cat will also make a perfect partner for the Horse. She will cope with his likes and dislikes, furnish his home comfortably and flatter him by whispering sweet nothings. The social Goat has every bit as good chance as the Cat to provide the Horse with a perfect marriage partner.

COMPATIBILITY OF HORSE IN MARRIAGE

Rat
Buffalo
Tiger
Cat
Dragon
Snake
Horse
Goat
Monkey
Rooster
Dog
Pig

Lady Goats have a warm and gentle sense of humour that attracts the Horse, and her gatherings, built around those he most enjoys, will be a talked-about delight. The lady Pig is also a splendid home maker, but the Horse's independence will suffer just a little when weighed down by all those home baked chocolate cakes, cheese flans and steak and kidney pies – he'll hardly be able to get up from the table to read the kids a goodnight fairy tale.

Roosters and Horses generally get on very well in married life. Both love the garden, and apart from the occasional misunderstanding with regard to the Horse's pretty young secretary, all should run fairly smoothly. The Dog, once wed, will do everything he can to express his loyalty and devotion, and the Horse will not abuse the Dog's open-hearted trust. But the Horse cannot help himself when he falls in love, and so the Dog must not pry too deeply into the Horse's personal affairs. The bewitching Snake is happy for the Horse to dominate in most matters, and will make a good partner once the Horse respects her need to keep silent once in a while. But will the Snake respect the Horse's need for independence? A fifty-fifty chance would be too generous.

The Tiger is impetuous, and might become besotted by the charm and beauty of the female Horse. He'll whisk her off and marry her, and then face the fact that they are both creatures capable of great personal change. The Dragon is easily adaptable, but very full of himself. He might easily fall for the lady Horse in a big way, but she will seldom give the Dragon her devoted attention. Generally speaking Horses and Dragons should avoid marriage, but when it goes well, nothing can stand in the way. Like a rosebed in a drought, the Horse/Dragon marriage will need a great deal of attention.

The Rat will begin married life with a Horse full of good intentions, but he is, like the Horse, easily led. Both know this, but it is not the wisest basis for a marriage. No Rolls at the front gate for the Horse and Buffalo either, if they can avoid it. The Buffalo likes to be the boss at home, and so does the Horse. A master cannot have two servants, nor a home two masters. Oh dear.

The Horse and Monkey will not quibble over who wears the trousers, and enjoy each other's jokes, but they will compete day and night for the mirror, and their marriage will end up in a conflict of vanities.

HOW YOU WILL BE INFLUENCED IN THE YEAR OF THE HORSE

A YEAR FOR ELEGANCE AND FREEDOM

Of all the twelve signs, only the Horse is not guaranteed good fortune in his own year, and in the year of the Fire Horse it can even be a positive disaster (*see* page 139). But again if the fates smile on the Horse, he will experience unparalleled success, and whatever winds of change blow, will certainly be blowing in his favour. An equally splendid year for the Horse's sometime companion in the meadow, the capricious Goat. Invitations to thrilling parties will come flooding through her letterbox, and should she care to work a little she'll be amply rewarded for her efforts. The Buffalo will also have his work cut out. When the corn is ripe in a Horse year, it grows high and plentiful, but the resolute Buffalo will not complain about the extra hours.

As in all years, Dragons do their own thing and the Horse year will not prevent him from leading his carnival parade. It will, in fact, encourage the spectacle. Like the Goat, the well-mannered Cat will enjoy a full social calender, but don't ask the cat to go cross-country running. The sensuous Snake will quickly cotton on to the fact that the Horse year is rich with affairs of the heart, but she won't take kindly to all the odd hours the Horse asks her to work. The talkative Rooster adores to be seen in fashionable circles and this year she'll have ample opportunities. And who knows, the Rooster might even let her hair down and have a frolic in the hay. One way or another, a good twelve months for the Rooster, whose bank balance will be in the black for a change. The Tiger will also see an upward trend in his finances, but with

157

Rat	☐
Buffalo	😊😊😊😊
Tiger	😊😊😊
Cat	😊😊😊😊
Dragon	😊😊😊😊
Snake	😊😊😊
Horse	☐
Goat	😊😊😊😊😊
Monkey	😊😊
Rooster	😊😊😊😊
Dog	😊😊
Pig	😊😊

so much easy-going romance in the air, the Tiger's volatile heart might find itself overstretched.

The Monkey's gift for hogging the stage will not win him many friends this year and there will be many clashes of vanity. But the artful Monkey will make out; he always does. Trouble for the cheerful Pig, who, in spite of all his hard and honest work, will find the Horse year too much in terms of fickle romance. Pigs like a bit of fun, but they take themselves a trifle seriously when they fall in love. The Dog, so loyal, will find no one takes his devotion at all seriously, or his defenceless trust. But one or two might love him a wee bit; it's that kind of year. As for the opportunist Rat, the charm he uses for his socially mobile life will work against him. Time for the Rat to tighten his belt.

FAMOUS HORSES

Arts
Samuel Beckett
Leonard Bernstein
Sir John Betjeman
Chopin
Catherine Cookson
Degas
Jack Higgins
Harold Pinter
J B Priestly
Rembrandt
Segovia
Andy Warhol
Vivaldi

Sports
Zola Budd
Willie Carson
Chris Evert
Brough Scott
Peter O'Sullivan
Freddie Trueman
Mike Tyson

Industry/Politics
Lynda Chalker
General Gaddafi
Billy Graham
Neil Kinnock
Kruschev
Lenin

Tiny Roland
Willie Whitelaw

Royals
Princess Margaret
Lord Snowdon
Duke of Windsor

Show Biz
Rowan Atkinson
Tony Blackburn
Ronnie Corbett
Sean Connery
Billy Connolly
James Dean
Clint Eastwood
Samantha Fox
Sam Goldwyn
Bob Hoskins
Spike Milligan
John Travolta
Joanne Woodward

Pop
Ray Charles
Paul McCartney
Alan Price
Paul Simon
Stephen Sondheim
Barbra Streisand

THE GOAT

1907	February 13th to February 1st	1908
1919	February 1st to February 19th	1920
1931	February 17th to February 5th	1932
1943	February 5th to January 24th	1944
1955	January 24th to February 11th	1956
1967	February 9th to January 29th	1968
1979	January 28th to February 15th	1980
1991	February 15th to February 3rd	1992

My men, like Satyrs grazing on the lawns, Shall with their Goat feet dance the antic hay.

Christopher Marlowe

THE YEAR OF THE GOAT

The Goat's year will begin, continue and end on a note of total accord, for in the eyes of the Chinese, the Goat is seen as a harbinger of peace. Wars and international crises started in other years will find that their strength has been spent by the time they reach the Goat's year. Both personal and universal feuds will be resolved when faced with the Goat's power to calm and pacify as the countless examples testify. January 1919 saw the Peace Conference in Paris, and on June 19 of that year, the Peace Treaty with Germany was signed at Versailles. In 1955 the World's leading scientists appealed for the renunciation of war because of the possible effects of the hydrogen bomb. In 1967 an International treaty was signed in Washington, banning nuclear weapons from outer space, the Moon, and other celestial bodies.

There will be plenty of scandal and gossip, however, and lots of squabbles. In May 1979 former Liberal leader Jeremy Thorpe went on trial at the Old Bailey, accused of conspiring to murder Norman Scott, his alleged lover. No big fights, to be sure – just a string of petty quarrels which are soon over and even sooner forgotten. But if there are no big punchers in the Goat's year it doesn't mean that sport gets left out in the cold. Although the Olympic Games are never held during the Year of the Goat, open any record book and you'll find it full of athletes who have excelled. The American miler, Jim Ryan, ran a world's best in 1967. In 1979 Seb Coe produced two magnificent performances: he set a new world record for both the 1,500 metres and knocked three seconds off Jim Ryan's fastest ever mile.

This is a splendid year for looking up old friends and visiting members of the family in far away places. It is, in fact, a good year for family life in general; a time to get married, have children and enjoy a little fun if it comes along. But don't go out of your way for it. It's a year to fill your home with beautiful objects and paintings; to line your shelves with leather volumes; throw Turkish rugs on your floors and fill your wine cellar with vintage clarets and the best port money can buy. In the year of the Goat there will be much wonderful music composed and played, and the theatre will see its finest actors and actresses performing in unforgettable productions. In 1955, the film *Rebel Without a Cause* introduced the world to James Dean, who added a new dimension to cinema acting. That same year the Vienna Opera House reopened, and the Soviet Union staged a performance of *Hamlet*, the first since the end of Tsarist Russia.

This is not the year to make plans or to design long term projects. Talk peace, but don't invest your life's savings in an industrial enterprise. Leave the stock market alone. Drink chilled wine in the long hot summer, eat lots of chocolate cake and gossip till dawn. The year of the Goat is one in which we should be guided by our instincts, and let them lead us to the Good Life.

THE GOAT PERSONALITY

'Time for peace and pleasure, enter the charming and capricious Goat.'

Of all the twelve signs of the Chinese horoscope, the Goat is the most uniquely feminine. Although universally respected for her shy and gentle manners, and her open sense of humour, the Goat is acclaimed above all as the Bringer of Peace. Nothing in the Goat's make up is hostile, and in so far as she shows aggression, it will only be as a means to restore harmony, peace and balance. But if you do bump into a Goat in a rage, you can be certain that her anger will be directed towards injustice. Wherever it is found, either in the wide and complex world at large, or in the confines of the home, the Goat is quick to react against conflict. For her, both the world and her home are of equal importance in matters of broken harmony, and nothing upsets her need for peace and content-ment more than voices singing out of tune. As a kind of umpire, checking the Great Game we all play is played according to the rules, the Goat is at the heart of things. And no one loves to be at the centre more than a Goat; she takes to being the main attraction one might say, as ducks take to water. And there is no doubt that her love of the spotlight is the reason why the Goat makes such a fabulous hostess. No one puts on a more glittering show when entertaining. Only a Goat arranges her table with such artistry, has silver that

164

gleams so bright and flowers that smell so sweet. And if you have some epicurean whim, there isn't a hostess on earth who will take greater care to ensure it is served exactly to your taste. If you want an omelette without eggs, you only have to ask the Goat hostess and it will be yours. And Mr Goat is no third-rate party giver either. For a classic example we need to look no further than the extravagances of the late Shah of Persia. Shortly before he was deposed, he spent billions building a city of gold in the middle of the desert and invited the world's most important, rich and influential people to share in what was estimated as the most expensive party ever thrown.

As well as his concern for plenty of bubbly and chin wagging with the in-crowd, the Goat has a highly developed artistic sense, and is born under the sign of art. Indeed the list of Goat celebrities include a high proportion of wonderfully talented, artistic people. If you were born in the year of the Goat, you share your sign with Herbert Von Karajan, Rudolph Valentino, George Harrison, Duke Ellington, Buster Keaton, Franz Liszt, Robert Graves, Marcel Proust and William Turner.

Although the Goat has a great natural flair for any kind of artistic enterprise, whether it's perfecting the *pas de deux*, or baking a spinach soufflé, the Goat's genius is of the wayward variety. There are none of the heavy intellectual overtones as found in the Buffalo's creation, or the drama of the Tiger's artistry. The Goat's art is one of gentle reflection, and it is perhaps why the Goat expresses herself best when engaged in an artistic partnership, where another hand can act as a stabiliser and guide. The great composer Felix Mendelssohn enjoyed only a short life but wrote much music of lasting beauty. His father was an essential figure in Mendelssohn's career, treating him first as a son, and then as a kind of super-client, arrranging his tours, publishers, holidays and just about everything else. And what of the Goat Mick Jagger? His song-writing royalties have always been shared equally with Keith Richards (also a Goat), who many believe has helped Jagger more than anyone to keep the Stones rolling for so many years.

The Goat's ability to work easily with others is, I'm certain, the key to unlocking his temperament. Left to roam freely, the Goat will wander in your neighbour's field, and your neighbour's neighbour's field. Sometimes he'll eat everything in sight, including the old mattress and car tyres. The next day it will be your prize marrow. It is therefore in everyone's best interest, including the Goat's, that he be tethered. A rope around the Goat's neck removes their inbuilt craving for security, and in addition, leaves them free to enjoy their immediate surroundings in a way they would not normally do if left to their own devices.

The word 'enjoyment', of course, is one placed very high on the Goat's list of most used words. And she has every right to enjoy her pleasure, for few can both give and receive with such good grace and charm. There are also few animals with quite such an extraordinary sense of humour, as the Goat Groucho Marx illustrates. But here, too, there is something of the Goat in need of a firm guiding hand. On the screen Groucho Marx was the hero of every plot, leading his hapless brothers in and out of a million wild and improbable scrapes. But in real life, Groucho was, according to his many biographers, a sad and lonely figure who was in desperate need of security right up to the very end. His romances and marriages collapsed more often than a clown's baggy trousers, and to this day there is still a dispute as to who is the rightful heir to his mammoth estate. And it might well be said that for every great Goat actor, you can bet your bottom dollar that there is strong support waiting in the wings. For every Laurence Olivier, there's a Vivien Leigh to give the performance that bit extra. Sir Larry was a classic Goat, and so is the dancer Anthony Dowell – a performer full of grace and subtle movement. And while on the subject of dancers, there are those who say the Goat Margot Fonteyn was never more nimble on her delightful feet than when Rudolph Nureyev (a Tiger) was by her side.

Because Goats tend to ponder a great deal before acting (or not bothering to act) they are very often poor decision makers and should not be left to make important decisions on their own. Fretful and whimsical, the Goat hates to commit himself, and will often wait for others to decide before acting. The trick, as the Goat sees it, is to let others do the worrying while they get on with life's big issue – having fun! This frequently has the effect of causing the Goat to become moody when the choice has been made against her wishes. But being a Goat, you'd never know you had made the wrong choice until it was too late. And when things go bad for a Goat, they really go bad. They are not good at coping with personal reversals, and are easily put off a project if the going begins to look tough. What is more, Goats cannot bear any kind of personal criticism. Tell a Goat that her lipstick is a tiny bit the wrong shade, or her watercress soup's on the thick side and you can cross yourself off her guest list! The Goat is far too polite to say anything there and then, but she won't forget. And while on the issue of guest lists, do not make the mistake of turning down a Goat's invitation, however casually it might appear to have been made. Rejection looms very large in the life of a Goat, and again exposes their basic sense of insecurity. A very noticeable characteristic of the Goat is his tendency to worry, almost fret, over trivialities.

Goats hate any form of restraint, and will fight shy of any role that imposes regularity and schedules. To be tethered to what a Goat finds agreeable is one thing, but to be harnessed to a routine is the Goat's idea of purgatory. Goats steer well clear of the Services, military or civil – unless of course, the job comes with a large house, servants and pots of money. And as a rule, Goats are best advised avoiding any form of commerce. In particular they should not apply for the job of salesman. They get easily flustered, and it is then that they might snap just a little. Remember, they have very sharp teeth, and a pair of back legs that can pack a hefty kick.

The really insecure Goat, the one who knows it, will need

167

a great deal of support. To be thought well of causes such Goats to introduce a false note in their behaviour; to have a pronounced social awareness. However much she puts into the preparation of food for a dinner party, even more care and attention will have gone into the composition of the guest list, which will contain as many fashionable and famous names as she can muster. And there in the centre of all these bright and witty people is the Goat herself, the very hub of it all. This in turn leads us to be cautious when the goat gives us her seemingly well-informed opinion of the current theatrical hit, or some other fashionable event. Her intention will not be to inform us, but to create an impression, which leads us to ask if the opinion she expresses so confidently is her own or her favourite reviewer's? And when we look through her bookshelves, aren't all those books in the bestseller lists? And the new oil painting over the fireplace, her choice or the Bond Street dealer's?

In the Goat's home there will be no shortage of bric-a-brac. There'll be etchings, records, videos, knick-knacks, heirlooms, junk from the local shop, junk from Christie's, hallstands, mirrors, old chairs with the stuffing coming out, sofas from Harrod's, Victoriana, art nouveau, art deco, wall hangings, coffee tables, coffee table books, cats, dogs, hamsters and children – lots of them. No one is more acquisitive than the Goat, and it is a trait that runs through both male and female alike. No matter what the cost, or whether she really wants it, the Goat will take her momentary fancy home. The lady on the package tour with the sombrero, castanets, and plastic bag bulging with duty free is almost certain to have been born in the year of the Goat.

As the French author Paula Delsol tells us in her book *Chinese Horoscopes*, the Goat enjoys what the Japanese call I-Shoku-Ju, which, roughly translated, means the love of the senses: food, clothes and comfort. No wonder there are always a handful of slimming books in the Goat's bookcase. But a life centred on its superficialities, however agreeable, can only spell trouble when dealing with serious matters. It is here that the Goat shows herself at her most fickle. In matters of love, as with everything else, Goats do not know the meaning of self-denial. When in love with a Goat, you will want to know her true feelings. But because she never wants to be thought ill of, and has an in-built desire to preserve peace, the Goat will often back away from her real feelings. When you ask simply, 'Do you love me?' the Goat will invariably give you the answer she imagines you want to hear. The same might be true for her opinion of your latest sonnet, your new car or your holiday snaps. This kind of detached response is perfect for an actor, whose lines are fiction to begin with, but in everyday life it can lead to insurmountable problems. Lucky, then, that the Goat has a remarkable gift for getting out of tight spots; namely, her immense charm. And make no mistake, the Goat can really turn on the charm when she wants something. What is more, if it's a man the Goat is interested in, he will soon know it. By flirting, pouting, throwing moods, even throwing off her underwear, the lady Goat will get her man. Her only problem is whether she really wants to keep him. With the wayward and coquettish Goat, it's always difficult to tell.

When a Goat does settle down, her family completely dominates her life, and she'll devote every ounce of her considerable energy in making sure her husband and children are contented.

Not much will escape her maternal eye, and no child of a Goat mother will be sent to school with holes in his shoes or a dirty shirt collar. And her husband won't exactly leave home looking as if he'd spent the weekend swilling out the pigsty. But for all her concern about family appearances, the Goat mother will not become a housemaid. Husbands and children can do their own ironing and clean their own shoes. She'll be there at inspection time, making sure that everything is tickity-boo, but that's her last line of commitment. Self-help is the by-word in the Goat's home.

Although Goats tend to leave their homes while still young, they have a curious habit in later life of moving close to their parents. One Goat lady I know married, had two children, and lived close to my own home. As her children grew she decided a bigger house was needed and started looking around. With the whole of London to choose from, she moved one door away from her mother. Another Goat lady, who is a friend of my wife, goes to live in her mother's house every weekend. And my uncle Edward lived in his mother's house from the day he was born until the day he died, aged eighty-five. The most extraordinary case of a Goat clinging to family ties concerns a former girlfriend. No matter where she was, she'd phone her mother at least once a day, even when she had nothing at all to say. We knew each other for seven years and she never once broke the habit. Many years after we had gone our separate ways, I bumped into a mutual acquaintance who told me that my former girlfriend had married and gone to live in Italy. I asked if she still phoned her mother, and was told that in order to avoid the wrath of her Italian husband, she would go to Milan station with a handful of change, and use the public phone to call her mother. She did this, I understood, *every single night.*

In spite of the Goat's desire for security, plus the fact that she is impressionable and easily led, the Goat lady is very much the boss in her own home. Not the one to make the choice, the Goat will subtly influence all the important decisions. Somehow the choice of where the family Goat takes its holidays, the type of car, the school its children go to, all of these home-based decisions will ultimately require the final approval of the lady Goat. It is therefore imperative that the Goat marries someone who is both strong and adaptable. He most certainly will need a strong head for drink with all those late night parties.

Because Goat ladies are easily impressed, they in turn like to impress, and their clothes often mirror this attitude. Even the most conservative Goat lady will aim to wear the kind of outfit that will win not only the admiration of her own man, but everyone else's. No matter what they dress up in, whether it's a leather mini-skirt or a see-through blouse, the Goat lady will put her need to be noticed top of her list and the need to feel comfortable way down at the bottom. Goat men, on the other hand, dress very much to suit themselves. If they work in a job where they can wear what they like – and most Goats do – they'll go in for shabby old corduroys, heavy tweeds and colourful woollen neck-ties. You might well find a Goat in second-hand clothes – the well worn feel and quality appeals to the Goat, as do spotted handkerchiefs tied into a cravat, and open sandals when the weather's fine. And Goat men very often wear their clothes until they fall apart at the seams.

When choosing a profession, Goats should stick to the world of the arts, although if they do decide that they are mountain Goats, and care to climb Everest, they will be in good company. Sir Edmund Hillary was a Goat. But there are a few pitfalls facing the lady Goat, and her innocent love of *la dolce vita* could easily find her serving drinks to tired businessmen in a Soho club, if you get my drift. However, the Chinese believe that a Goat in the home brings good fortune as the Goat has a pure heart. This means that he will always have money, although he will not necessarily always be wise in the way he spends it. But once a Goat gets the hang of finance, he will exercise great shrewdness in his business dealings.

The first of the Goat's three phases of life will find the young Goat clinging to the family, and she'll be one of those children who will be quick to use her tears to get her own way. But her fickle nature will lead her to want her own life and she'll leave home while still very young – coming back every time she gets into hot water. Driven by her senses, the Goat will suffer complications, especially in matters of love. But she is not foolish and quickly learns from her mistakes. Once the Goat realises that her own patch of ground is no greener than the patch on the other side of the fence, she will settle down to a long and contented final phase, and will be visited often by her large and loving family.

GOAT AS PARENT

The mother Goat and her daughter kid will have an almost perfect understanding, as both are aware from a very early age just what trouble a capricious heart can get them into. There will be no moralising between them, nor will there be any great competition, just a regular session of exchanging notes. The Goat mother's view of her baby Pig will not be very different, and she'll encourage the social side of his character so that he learns to play as well as work. 'Thank you very much,' says the Pig in genuine gratitude. The Horse daughter will also grow up contentedly in a Goat's home; nice clothes, good school, riding lessons . . . The baby Cat will also enjoy life with a Goat as a parent. He is an artistic child and the Goat father will do his best to encourage his talented son. But Kittens need a lot of pushing to get them off on the right foot.

The Goat father will adore his Monkey daughter, but she'll suffer from his over-indulgence in later life. Alas, we cannot trick our way out of every tight corner, not even if we are the cleverest of Monkeys. Snake children have a slight chance of happiness in the house of a Goat parent. They mature very slowly and the Goat mum insists her Snake daughter glitters at every social function – often put on for the daughter's benefit. Nevertheless, the Goat mother will support her Snake offspring, even though she might receive a small return for her investment.

On the other side of the coin, the Dragon son can do no wrong in the eyes of his Goat mother. The problem facing parent and child here is how to introduce some kind of critical appraisal. All that showing-off might get the Dragon somewhere in life, but what if it doesn't? The reverse is true for the young Buffalo. He's such a solitary child, and to get him to say anything to all the high-spirited guests the Goat

172

COMPATIBILITY OF GOAT PARENT AND CHILD

brings home ... well! Young Tigers will be happy enough to say a few polite words to the Goat's friends, and even amuse them. Tiger children can be very cute. But they'll grow sick of the rich sponge cakes and lack of adventure.

The baby Rooster *thinks* she likes the Goat's somewhat shambolic home life, but great method burns within her young heart, and a sense of what is right and wrong is also deeply etched there. The Dog child will form a good relationship with the Goat parent. Son or daughter, the young Dog will love and be loved by the Goat, and the love will grow stronger as they all grow older. Dogs will visit their Goat parent in old age, and never reproach them for having low horizons. The young Rat can get nothing from a Goat parent but more of what he has already. He might like it, but it won't do the Rat child any good to throw his charm around. To be truly successful, the baby Rat must be given the kind of tools the Goat doesn't own.

GOAT IN BUSINESS

Goats, broadly speaking, are at their best when involved in some way with the arts, however tenuous the connection might be. It therefore follows that they should steer well clear of business, especially the industrial areas. A partnership of two Goats is not a good idea, as both need a strong hand to help produce their best. But an escort agency might work out all right. A steadying influence will be found under the practical and hard working Horse. The Goat and Horse are natural partners in many fields and the world of commerce is no exception. The honest Pig might not tether the Goat, but he will make sure that the work gets done, even if he has to do a bit extra himself.

If the Goat is an actor or an actress, or someone who works for a fee rather than a wage, he or she would be well advised to find themselves a Cat for an agent. They will sniff out the best jobs and ensure that the Goat gets the top price. The Dragon is a strong leader, and the Goat will be quite happy to follow the Dragon's great schemes. But if the Goat sits in the driver's seat he'll change directions too many times for the Dragon. The Goat's on/off attitude will exasperate the Dragon who will sell his shares and move on.

The opportunist Rat sounds like a good bet to partner the Goat, but they both have a very different method of arriving at the same goal. Rats grab, Goats lay traps, and in business it does not pay to have a divided front. But Rat and Goat can make money – a firm of liquidators, perhaps, or auctioneers?

COMPATIBILITY OF GOAT IN BUSINESS RELATIONSHIPS

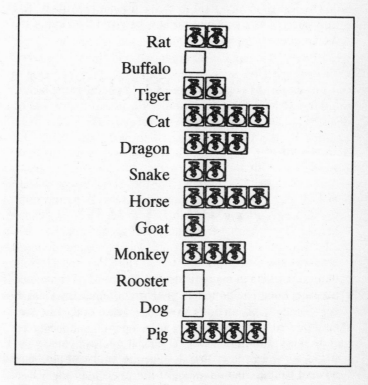

The Tiger has plenty of schemes up his sleeve, but he'll want the kind of firm commitment and instant action that the Goat is seldom happy giving. The Monkey is good with money, and takes his time deciding on the best investment. This is good news for the indecisive Goat. But he must be careful how he deals with the profits the Monkey so carefully accrues. No wild spending. Spending the profits is a problem facing the Snake and Goat as partners. The only partnership for these two would be one financed by a trust, so the money would never be theirs to spend. Perhaps they should run the British Museum.

The resolute Buffalo knows how to get the Goat working, but the Goat has his own pace and his own very specific ideas about work and leisure being quite separate. Nothing but prolonged and bitter arguments here. There is no point in a Rooster teaming up with a Goat, even if they are good friends. The Rooster is well organised and thinks positively. Why can't the Goat stick to one thing at a time? The Dog is not cut out for the wheeler-dealer side of commerce, which is the only aspect a Goat can handle. No routines, just lots of deals. The Dog is the complete reverse. He'll be driven bonkers by the Goat's wayward approach, and be at the double vodkas to steady his nerves before you can say Jack Russell.

GOAT IN LOVE

Goats are no strangers to the complex affairs of the heart, and generally speaking don't have a great deal of control over them. This can obviously lead to all manner of complications, and in many ways hinders the Goat's, if you will pardon the expression, 'joy of sex'. For the partner who will give him least problems on the emotional front, the Goat might well fall in love with the sensuous Cat. She has a comfortable home and a very comfortable bed. But the Goat should at all times avoid animals with a highly developed sense of morality. The Rooster, in spite of his boasting, is deeply conservative in all matters concerning love, and will not go along with the Goat's capricious attitude. The anxious, loyal Dog won't care for it much, either.

The Buffalo shares the Rooster's strait-laced views on sex, but in this case that won't be his problem. When the Buffalo does actually manage to get the fires of passion burning, he'll have found to his dismay that the Goat has nibbled through

COMPATIBILITY OF GOAT IN LOVE

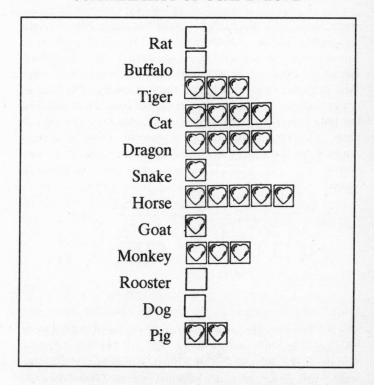

her tether, and is in someone else's meadow. As for the Rat and Goat 'getting it all together', the chances are very slim indeed. They both prefer someone else's hayloft, and would never know where they were supposed to meet. There'll be no problems with the sexually easy Horse, and he'll charm and be charmed by the Goat. A perfect partnership so long as the Horse remembers not to use up all his stamina showing off in the five mile chase. Pigs are not complicated lovers, but come unstuck when they fall too heavily. The Goat might enjoy having a moon-eyed Pig at her elbow day and night. There again, she might not. The Tiger is hot blooded and passionate, and will be quickly taken in by the Goat's promises. But the Goat must be careful to keep them.

There will be no long term conclusion to the Snake and Goat, at least, no long term passion. The Snake's love is too mysterious for the fickle Goat, and has so many strings attached. The playful Monkey won't bother with strings, and the Goat might think that this suits her at first. But what happens when she dials the Monkey's number and finds there is no answer? The fiery Dragon will seduce the Goat in a twinkling and they will enjoy love uncomplicated by guilt, but both enjoy quantity as well as quality. Who will grow tired first? To have an affair, someone has to make the first step, unless, of course, both lovers are clairvoyant. This won't be the case when two Goats fall in love. It will be fine so long as one of them declares an interest.

GOAT IN MARRIAGE

Once a Goat decides to settle down, for however brief a time, she becomes the perfect home maker. The glass-fronted walnut cupboards will be full of beautiful china and the wine cellar will never be short of good wines. Goats have an instinct for the Good Life, and will quickly fall in with any spouse who will help provide it. The intelligent and industrious Horse knows all about Georgian candlesticks and has the energy and know-how to deal with the Goat's need for security. For a marriage to last, the Goat need look no further than the Horse. A good partnership, too, when the Goat marries the refined and equally socially conscious Cat. Both love a comfortable home and adore children. The Monkey might well walk down the aisle with the Goat. But they have very strong opinions, both of themselves and just about everything else. Silly to break up a marriage just because they can't decide which wallpaper to put in the

COMPATIBILITY OF GOAT IN MARRIAGE

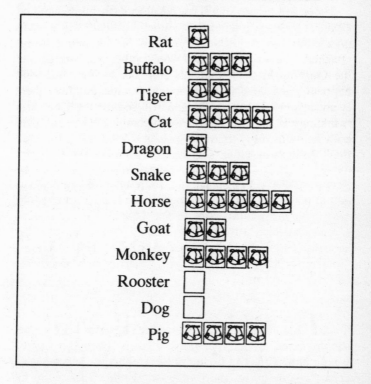

downstairs loo. The lady Rooster might well decide that the pattern on the wallpaper is the most important thing in the world, and could even come to blows over it. Goats and Roosters are not a good idea when it comes to setting up home. Snakes, especially males, will find an ideal companionship with a lady Goat. But it will help the Goat if the Snake husband has a well paid job, and it will help both of them if they become Jehovah's Witnesses – they have such romantic inclinations ...

A Goat marrying a Pig will not find his mind bothered by the way the home should look. The Pig will just get on with it, and it will be just the way the Goat likes it. A lady Goat might easily marry a Buffalo – after all, he's so strong and resolute. Both like children and secluded gardens to sit quietly in on hot summer days. But the Buffalo is a bit of a bore at party time. The Goat should avoid the Dog, who is a terrible pessimist, and his pessimism will only magnify the Goat's own deep-rooted insecurity. The Tiger will cut a dash alongside his charming Goat wife. But Tigers crave adventure, and the Goat can hardly hold her soirées in a tent in the middle of the jungle. Rats are warm hearted, and love society. They will easily marry a Goat, and just as easily wander off. And that will mean both partners having fun on the side. The marriage of two Goats will only work if the pasture is filled with instant grass. Both take what's going and do not plan. But a big family might keep two Goats together – or drive them further apart. The Dragon has great ideas about himself, as a husband and anything else he turns his hands to. But in marrying the Goat he will only be making a mistake, for her as well as himself. Dragons make decisions. Goats avoid them.

HOW YOU WILL BE INFLUENCED IN THE YEAR OF THE GOAT

A YEAR FOR PEACE AND LOVE

Bliss for the Goat! A mixed year for workers, but the shirkers do just dandy. The go-getting Rat can't believe his luck after the previous truly miserable twelve months. The Goat's year is a veritable cornucopia of delights for the opportunist everywhere, and the only problem facing the Rat is, will he

Rat	
Buffalo	
Tiger	
Cat	
Dragon	
Snake	
Horse	
Goat	
Monkey	
Rooster	
Dog	
Pig	

eat too much? Careful fat Rat. The social Cat will be given ample opportunity to live the life just how she wants under the influence of the equally socially inclined Goat. A fine year for Cats, but they must remember to get their beauty sleep.

The popular Horse will recover from his own year, should it have been a disaster (with the year of the Horse it is impossible to know). He'll get along well as long as he confines his practical skills to hanging paintings and opening the wine. And while there are plenty of parties, the merry Pig won't mind. He'll be there with his jokes and smiles and quickly-emptying glass. The Pig's one setback is in choosing which of the gilt-lined cards that decorate his mantelpiece he'll have to say 'sorry' to. The Monkey will take what's on offer – when doesn't he? And it will be fine until he realises he's the one who has to foot the bill.

There are two Roosters: the spendthrift type and those who save every penny. No matter which, they'll be footing *all* the bills in the Goat's year, and neither sort will do it graciously. The unpredictable Tiger will love everything that's going during the first few months, but as he begins to realise that it's all fun and games, he'll grow bored and restless. The subtle Snake will enjoy the flood of artistic achievements but will not find the sexual competition much fun. In fact, she'll loathe it. But sex wars never worry the dutiful and hard-working Buffalo. Nor does sex peace. He's simply not interested. Cocktail parties are neither for the Buffalo nor the loyal, idealist Dog, and both he and the Buffalo might as well move into a quiet corner and wait till the Goat's party guests start asking for their hats and coats.

The Dragon doesn't usually have a bad year, but when he does, this is it. The leader of the carnival goes around puffing fire and filling the air with his flames. The poor old Dragon; he glitters, he seduces, he stimulates, but no one pays him the least bit attention. Well … maybe just one.

FAMOUS GOATS

Arts

W H Auden
Peggy Ashcroft
Jill Bennett
John le Carré
Leslie Caron
Enrico Caruso
Margot Fonteyn
Robert Graves
Franz Kafka
Buster Keaton
Ben Kingsley
Franz Liszt
Proust
Mendelssohn
Iris Murdoch

Daphne du Maurier
Lord Olivier
Leslie Thomas
Seurat
Turner

Sports
Arthur Ashe
Boris Becker
Ian Botham
Bobby Fischer
Paul Gascoigne
Sir Edmund Hillary
Billy Jean King
Olga Korbut
Victor Korchnoi
Steve Ovett

Industry/Politics
Terence Conran
Mikhail Gorbachev
John Major
Rupert Murdoch
Mussolini
Cecil Parkinson
Eddie Shah
Norman Tebbit
Lech Walesa

Royals
Shah of Persia
George VI
Richard II

Show Biz
Diana Dors
Shree Bagwhan Rajneesh
Buzby Berkeley
Cilla Black
Larry Hagman
Frank Muir
Ned Sherrin
Rudolph Valentino
John Wayne
Lord Weidenfield

Pop
Jack Bruce
John Denver
Lonnie Donnegan
George Harrison
Mick Jagger
Billy J Kramer
Keith Richards
Scott Walker
Paul Young

THE MONKEY

1908	February 2nd to January 21st	1909
1920	February 20th to February 7th	1921
1932	February 6th to January 25th	1933
1944	January 25th to February 12th	1945
1956	February 12th to January 30th	1957
1968	January 30th to February 16th	1969
1980	February 16th to February 4th	1981
1992	February 4th to January 22nd	1993

Some Monkey's queer grimaces,
Forestalling human faces,
Fill the gaps and spaces
That link two ancient races.

Leon Underwood

THE YEAR OF THE MONKEY

If you regard yourself as a wilting flower, then the hyperactive year of the Monkey is definitely not for you. Everything is up for grabs, and it's a case of first come first served. And if there's to be a rule, it will, I am afraid, be the rule of anarchy. Under the influence of the mischievous Monkey, anything can happen, and almost certainly will. You will wake up each morning and read the newspaper headlines with growing disbelief. In 1920, Americans woke up to find prohibition had been introduced, and in 1968 slumbering Parisians opened their bleary eyes to find the streets full of rioting students – the most serious of its kind since the last century.

The accent everywhere will be on trend, on posture, on novelty: Monkeys love fun. But in spite of its superficiality, the Monkey year will give birth to a great many discoveries and there will be great strides made in the fields of science and technology. It's a time for new ideas, new methods, new worlds. Britain's first atomic power station was opened in 1956, and in the same year the House of Commons rejected a motion to retain the death penalty.

The year of the Monkey is not one in which to sit around and contemplate your naval, not unless that's the current trend. The secret is to take chances, to take risks, to deal and double-deal. In 1968 there was an almost unprecedented rush on gold, and at one point the Stock Exchange closed down. In 1980 Lord Thomson put *The Times* and *The Sunday Times* up for sale.

One way or another, political issues will be settled. The

Hungarian uprising was finally squashed by Soviet troops in 1956 and later that year Pakistan proclaimed itself an Islamic republic. Nothing that happens in the year of the Monkey will be pint-sized or insignificant. Senator Robert Kennedy and the Reverend Martin Luther King were both assassinated in 1968, and in 1980, John Lennon was gunned down outside his New York apartment.

The trick to learn in the year of the Monkey is not to run against the tide. It is not a time for moralists or stick-in-the-muds. In 1968 the Pope issued his encyclical banning of all methods of artificial birth control, and found it met with a largely hostile reception. Evangelists should talk less to their flock, and more to their tax lawyers. But the world of popular entertainment will flourish, and there will be many new stars in the galaxy of sport, music and cinema. The very first public broadcasting station was opened by the Marconi Company in 1920. The greatest popular entertainer of all time made his disc debut in 1956: 'Heartbreak Hotel' was the title of the record that was to introduce Elvis Presley to a public who continue to buy his albums in millions.

The Monkey's year will begin and end in a restless pursuit of fun and profit. But if things don't work out, don't expect to hang around and mope. The Monkey just swings skilfully, effortlessly, onto the next branch. And do not expect the Big Love Affair to last a lifetime. Those who are lucky at cards are often, so it is said, unlucky in love. There'll be plenty of five card poker in the year of the Monkey, but the luck will, I'm afraid, run out at the bedroom door.

THE MONKEY PERSONALITY

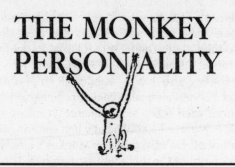

'Roll the dice and throw a six.
Enter the wise and clever Monkey.'

It is an inescapable fact that of all the animals, the Monkey bears the strongest resemblance to Mankind. Whether you accept Darwin's theory of evolution, or throw your lot in with the Bible thumping fundamentalists, there can be little doubt that when we come face to face with a Monkey, we in some senses see ourselves. And once we have examined those born under the sign of the Monkey we will discover a sobering truth; Monkeys are blessed not only with the very best Man has to offer, but also, sadly, his worst.

On the credit side, the Monkey has great wisdom. He has a high regard for knowledge and has an extraordinary power to reason out the most complex of problems, seemingly with no effort. He knows the rewards that this world has to offer, and that wealth and power are the means to achieve them. Not one to pick up the sword to attain his goals, the Monkey instead uses his logic, his wit, and his intuition, which seems to tell him the precise time to act. Utterly charming, resourceful, with an overwhelming conceit that we invariably forgive, the Monkey will go as far as it is possible in whatever field he chooses. And if the Monkey has a foundation stone on which all his enterprises are built, it will be engraved with the two words: *Wit* and *Wisdom*. If you were born in the year

188

of the Monkey, you share your sign with: Leonardo da Vinci, Liz Taylor, Sir Christopher Wren, the great escapologist Harry Houdini, Bette Davis, Peter O'Toole, Charles Dickens, Ronald Searle, Diana Ross, Rod Stewart and Koo Stark.

The Monkey also has a wonderful gift for figures and you'll find his mathematical genius popping up in areas as distinct from each other as commerce, science, architecture and music – you need a cool head when counting the beats to a bar. But of all his qualities, the Monkey's closest link with Man is to be found in his sense of humour. His wit is not caustic or blunt, bawdy or cynical. What it does is bubble with a mixture of very gentle rib tickling and the purest wit. At its best, the Monkey's wit resembles the subtle sayings of Eastern sages. You can quite easily picture the wise old Monkey sitting under the shade of a Lotus tree, surrounded by enchanted admirers, and hear him telling the assembly, 'He who plants a forest in the morning cannot expect to saw planks in the evening.' Or, 'Those without shoes should think of those without feet.'

Bearing in mind these ancient proverbs, it is not surprising to learn that the Buddha himself was a Monkey.

But if the irresistible Monkey mirrors all our finest qualities, how far does he go in aping those we respect least? Certainly you will look long and hard for any deeply felt scruples, and you might as well find the proverbial needle in a haystack as discover a Monkey with a strong ethical code. It is just not part of his make-up. Crafty, shy, sly, artful, these are the words used in describing the Monkey's inferior side. Sharp practice is very often the Monkey's stock in trade, and success his only goal. And if the Monkey has a tool it is deception, which he uses as mechanics use a universal spanner.

However, it must be said that the Monkey has such guile, such a highly developed sense of his own superiority that he is very often unable to distinguish fact from fiction. He will, on many occasions, believe his fabrications to be the real thing. After all, the Monkey is born under the sign of fantasy.

Arrogant, and having little or no respect for the opinions of others, the Monkey will often get clean away with his tricks. And strangers are easily taken in by the Monkey's fast talk. Only those who live close to the Monkey know how to catch him. In this respect, the bushmen of the Kalahari desert in Southern Africa have got the Monkey's number, tricking him in true Monkey style. They do it simply by relying on the Monkey's greed. First the bushman digs a tunnel in a mound of earth roughly the length of a Monkey's arm, and at the end of it, he makes a slightly larger hole. After making sure that the tunnel is only wide enough for a Monkey to place an open hand through, the bushman deposits a pile of sugar in the hollow. When the Monkey puts his arm in and grabs the sugar, his fist naturally has to shut. But with his fist closed around the sugar, it is too large to pull out through the tunnel. Rather than let his prize go, the Monkey foolishly, avariciously, holds on. Even when the bushman appears, the Monkey will never let go. That sugar is his! Poor, misguided Monkey. So the lesson is quite clear when dealing with a Monkey: don't try to win an open confrontation, he is the world's number one smart alec. A war of words will get you nowhere. Just offer him some sweet wine and a huge helping of chocolate fudge cake, and wait till he's too drunk or fat to fight.

The combination of a sharp mind, opportunism and thrift provides the Monkey with all he needs to become a candidate for the super tax league. Indeed, the Monkey may pile up treasures for himself, and do so with the kind of panache that will always hit the headlines. And Monkeys seldom specialise, preferring always to diversify their talents as much as possible. They might make their first million late in life, like the famous American primitive painter, Grandma Moses, or before they leave their teens – remember Bjorn Borg?

Fundamental to the Monkey's prosperity, and equally essential to his great social adaptability, is his quite extraordinary memory. Buffaloes, Dogs, Pigs and Snakes can all be relied on to dredge up some half forgotten fact at the drop of a hat, but no other animal can lay claim to having such a remarkable gift as the monkey's memory. And it is perhaps no accident. The Monkey, for all his quick wit and craft, is usually insecure at heart. He needs to be shown love openly and craves attention. It is here that a good memory is not just a blessing, but an essential piece of equipment. After all, if he can immediately remember your name, little details about your likes and dislikes, facts about your private life and so on, he is well on the way to winning you over. How fascinating you must be for the Monkey – such a charming creature – to have taken so much trouble to have remembered all that about you; *you* of all people! But flattering you by remembering the name of your eldest son, the school he goes to and how high he came in his mock GCSEs is all part of the Monkey's bag of tricks. It is, in effect, a confidence trick in the fullest sense. The truth is that the Monkey's memory is second nature, and moreover, he is the same warm hearted, smiling, laughing, fun loving, fun person with every single person he meets. No matter who it is: taxi driver or oldest friend, stranger or relative – all are one to the Monkey in search of security. Never one to be weighed down with compassion, the Monkey's motto might easily be that of con men everywhere, 'here come the mugs'.

An outstanding memory is of course essential if you want to become a linguist. The present Pope, John Paul II is a Monkey, and I understand he speaks six languages more or less perfectly. Fred Housego, the taxi driver winner of *Mastermind* is a Monkey, and so was the original Memory Man, Leslie Welch.

A Monkey friend of mine, Barney Bates, is a freelance pianist who plays in my jazz band. He worked for years with Acker Bilk and his Paramount Jazzmen, and has stored up in his mental filing system an incredible number of standards, blues, pop songs, work songs, hymns, chants, rags, waltzes and heaven knows what else. I was once told that during an evening session, playing solo piano, his fingers improvised on over 120 different numbers: Barney did so without a single note of music, a wrong chord, or even batting an eyelid. It was just another night to him.

Allied to the Monkey's astonishing power of recall is his avid thirst for knowledge. No matter whether it is a piece of junk mail that has just fallen on the doormat, or the latest Pulitzer Prize novel, the Monkey will read it avidly, and very often without a hint of judgement. For the Monkey, knowledge is simply knowledge, to be stored away for use on a future occasion. Moral issues are not his concern in this respect. And his appetite for new experiences will lead a Monkey to try anything once. Just watch the Monkey at the table, dipping his finger into everyone else's pie. If it is new, if he's never had it before, you can count on the Monkey to be in the front of the queue of those wanting to try a sample. And the Monkey won't stop at your summer pudding. So watch out if he takes a fancy to your wife (or husband).

In commerce, the arts and sciences, the Monkey's combination of a retentive and attentive mind, plus his never ending quest for new experiences, makes him a formidable opponent. But in spite of his remarkable memory and thirst for knowledge, the Monkey is seldom an originator. Just think of those crowds in front of the Monkey cage at the zoo. They stand there pulling faces and before you know it, the Monkey is doing the exact same thing. All the tricks the chimp learns for his comic tea party he learned from us. Of course, there are exceptions. The first painter ever to cover his canvas with coloured squares, Piet Mondrian, was a Monkey. So too, was the greatest original in all jazz, the alto saxophonist, Charlie Parker. He revolutionised jazz in the forties and influenced millions of musicians. Yet Charlie Parker always claimed his highly original style was modelled on a long forgotten player whom he'd heard as a young man in his home town of Kansas City. And how original is Roy Hattersley, or Shirley Conran? Like rag and bone men, Monkeys take a little from here, a bit from there and often without the faintest idea that they are doing it, sell the goods off as their own. I remember telling my young Monkey sister-in-law an idea I had to throw a swanky dinner party, complete with waiters, buckets of champagne, and guests in full evening dress. But it would all take place in a rented bedsit in the most dreadful area of Earls Court, and when the silver lids would be lifted, all my guests would find to assuage their appetites would be piles of bangers and mash. Some time later I heard the same idea told back to me by her aunt, who in turn had been told it by my sister-in-law, who had apparently given the impression she had just thought of it.

Put without frills, what the Monkey tends to offer is frequently a touch superficial. But however skin deep his knowledge is it is nevertheless extremely broad. And his stories, whatever their source, always hold our attention. No one tells a tale better than a Monkey, or laces it with such charm and wit. And it must be emphasised that the Monkey has a terrific sense of humour, one that gets him both into and out of his fair share of scrapes. Whatever else, there will be no shortage of near misses and close calls in the fast and furious life of the Monkey.

Once the Monkey has decided on a course of action, he must act at once. If a Monkey is kept waiting, he'll quickly move on to something else – and there are always plenty of options, he makes sure of that. I knew a Monkey who planned to go to the United States, but got fed up with waiting around for her visa and went to Israel instead. She came back to England and applied to go to art school, but she'd left it too late to do any work for her portfolio and got turned down. She then went back to Sussex University (where she had planned her American trip), thought about becoming a flying doctor, applied for an American visa ... The one thing you can say about a Monkey who stares defeat in the face is he'll admit to it. There'll be no false heroics. This has the advantage, of course, of conserving the Monkey's energy, and gives him time to prepare to strike again.

Because Monkeys must experience everything, and given the chance, all at once, they adore travelling. The open road holds up the endless promise of ever new and increasingly wonderful adventures. This is particularly true of young Monkeys, who dominate the autoroutes of the world with their hitched thumbs and engaging smiles. An old chum of mine from the pop explosion of the Sixties is the Kinks leader, Ray Davies. He has been on the road solidly since 1964, and to my certain knowledge has travelled the globe a dozen times.

But if it seems that Monkeys have more going for them than most, that too is perhaps a result of the Monkey's cunning. For all his artfulness and acumen, the Monkey finds little joy if he or she falls in love. For many, the heart poses no end of threats, but not for the Monkey. If anything, Monkeys treat love far too lightly, seeing it as just another game in which they hold all the aces. But love is not like a game of poker. No matter whether it is a life-long commitment or a casual affair, there can be no winners or losers in love. What is needed is a mutual respect and the constant necessity to share – the two qualities that the Monkey has in short supply. Try as he or she might to settle down, the ever present need to try out new experiences will exert itself. No one will ever fully satisfy him, because the Monkey never really wants satisfaction. A tendency towards casual affairs may sometimes lead lady Monkeys off the straight and narrow, and if they are not extremely careful, onto the streets. And I know several lady Monkeys who have absolutely no regrets at having become high-class mistresses.

For all his excesses and acquisitiveness, the Monkey is capable of great charity. He will genuinely rejoice in your successes as well as commiserate in your failures. And when the Monkey calls, he will never come empty-handed. Even if it is no more than a valueless trinket, there'll always be a little gift especially for you. And when you find a postcard on your doormat from some far flung corner of the globe, it will be a Monkey who was wishing *you* were there. How the Monkey loves to please. How considerate.

Monkey ladies often have fair and sensitive skin. Their

faces redden easily and they tend to suffer minor skin complaints. They dress almost entirely to impress, and spend a lot of time on their very beautiful hair (they would like you to believe that it grows so beautifully naturally). But although they dress to knock you dead, they do it with taste. Indeed, in the years when the world of fashion talked about the best dressed woman, the Duchess of Windsor, a Monkey if ever there was one, held the title for fifteen years on the trot.

The Monkey male is neat and dresses without much interest in trendy fashions. His work room will be functional and even sparse, resembling in some cases, a monk's cell. But if two Monkeys get together, the Monkey mansion will end up a shambles. But whatever the state of the living room, two Monkeys make a splendid marriage, and are high on the list of all time great combinations. However, Monkeys will not be heartbroken if Mr Right never comes along. I know a Monkey lady who has four different children from four separate relationships – two lawful husbands and two live-in hubbies. She could charm rain to fall on the Sahara, that one!

Whatever the Monkey chooses as his first profession, it will in all likelihood not be the one for which he becomes famous. World champion snooker player Ray Reardon was a miner and a policeman before becoming a household name in the snooker field. And the painter Paul Gauguin was a bank clerk before he packed up his paints and set sail for the South Seas. Monkeys change their husbands and wives almost as often as they change jobs. Ethel Merman was married four times, and Rex Harrison has been married to six different women. But should a Monkey stick to a job, he would be well advised to choose a post in which he can employ his agile mind, power to organise and phenomenal memory. Monkey ladies make exceptional personal secretaries. Often they exert more influence than their boss, carving out a small autonomy within the framework of their organisation. In this position they can exercise the maximum control with the minimum of responsibility. The boss will carry the can for the bad deals as well as take credit for the good. But that won't bother the Monkey, who will herself know the real power behind the throne. And as a dealer in sharp practice, the Monkey has no rival. 'Softly, softly, catchee Monkey', is one saying. 'Softly, softly, clinchee deal', is another.

The three phases of a Monkey's life will be marked by an unsettled childhood, with his youthful blend of artfulness and sense of superiority constantly placing him on the wrong side of authority. But his brushes with power will toughen him up for the middle period of his life in which he'll be on the receiving end of some pretty hard knocks. He'll make a name for himself, no doubt, but his home life will never be as stable as it might and there will be many out to play him at his own game. Old age will be kinder to the Monkey, but the thirst for knowledge and new experiences will never leave him, no matter what age he lives to. I have a suspicion that those old age pensioners photographed holding university degrees are all born in the year of the Monkey. But the Chinese warn that all Monkeys are in danger of dying a sudden death a long way from home. Monkey, be warned!

MONKEY AS PARENT

The Monkey will often become a fine parent, presenting his children with one of the most important of all tools – an inquiring mind. A child under the roof of a Monkey will never lack stimulation, and will be given every encouragement to learn whatever he desires. And there will be no shortage of affection and love that comes direct from the heart. Even if the Monkey parent gets divorced, the children will always come first, no matter what. The baby Rat, especially a boy, will get all he asks from his mother Monkey, and will seize every opportunity that's offered him with both hands. The young Pig will also flourish against the Monkey's

COMPATIBILITY OF MONKEY PARENT AND CHILD

warmth and intelligence. And a Cat child will never be bored. With so much clever conversation to keep her mind occupied the Kitten will not be so easily frightened by every door that's slammed shut by a gust of wind. And Daddy Monkey will be so proud of his Cat daughter's artistic achievements. He'll also delight in the talents of his daughter Goat, but won't be so thrilled when the young lady starts to play him at his own tricks.

The Horse daughter will have no time for a Monkey mother who spends all her time in front of the mirror, more so since that's where the baby Mare wants to be. But at least they'll be able to swop clothes. Vanity, however, is not the problem facing the Buffalo in the Monkey parent's home. He is not over-enthusiastic about his father Monkey's less than modest ways, and wonders where is the substance to what he is being told? But if nothing else, the Buffalo infant will be loved, probably because he *is* so critical. Monkeys like any kind of lively mind, but the young Rooster will expect high standards from her Monkey parent; nothing the Monkey can do or say will sway her to an easier manner. Jokes are fine in their place, but the Monkey father really oughtn't to laugh at his Rooster daughter's upright opinions quite so openly! There'll be no laughter at the baby Tiger, whose vigour and daring will win approval all round, though the Tiger must learn when not to interrupt her Monkey mother when she's on the phone. The Monkey father might find his Snake son a little silent, even withdrawn, but he'll forgive this trait in his Snake daughter – she is so lovely, so bewitching ... even the Monkey is enchanted. There isn't a Dragon son born who doesn't expect his parent to be fascinated by his every word. And with the Monkey as a parent he'll have a captive and doting audience. But is it really healthy for the darling Dragon to be showered with Oscars at such an early age? He could grow up to become a monster.

Unfortunately for the puppy Dog, there'll be plenty of criticism coming his way. Too much, usually. He can find no substance in his father's advice, no calls to a more perfect world. Dog children want ideals from their Monkey dad, not six ways to win at cards. Baby Monkeys, conversely, want nothing else from their Monkey parent. No wonder Monkeys are so full of tricks.

MONKEY IN BUSINESS

There can be no doubting the Monkey's great ability to make money, and make the most of himself while doing it. For as much as the Monkey enjoys having a stable bank balance, he enjoys doing it in style almost as much. Better working as an individual, the Monkey nevertheless pairs up well with the assertive and flashy Dragon. Both love the big time and will give each other a leg up as they climb the social and financial mountains. If the lady is a Monkey she will make an excellent personal assistant to a Dragon boss. And the grander his position, the better for both of them. The Pig also likes the headlines, and is another first-rate bet for a Monkey businessperson. He'll work long hours quite happily while the Monkey charms the clients with expense account lunches. If the Dragon and Monkey go into advertising, the Pig and Monkey should run a mini-cab company. As for the other animals, only the Goat and Rat have anything like a chance of succeeding alongside the superior Monkey, who really is jolly clever when he wants to be, and very ambitious. The Goat will quickly learn the Monkey's stock in trade (charm and attention to detail) and might even learn enough to go it alone. If she does, she'll take the Monkey's tricks with her. The Rat is quick to sniff a bargain, and starts the bidding long before most of us are out of bed. But the Rat will want a deeper financial commitment than the Monkey is usually prepared to give, and you can't bid with one tight fist when the opposition gets tough.

On the subject of who invests what, and when, it is difficult to see how a pair of Monkeys could get along running a business. Perhaps they should forget about commerce and stick to writing comedy scripts. The Tiger's bright ideas will stimulate the Monkey, and he's intelligent enough to capitalise on them. However, he is an idealist at

COMPATIBILITY OF MONKEY IN BUSINESS RELATIONSHIPS

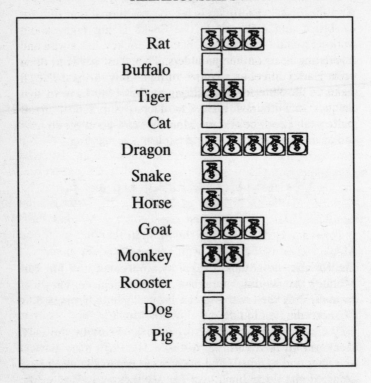

heart, and might easily resent the Monkey's somewhat 'personal' ethics. The honest Dog will positively reject any notion of double dealing, and the Monkey might well turn up for work one morning and find the tax inspector, VAT man and the Fraud Squad waiting on the doorstep. The Dog will have no truck with shady deals, and nor will the high-handed Rooster. When the Rooster says the cheque is in the post, she is telling the truth. The sensitive Cat should also avoid partnering a Monkey. The Cat's strength is in his methodical approach – slow but sure. But the Monkey works any odd hour, and there will again be a conflict over investment.

Not much can come from a Monkey setting up shop with a Buffalo. The Monkey uses his wits more than his muscles. And the Buffalo's attitude is far too traditional and dull for his bright and agile mind. The Snake is not crazy about working round the clock and, like the Monkey, has a wise and calculating head on her shoulders. Their best bet is to open up in Harley Street as a couple of high-class shrinks. They'll make an absolute fortune as long as they both have to sign cheques to withdraw cash. The Horse is practical in all matters, and both he and the Monkey like a good gossip now and again. Perhaps they should publish a society rag.

MONKEY IN LOVE

The Monkey usually has to face a complicated love life, full of affairs that promise more than they ever achieve. They will get away with whatever they can and will need a firm hand to bring out the best in them.

The male Dragon will easily win the heart of the lady Monkey, only it will be a bit *too* easy. The Pig is a jovial chap who likes nice soft beds and buckets of bubbly. He won't find a lady Monkey turn him down, but she must make her secret phone calls well out of earshot. Pigs don't like to be two-timed.

The Buffalo will be enchanted by the lady Monkey's bright conversation and wit. He will be put at his ease and open up his heart. 'Tell me more at my place,' says Miss Monkey. The problem is that is all the old-fashioned Buffalo will probably do. Mr Monkey will adore the lady Cat's soft skin and sensuous ways, but she will not trust the Monkey, and without it relationships do not normally last. If the Cat is uncertain as to what the Monkey tells her, the Rooster will positively disbelieve it. The trouble for the lady Rooster and

COMPATIBILITY OF MONKEY IN LOVE

Rat	♡	♡	♡	♡	
Buffalo	♡	♡	♡		
Tiger	♡	♡			
Cat	♡	♡	♡		
Dragon	♡	♡	♡	♡	♡
Snake	♡	♡	♡		
Horse					
Goat	♡	♡	♡		
Monkey	♡	♡	♡	♡	♡
Rooster	♡				
Dog					
Pig	♡	♡	♡	♡	♡

the Monkey is that she sees through him after it is too late.

The Snake is wise as well as beautiful, and the male Monkey will fall for her big eyes and bewitching smile. He'll do everything he can to please her, but might find her reluctant to give him time to himself. Take care Monkey. The Tiger might easily be taken by the lady Monkey's charm, and if he falls for her he'll fall in a big way. But any affair involving such two volatile creatures is destined to be short and sweet. Nothing is forever in the lives of Monkeys and Tigers – not diamonds, not promises, and not long drawn-out relationships.

The Horse knows all about vanity and it is difficult to see

how a Horse and Monkey could have anything at all in common apart from self-interest. Even if two such self-centred lovers got together, what on earth would they do? The faithful and guileless Dog is in a similar fix, but for different reasons. In his case, enchanted by the Monkey's wit and charm, he'll just sit mesmerised. On the other hand, the pleasure-seeking Goat can easily handle the Monkey's tricks, and what's more she'll give as good as she gets. But she won't like being made a fool of. The Rat is another creature who knows how to use his charm, and the lady Monkey might well go along with him.

There will be no shortage of passion from the Rat. But will the Monkey be so open-hearted twenty-four hours a day? As for two Monkeys in love, it's a case of smiles all round. Lots of them.

MONKEY IN MARRIAGE

Two Monkeys; the perfect match. Wise, sociable and witty, they complement each other in every respect. And their little tricks cancel each other out.

Whereas the faithful Dog is no lover for the Monkey, he is a good bet as a husband. He will protect the Monkey from extremes and in return, she'll help him to laugh at himself. But the Monkey must be careful when laughing at her Buffalo hubby. He might think she is ridiculing him. The Monkey might easily marry a Cat, who is amused in only the way Cats can be by his wit. But Monkeys adore to travel, and Cats love their homes. A red light here, I'm afraid.

Mr Monkey will make the Tigress feel responsible as a result of his odd hours and even odder tricks. But it is an adopted role, and she'll grow resentful of it. The Snake and Monkey can make a match. Both are wise over money, but

COMPATIBILITY OF MONKEY IN MARRIAGE

Rat	🐵🐵🐵
Buffalo	🐵🐵
Tiger	🐵🐵
Cat	🐵🐵
Dragon	🐵🐵🐵🐵🐵
Snake	🐵🐵🐵
Horse	□
Goat	🐵🐵🐵🐵
Monkey	🐵🐵🐵🐵🐵
Rooster	□
Dog	🐵🐵🐵
Pig	🐵🐵🐵🐵🐵

both cannot help wanting to possess what they love. More giving needed here to make it last.

Rats are generous and passionate. The best pairing is a Monkey man and a lady Rat. Both know a good thing when it comes along, but they must make certain the good thing is not another Rat or Monkey. The Goat makes no bones about what she wants from marriage – a big family and plenty of fun. Monkeys also like to enjoy themselves, and their families. Nothing will go wrong so long as the Goat and Monkey have fun *together* occasionally.

The lady Rooster's idea of fun, though, is a spending spree and the Monkey won't approve. The latest creation from

Paris is not a sound investment for the Monkey's carefully invested income. However, money won't be the bone of contention should the Monkey ever marry the Horse. It will be a case of vanity splitting them up. No wedding bells here. But ding-dong for the Pig. She'll provide the home, and when times are bad, her goodwill and self-esteem will help them both. Chimes from the steeple for the Dragon, too. He will be utterly enchanted by his Monkey wife, who will do everything she possibly can to keep his powerful gaze centred on her. And she'll never be short of compliments (how cleverly she engineers them). Roll on the Golden Wedding celebrations.

HOW YOU WILL BE INFLUENCED IN THE YEAR OF THE MONKEY

A YEAR FOR FUN AND FANTASY

A five-star year for the Monkey, and apart from the resolute and responsible Buffalo, who cannot take the Monkey's games at any price, it's by and large a better than average year all round. The Rooster, though, shares the Buffalo's high principles and is also deeply conservative. The only way for the Rooster to make anything of the Monkey's year is to keep away from arguments and her nose to the grindstone. The honest and loyal Dog gets tricked into the idea that he can play the same game as everyone else, but after a promising start is quickly disillusioned. It's all too fanciful. Sensitive and refined, the Cat will nevertheless give the more outrageous schemes a try. But where is the method to it all? The truth is there isn't one. And the question the rebellious Tiger will ask is, 'What on earth am I rebelling against?'

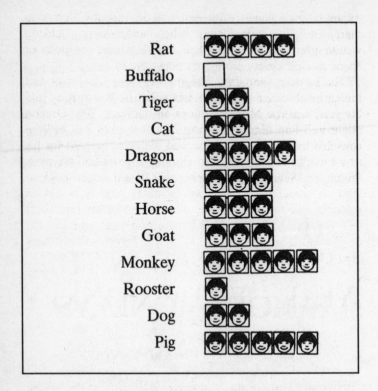

Rat	🐵🐵🐵🐵
Buffalo	⬜
Tiger	🐵🐵
Cat	🐵🐵
Dragon	🐵🐵🐵🐵
Snake	🐵🐵🐵
Horse	🐵🐵🐵
Goat	🐵🐵🐵
Monkey	🐵🐵🐵🐵🐵
Rooster	🐵
Dog	🐵🐵
Pig	🐵🐵🐵🐵🐵

Although not a disastrous year for the Cat or the Tiger –
far from it – both will end up joining the Dog in wondering
why it all went wrong? A much better year for the Rat,
however, who faced lean times during the previous twelve
months. He'll quickly latch onto the Monkey's mood and
make the most of well-stocked cupboards.

There's plenty of craft and cunning in the air, lucky Rat.
The wise Snake likes to move thoughtfully and feel her way
carefully – the Monkey swings high in the trees. If the Snake
doesn't try to play the Monkey at his own game, she will end
up with a reasonably healthy bank account. But it won't be
easy money. The independent Horse must also take life as he
finds it, and use his practical skills in making sure he isn't

duped over financial deals. Not a good year for Horses to marry, or fall in love. On the other hand, Goats would do well to marry in a Monkey's year. But they must not invest or spend a single penny more than they have to.

The boastful, parading Dragon will shine as always, but the carnival leader must remember that he has already had his year, and the Monkey enjoys an audience. The Dragon might well find himself the butt of a few jokes, but he'll be consoled by the wage increase and the price he paid for his new car. The honest and hard-working Pig will find life plain sailing, and whatever he touches will turn if not to gold, at least to something almost as valuable. And it is also a splendid year for Pigs in love. As for the Monkey himself, it will be smiles all round, from the bank manager to the magistrate. It would be hard to find a bigger success story than a Monkey in a Monkey's year.

FAMOUS MONKEYS

Arts
Ray Bradbury
Cartier Bresson
Dave Brubeck
Lord Byron
Alistair Cooke
Charles Dickens
F Scott Fitzgerald
Ian Fleming
Antonia Fraser
Paul Gauguin
W S Gilbert
Arthur Hailey
Osbert Lancaster

Jane Lapotaire
Charlie Parker
Nigel Kennedy
Beryl Reid
Modigliani
Ronald Searle
Johnny Speight
James Stewart
Isaac Stern

Sports
Bjorn Borg
Donald Bradman
Sebastian Coe

207

George Graham
Stephen Hendry
Tony Jacklin
Clive Lloyd
Dan Maskell
Brian Moore
Ray Reardon
Bryan Robson
Martina Navratilova
Tessa Sanderson

Industry/Politics
Lord Forte
Rocco Forte
Roy Hattersley
Roy Jenkins
Glenys Kinnock
Nigel Lawson
Pope John Paul II
Marcia Williams
Lord Young

Royals
Duchess of Windsor
Princess Michael of Kent

Show Biz
Michael Aspel
Bobby Ball
Carol Barnes

Hywell Bennett
Frank Bough
Yul Brynner
Roy Castle
Bette Davis
Jerry Hall
Richard Harris
Rex Harrison
Harry Houdini
Fred Housego
Kylie Minogue
Robert Morely
Peter O'Toole
Angela Rippon
Omar Sharif
Koo Stark
Liz Taylor

Pop
Johnny Cash
Joe Cocker
Roger Daltry
Ray Davies
Jason Donovan
Bobby Gentry
Dave Gilmour
Bob Marley
Tim Rice
Diana Ross
Rod Stewart
Mary Wilson

THE ROOSTER

1909	January 22nd to February 9th	1910
1921	February 8th to January 27 th	1922
1933	January 26th to February 13th	1934
1945	February 13th to February 1st	1946
1957	January 31st to February 17th	1958
1969	February 17th to February 5th	1970
1981	February 5th to January 24th	1982
1993	January 23rd to February 9th	1994

Pope John Paul II (Monkey)
The Monkey has many followers

Mary Quant (Rooster)
The Rooster loves putting on a show

Duchess of Windsor (Monkey)
The lady Monkey
usually gets her own way

Ken Livingstone (Rooster)
Spendthrift Roosters are not rare

Diana Ross (Monkey)
There isn't a Monkey who
doesn't love the limelight

Steve Davis (Rooster)
The Rooster is methodical and
well-organised

Winston Churchill (Dog)
There is no one more loyal
than the Dog

Elton John (**Pig**)
The Pig loves life,
and loves dressing up

Joanna Lumley (Dog)
The perfect Dog lady –
beautiful and intelligent

Woody Allen (Pig)
Pigs often have the talent
to amuse

Mother Teresa (Dog)
The very essence of the
Dog's idealism

Maria Callas (Pig)
Once in love,
the Pig gives everything

Prince Charles (Rat) and Princess Diana (Buffalo)
The Bufffalo always wears the trousers in a Rat's home.
But the charming Rat finds it difficult to settle down

Jackie Kennedy (Snake) and Aristotle Onassis (Pig)
Snakes can become anything they desire –
at the expense of another

Eric Morecambe (Tiger) and Ernie Wise (Buffalo)
The Tiger has the ideas and the Buffalo puts them into practice.
But the Buffalo is always the stronger

COUPLES

Princess Margaret (Horse) and Lord Snowdon (Horse)
Horses are fiercely independent, and two under the same roof
will often spell disaster

Fred Astaire (Pig) and Ginger Rogers (Pig)
Pigs are often at their best when forming a partnership.
Two Pigs can have the moon

John Lennon (Dragon) and Yoko Ono (Rooster)
The Dragon inspires the Rooster and the Rooster keeps the Dragon
on the straight and narrow. The best of all unions

Clark Gable (Rat)
The Rat's charm personified

Napoleon (Buffalo)
When a Buffalo decides to conquer
the world, watch out!

The Queen Mother (Rat)
The warmth of the rat is obvious
in everything she does

Margaret Thatcher (Buffalo)
There is no alternative

Andrew Lloyd Webber (Rat)
The world of the theatre is just ripe
for the Rat's opportunism

Bertrand Russell (Buffalo)
Whatever he believed,
he did so with conviction

Beethoven (Tiger)
The bravest Tiger of all,
and the most brilliant

Ingrid Bergman (Cat)
The most beautiful of Cat ladies;
sensuous and subtle

Marilyn Monroe (Tiger)
The classic lady Tiger;
lived hard and died young

Malcolm Muggeridge (Cat)
The Cat has a nose for good gossip

Terry Wogan (Tiger)
Typical Tiger ideas man –
they seem never ending

Selina Scott (Cat)
The Cat very often gets the cream

Martin Luther King (Dragon)
The Dragon's self-belief is everything

Princess Grace (Snake)
The essential lady Snake
has beauty mixed with wealth

Esther Rantzen (Dragon)
Is there anything beneath
the Dragon's bright facade?

Picasso (Snake)
The Snake's art is often a mixture
of wisdom and wit

Geoff Boycott (Dragon)
The perfectionist Dragon
at the wicket

John F. Kennedy (Snake)
The complete male Snake;
intuitive and influential

Chris Evert Lloyd (Horse)
A typical example of the practical
and beautiful horse

Margot Fonteyn (Goat)
The lady Goat is so full of artistry

Barbra Streisand (Horse)
Witty and elegant –
the perfect female Horse

Mick Jagger (Goat)
The successful Goat always knows
what his public wants

Paul McCartney (Horse)
The hard-working Horse
can have everything

Herbert von Karajan (Goat)
The artistic Goat
has many masters

The crown of red
set on your little head
is charged with all your fighting blood.
Elizabeth Bishop

THE YEAR OF THE ROOSTER

The Cock crows and the world awakes to find the streets filled with men on the march. It is a time for military parades and gleaming brass helmets; trumpets and drums will be the order of the day. It is a time for important public events, celebrations, and shows of strength. And when the military stop their strutting, there will be no shortage of civilians taking to the streets. In 1981 100,000 rallied in Trafalgar Square to support the People's March for Jobs. Later that year, 6,000 coloured people marched through London as a protest against the Deptford arson attack. The Rooster's parades, though, will not be like the Dragon years – there'll be no frivolities, no firecrackers.

The year of the Rooster will be full of big, expansive and impressive events. In 1969 Concorde made her first flight, *Queen Elizabeth II* set sail on her maiden voyage and Aldrin and Armstrong became the first men to set foot on the Moon. This is the time for Royalty to make its presence felt, adding its support to an all-pervading air of public order and firm, moral leadership. The Queen's Christmas Day message was televised for the first time in 1957, and in 1981, 800 million people watched the wedding of Lady Diana Spencer and Prince Charles.

Whatever the events on the royal stage, the military will never be far from the headlines, and there will be many a military coup or intervention. It will also be a time for new political parties forming themselves, not to bring about great new changes, but to restore old orders. In 1981 the Polish

Prime Minister was replaced by an army general, and the same year in Britain saw 'the gang of four' form the Social Democrats.

The Rooster's year will not be one for idlers and skivers. There's work to be done in the barnyard and the influence of the number one organiser will be felt everywhere. Day-dreamers will have their day, but they won't have it often, and it won't last long. Don't expect to get rich in a hurry. All the effort and hard work, the tough line policy on thrift and careful organisation does not necessarily mean a full basket of eggs. ICI made a record loss of £121 million in 1981, and Sir James Goldsmith's *Now* magazine closed down after losing £6 million.

The Rooster's year is one for a return to old-fashioned values, and there will be a big accent on high standards of morality. It is most certainly not the best of years to embark on a passionate love affair. Get married, join the army, or become a nun, but don't fool around. And don't try to get rich from video nasties or clip joints, you'll probably end up in jail. Nor should you attempt to lie your way out of trouble. The Rooster has no time for liars, cheats, or any other kind of anti-social behaviour. The Yorkshire Ripper was sentenced to life imprisonment in 1981.

Behave honestly, show candour and work hard, and the year of the Rooster will bring its own very special reward. You might not grow fat – you might even go broke – but you might well grow to respect the importance of straight-dealing.

THE ROOSTER PERSONALITY

'Polish your buttons and step lively. Enter the candid, no-nonsense Rooster.'

Whereas some animals display either strong masculine or feminine characteristics, those born under the sign of the Rooster will find the edges between the two sexes less well-defined than most. In fact, there is such a strong overlap that the Rooster is known variously as both the Hen and the Cock. But whatever we call him, there can be no uncertainty about the nature of the creature we are dealing with. The moment the Rooster walks into a room we are immediately made aware of his or her presence. And there can be no doubt that the Rooster's first job of the day may be an important clue as to his instantly recognisable personality, and his ability to impose it on all those around him. As the 16th century naturalist, Laurens Andrewe, wrote: 'The crowing of the Cock is sweet and profitable; he waketh the sleeper, comforteth the sorrowful and rejoyceth that the night is over.'

Whether the Rooster is tall or short, fat or thin, he will make no effort to disguise his extreme qualities. Roosters do not go in for falsehoods, pretence, games-play or confidence tricks. The Rooster is what he is, take him or leave him – which is usually slap bang in the centre. If you have invited a Rooster to your party and there's no one in the middle of the action you can bet your last cent that he hasn't arrived. No matter what the occasion, a Private View or a Public

214

Meeting, you'll never miss the Rooster's entrance.

Generous, and with the odd exception that proves the rule, the Rooster is honest to a fault. Methodical and organised, Roosters plan their lives with the precision of a watchmaker. And you have only to have kept a chicken or two to know that nature's early morning alarm call is deeply conservative and set in his ways. As soon as dusk settles, hens everywhere rush home to roost. Off the ground they believe that they are safe from predators and feel protected by their numbers (and in most cases they are correct in their belief). Like doing the daily crossword, or eating the same lunch, the Rooster's ritual of roosting is one she'll perform every day of her life, providing another insight to her vibrant and expansive personality.

If you were born in the year of the Rooster, your famous fellow Roosters are a mixed variety of geniuses, every one an original and every one his or her own boss: Wagner, Tommy Cooper, Peter Ustinov, Bianca Jagger, Frankie Howerd, Harry Secombe, James Mason, Dirk Bogarde, Mary Quant, Douglas Fairbanks Jr., Benny Goodman and Joan Collins.

Chinese tradition has it that Roosters fall into two quite distinct types. Those born at sunup and sundown, between the hours of five and seven will be essentially extrovert in temperament. Bragging and boastful, a sunup/sundown Rooster will be that chap at a party who can't resist telling you about his first million, and the way he built up his business from a broken down company he bought for a song. This Rooster will be that hail fellow who shouts your name across a crowded bar and insists he buys you a drink, even if you don't want one. And he'll be the first to end up under the table; in spite of all their cock-a-doodle-doing, Roosters have no head for drink (nor can they say no).

The sunup/sundown Rooster is the chap in the office who's the first one to give you his advice, whether you've asked for it or not. I regularly play snooker with a Rooster who simply cannot stop himself telling me what my next shot should be. Very often, his kind of Rooster will be the first to complain about public morality, and his views on the way the country is being taken over by communists and left-wing revolutionaries will be given plenty of airing in public. With his reactionary political stance and puritanical morals, this Rooster is not one to be crossed. He says what he thinks, and sometimes says it without thinking. All Roosters are born under the sign of candour, but this Rooster in particular has no concern at all about the effect his frequently harsh criticisms have on those who stand up to him. The Rooster has spoken and that's that. If it hurts, that's not his problem. Facts must be faced, life is tough – too bad. And do not retaliate, and criticise this Rooster or question his methods, especially if you are only half certain of your facts. The sunup/sundown Rooster is always right. He believes in himself 200 per cent. Argue with him and he'll put up a fight – just think of a cock fight – and he won't let you off the hook until the point's been proved one way or another. 'Put your money where your mouth is,' he'll say, 'bet you I am right.' And you should think twice before entering such a wager. For all his boasting, the Rooster is very intelligent. Behind his façade of bragging, the Rooster has a keen mind. He learns fast and has in most cases, a long, long memory. In some senses, the Rooster views facts much like the grains of corn in the barnyard which he snaps up instantly and thoroughly digests.

Roosters not born in the hours of sunup or sundown, especially those born during the night, are very different – or at least they appear to others as so. They sit quietly in the corner of a room and seldom speak unless spoken to. They very seldom venture an opinion and even then it will in all probability be nothing more earth shattering than the way they deal with the greenfly that have invaded their beloved garden. Usually fair and soft-spoken, these Roosters will calculate to win your attention by their wilting flower act. By saying little and listening plenty, these Roosters will stand out in a crowd just as clearly as if they were wearing skin tight pink leotards and banging a bass drum. In their own subtle way, this type of Rooster is still after one objective – your full

216

and undivided attention. And when you hear them denying themselves the extra slice of lemon meringue pie: 'No, no, really, I'm on a diet. Can't you see I am every bit of a pound overweight', it's no different from demanding the biggest helping. Both comments take your eyes straight to the Rooster. Objective achieved.

Obviously, since only four hours determine the hours of a sunup/sundown Rooster, there must be fewer of them. Nevertheless, however introvert those Roosters born at other times are, all will have a degree of the sunup/sundown Rooster's temperament. Equally obvious is the fact that the extrovert Rooster *is* more noticeable and is almost certainly the reason he appears to come in greater supply. At this point I feel I must admit to having considerable personal experience with Roosters, and as a result, perhaps a little more insight. My mother is a Rooster, and so was Aunt Mary, who helped my mother bring me up in the difficult first years of the last war. Her generosity and kindness to me, treating me as if I were her own child, will remain etched on my heart forever. My wife, Tesse, is a Rooster, although I didn't know that when I married her, as my interest in Chinese horoscopes began much later. And throughout my working life, at *The Times*, *Private Eye* and *The Listener*, the three journals I contribute to regularly, I am surrounded by Roosters of all kinds.

Having met sunup/sundown Roosters and the others it is necessary to point out a further division. In this instance the split is to do with an aspect of Rooster life which is central to his or her daily existence – the thorny matter of finance. But as we shall see, the division is one that causes the two sides to face inwards. The two types are in some ways the commercial equivalent of the wise and foolish virgins.

Put simply, there are those Roosters who scrimp and save every single penny. With a single-mindedness and a method that is ruthlessly adhered to, these Roosters will never buy the smallest item without comparing the cost. When they buy a new filing cabinet for the office, it will be the best value in town; when they book a flight to New York, they will have paid the lowest fare; when they go shopping in the super-market, their basket will be full of every cut price, discount and bargain the shop has to offer. This Rooster's bank balance will grow slowly but steadily. And if you are like the Roosters Stavros Niarchos or Bernard Delfont, you will have built your fortune on nothing more than sheer grit and determination.

The thrifty Rooster's opposite number, as you may well have guessed, is the spendthrift. And as far as I have been able to discover, there is no inbetween. Roosters either save or they spend, and those who spend do so with not only their own money but everyone else's – the bank's, their spouse's, the credit card company's ... This type of Rooster lives each day engaged in idle dreams, building endless fantasies. They dream of new curtains, new carpets, schemes for turning the spare room into an *en suite* bathroom, turning the spare *en suite* bathroom into a conservatory; without a penny in the bank they will be happy to refurnish the house from the attic to the cellar in their mind. Such Roosters can't pass a clothes shop without going in, or leave it without taking half the stock with them. For them, the idea of shopping in the supermarket across town to save a penny on washing up liquid is quite simply abhorrent. Thrift is in their dictionary of non-expressions, alongside 'overdraft', and 'please settle your account at once'. Indeed, spending vast sums of money he didn't own is the charge constantly made against the most famous GLC leader in history, Mr Ken Livingstone.

But aren't the spendthrift and thrifty Roosters simply two ends of the same pole? I'm sure that they are, but much more important is the fact that both are astonishingly generous. Whether they owe a million or own it ten times over, you have only to ask a Rooster for a loan, and providing they have a high enough opinion of you, it will be yours. The loan, more often than not, will end up as a straight gift, no strings attached. Indeed, I have known the most thrifty of Roosters to act in an unbelievably generous, almost foolhardy, manner.

As well as being richly generous, with money and praise, the Rooster is the best organiser in the world. If you are looking for a new office manager and wish to avoid the sex discrimination act, then you might do a lot worse than advertise for a Rooster. If a Rooster answers, then in 999 cases out of 1000 you will get the office manager of your dreams. You will find your filing system works efficiently for the first time ever, your phone book will be up to date, your lunch appointments verified, your desk tidied, your plants watered, your pencil sharpened and your overcoat sent to the cleaners. And all that will be done before lunch! No one in the whole wide world is more methodical, or spends more of their time writing everything they do or plan to do down on bits of paper. The Rooster's handbag will be full of little books and folded envelopes and bus tickets with little messages and timetables and heaven knows what else scribbled over them. My Rooster wife is a bookbinder by profession and is typical in this respect. In her case, as our family joke has it, she even makes books in which she keeps details about the books she writes her seemingly endless lists in.

However, in spite of all the Roosters' verve, intelligence, acumen and great powers of organisation, they tend to lack initiative. In short, Roosters need to be inspired to achieve, or more importantly, to realise themselves in the fullest sense. The Chinese believe that Dragons inspire Roosters and that they form the best possible partnership. One of the most public unions between a Rooster and Dragon in recent times was that between the Dragon John Lennon and Rooster, Yoko Ono. Since his tragic death, Yoko Ono has gone to some lengths to express openly how Lennon's life and now, touchingly, his death has motivated her into a greater awareness of herself. But their union, as in all the most harmonious, was (is?) two-way.

But if the Rooster sometimes lacks initiative, he never lacks method, or the incentive to turn his powers of concentration into gain. No one who has ever watched a snooker match on TV can have failed to have been impressed by the painstakingly deliberate and methodical style of world champion Steve Davis. In his short career, this young Rooster has potted his way into the history books and earned himself a million.

The Chinese believe that there is a pronounced military streak in the Rooster, and it is true that Roosters love to dress up and swagger. The Nazi Goebbels was a Rooster and is reported to have adored strutting around in his uniform. On a different note entirely, but from the same tune, the former Archbishop of Canterbury, Robert Runcie, is a Rooster, and hardly a stranger to dressing up. But in the West the military parade has lost much of its appeal and we now see our heroes and heroines dressed in their uniforms on the stages of popular music. Dolly Parton, Pete Townshend, Blondie, half of Abba, Eric Clapton, Jerry Hall and Bryan Ferry are all Roosters. So is Erica Roe, the young streaker who hit the headlines when she ran onto the field at Twickenham, providing the rugger fans with a full frontal sight of her considerable charms.

Lady Roosters are invariably striking in their beauty, and have wonderful hair. They spend a lot of time and money in the salon, and are never happy until their hair is exactly right. They adore perfumes and have extremely sensitive noses. Again they fuss a great deal before finding a perfume that suits them. In spite of her great presence, a lady Rooster dresses in non-flashy, well-made clothes. Her wardrobe will be fashionable but not trendy; remember, the Rooster is an arch-conservative at heart. But a lady Rooster's handwriting might well give you a clue as to her birth sign's main characteristic, being positive, decorative and immediately recognisable. Although they love all kinds of social gatherings, they are just as happy having a night out with female companions as dating a chap, however honourable his intentions. After all, Roosters stick together in the hen-house.

Male Roosters tend to dress on the flash side, whether they wear a three-piece suit or jeans and a T-shirt. But clothes aren't so important to male Roosters, he's more interested in telling you how much he earns and what he spends. And he will expect you to be as candid. When you tell them, they will often seem uninterested, bored even. But they will have remembered every single word.

The Chinese word for Rooster is *Ji*, which means chicken, but there is nothing 'chicken' about the Rooster when they come face to face with an important issue. They are frequently brave beyond the call of duty, and when it is asked of them, will not shrink from taking a firm moral stance. This leads Roosters to take a high moral tone generally, which sometimes works against their best interests.

All Roosters love their gardens, and will grow plants and flowers wherever they live, even if it is only in a few pots on the windowledge of their top floor tower block. Plants grow firm and strong under the Rooster's green fingers, and when choosing a profession, the Rooster should bear this in mind. A job in the country is more suitable than one in the heart of a city. Because Roosters love their homes, they often become skilful interior designers, but any job that involves organisation, thrift and flair will suit them – especially if there is a house and garden involved. Whatever the job, whatever the vocation, truth and fidelity are the lights a Rooster lives by, and will in the end dictate either his success or downfall. And there will be no compromises in a Rooster's world, which leads them to promise more than they are often capable of delivering. Their grand gesture, so beautifully wrapped, has all too frequently a hollow centre.

The three phases of a Rooster's life will find the child happy and contented. They are bright and attentive children and learn quickly; the head prefect is invariably a Rooster. But the ensuing middle years bring problems. Love is something that the Rooster simply cannot organise, and however rich they become, a Rooster might have to face at least one failed marriage. In old age, the Rooster might very well become a solitary creature with no more than a garden, a few cherished friends and her great moral fibre to support her. And she will, of course, have her day-dreams.

ROOSTER AS PARENT

The Rooster parent will not be noted for his leniency, and will be quick to punish large transgressions and admonish small ones. But there will be no shortage of genuine concern for the child's wellbeing. The most effectual relationship between any parent and child is perhaps the one formed by the Rooster mother and Dragon son. The Chinese certainly consider it one of the most desirable. The Dragon son is ever anxious to please, and it is well understood by all those who know young Dragons that they perform their tasks as if they were religious rituals. However silly he may sometimes seem, the Rooster mother will never laugh at her Dragon son's strange ways, thereby injuring his considerable pride. Instead, she will encourage each and every whim, assisting him to achieve the greatness of which he constantly dreams. The young Buffalo will be encouraged in much the same way, but the communication between mother and son will not have the same warmth. The baby Buffalo does not crave love, only knowledge, and he'll have plenty of books to read in the Rooster's home.

The young Pig will receive all the attention he desires, and warmth. He's honest and hard-working, even as a child, and this will not go unnoticed by the Rooster father. Honesty and hard work, however, are not the qualities the Rooster father sees in his young Goat daughter. They will simply never see eye to eye; what is that girl of his up to when she stays out all night? And what are those pills in her bedside drawer? Poor little Goat. And the young Monkey will get nothing from his Rooster father but long lectures on being home before midnight. It's just as well the Monkey can climb in through the open bedroom window when the front door is locked and bolted.

The youthful Tiger needs to rebel in order to express

COMPATIBILITY OF ROOSTER PARENT AND CHILD

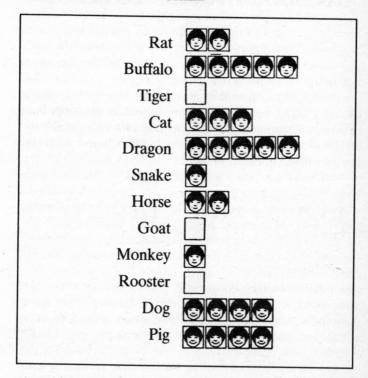

himself, but he finds no allies in the Rooster's home. He'll just find himself out on a limb. The beautiful Horse daughter will capture the heart of her Rooster father, and will be thoroughly spoilt. But the Rooster dad will want a bigger show of gratitude than the Horse daughter will ever be prepared to give. The young Dog will give his thanks often enough, and mum Rooster will be forever touched by her puppy. All will go well between them so long as the Dog does not become dependant; a Rooster parent likes to see their offspring stand on their own two (four) feet, however much they love them.

The Cat child is usually too detached for the Rooster's liking, and the Kitten's finicky ways will irritate the Rooster mother. The young Rat has enough charm to keep himself on the Rooster parent's right side. But baby Rat had better make sure his school report is up to scratch. The Snake boy lies in bed and dreams ... of nothing much – he takes an age to develop. The Rooster dad is up at the crack of dawn and works till dusk. No wonder tempers are frayed. The tension remains high when there's another Rooster in the coop. Baby Roosters start preaching from day one, and with the Rooster father or mother already doing their bit, confusion can be the only conclusion. And what a din!

ROOSTER IN BUSINESS

Oh dear, what a generally bleak picture facing the Rooster who wants to form a business partnership. But the question has to be asked: does the Rooster really want a business partner? I suspect that the firm answer is no, and that the Rooster is more than happy to run things on his own. But should he want the business notepaper to carry a second name, then the Rooster would be best advised to throw in his lot with either a Dragon or a Horse. Deeply practical, the Horse will buckle down to his tasks and do so without fuss. The Rooster will, in turn, add his own powerful sense of organisation to the partnership and both will prosper. The Dragon enthuses everyone he meets with his bright schemes. The Rooster will keep the books tidy and prevent the Dragon over-reaching. A very good commercial pairing, Dragon and Rooster. The Rooster's chum down on the farm is the solid and reliable Buffalo. Conservative to the bottom of their bootlaces, the Rooster and Buffalo might not get rich but they will certainly grow contented with their business enter-

COMPATIBILITY OF ROOSTER IN BUSINESS RELATIONSHIPS

Rat	☐
Buffalo	💰💰💰
Tiger	☐
Cat	💰💰
Dragon	💰💰💰💰💰
Snake	💰
Horse	💰💰💰💰💰
Goat	☐
Monkey	☐
Rooster	☐
Dog	☐
Pig	💰💰

prise. They should open a second-hand bookshop selling unfashionable authors and guides to historic homes and gardens.

The Pig is honest, reliable and hard-working as the day is long. But he loves a big boozy lunch, and although it is often for the good of the firm, the Rooster sometimes forgets this when he smells double brandies on his partner's breath. Unlike the opportunist Rat, whom the upright Rooster should avoid, the meticulous Cat will make the Rooster a very reasonable business associate. Astute in all matters of commerce, the Cat cannot help making a bob or two. But his pace might be different to the Rooster's, who works such terribly long hours when forced, and won't stand for any dilly-dallying.

The Snake has good ideas, and the Rooster has plenty of ways to sell them, but working together, Snake and Rooster might want too much too soon. Much the same can be said of the Tiger in terms of a chap with brights ideas. But his unpredictability will send the methodical and well-organised Rooster screaming up the wall. Not recommended.

The Rooster will have no joy in business with: (a) the Goat – too easily put off when the going's tough; (b) the Dog – too anxious, and worries over details the Rooster doesn't even notice; (c) the Monkey – too quick to put his hand in the till for a share of the profits. Unlesss it's a Horse or a Dragon helping run the show, the Rooster had better run it solo.

The Chinese believe that under no circumstances should Roosters form a business partnership. Although they have all the organisational skill in the world, two Roosters seldom muster enough initiative to turn their great schemes into reality. But if a pair of Roosters do find a way of working together, they will hit the jackpot. Dealers in dreams, perhaps? What about a couple of chart-topping song writers?

ROOSTER IN LOVE

There is no doubt about the fact that of all the animals, the Rooster has the greatest distaste for casual romance. Both Mr and Ms Rooster do not go in for passion-filled nights unless they bring the promise of a deep and lasting relationship. However, if the lady Rooster does say yes to a naughty weekend, you can be sure that she will come well prepared. She'll have the train times, the times of the hotel restaurant and a list of the local places of interest. She might easily have

COMPATIBILITY OF ROOSTER IN LOVE

Rat	☐
Buffalo	♡♡♡♡
Tiger	♡
Cat	☐
Dragon	♡♡♡
Snake	♡♡
Horse	☐
Goat	☐
Monkey	♡
Rooster	♡
Dog	♡
Pig	♡♡♡

your amorous advances worked into her schedule. In any event, her choice of Romeos are few. Her best bet is the Buffalo, who has such a lot in common with the Rooster, and whose low threshold of passion will suit her down to the ground. But the lady Rooster's great companion through life, the Dragon, pleases her less well in his informal role as lover. He is usually an extremely extrovert fellow when displaying his emotions, and the Karma Sutra is not on the lady Rooster's list of bedtime reading. But fortunately for the Rooster, the Dragon is attracted to all females of the species, and the fact that she needs to be wooed presents him with all manner of challenges.

On the subject of attraction, the male Rooster will certainly be attracted to the female Pig. She'll listen patiently as he tells her and everyone else in earshot what a good and clever fellow he is. She'll even put up with his terrible jokes. The lady Rooster will positively recoil from the Rat's shallow advances and obviously phoney flattery. And the fickle Goat's lack of candour will do nothing to win him the puritanical Rooster's heart. The female Cat will threaten the swaggering male Rooster with her sensuous charm, demanding he be more gentle and refined. Poor Rooster, those are not his qualities when in love.

The Tiger is passionate and adores any kind of romance, but if a male Rooster falls for a lady Tiger he will find her too intense during the first stages, and be made to feel a competitor – something he hates in terms of human relationships. The vain and beautiful Horse lady will mock the male Rooster after she has knocked him sideways with her wit and looks. The last thing she wants is to see her lover staring at her starry-eyed and helpless. And a love affair between the high-minded Rooster and unscrupulous Monkey can only end in disaster. Theirs is the meeting of two irreconcilable forces, but they might try just once before they realise their mistake. The Snake lady has enough charm and sexual mystery to entice a eunuch, and the poor old Rooster will come running. But once the Snake shows him her passion, he'll go flying back to the safety of the coop.

The well-meaning Dog will be happy to be loved by a Rooster, and her sense of order will bring out the best in him, but he'll worry for all the Rooster's optimism and his love will lose its way. A male Dog and female Rooster have the best chance of the two pairings. As for two Roosters sharing an affair of the heart ... well, not only Pigs might fly, but lead balloons and plastic ducks! Two Roosters in love is strictly for the birds.

ROOSTER IN MARRIAGE

The male Rooster very often creates an image of himself as being a bit of a lad with the ladies. But in almost all cases, he is, in fact, an old-fashioned fellow who places a secure and faithful married life at the top of his list of priorities. The Rooster, therefore, makes an ideal partner for all those who

COMPATIBILITY OF ROOSTER IN MARRIAGE

Rat	▨▨
Buffalo	▨▨▨▨
Tiger	▨▨▨
Cat	☐
Dragon	▨▨▨▨▨
Snake	▨▨▨▨
Horse	▨▨▨▨
Goat	☐
Monkey	☐
Rooster	☐
Dog	▨
Pig	▨▨

229

share the love of a home, garden and family. The male Dragon is capable of providing the female Rooster with most, if not all, her needs and together they make a splendid couple. The careful Snake, wise with money when the Rooster is not, will stabilise a marriage between them. The Rooster in her way will be brave when the need arises, and protect the Snake.

The male Rooster will court and win the lady Horse. They will in all probability have a large and happy family, and own a beautiful house. But the Rooster must not become over-attentive and allow his Horse wife her independence. Once married, the Rat relaxes and lets his wit have its head. Roosters love laughter, and there is a chance it could work out as long as the Rat's store of jokes doesn't run short. And he must remember not to keep telling the same old chestnuts. The Tiger has a rebellious as well as a romantic heart, and if Tiger and Rooster can find some mutual cause, the marriage might last; *Ban the Pill,* perhaps, or *Keep Britain Conservative.* On second thoughts ...

The jovial Pig might walk down the aisle with the lady Rooster, but he can be just a bit of a glutton at times. And no rude jokes at the dinner table, *please*! There will be no coarse humour from the anxious Dog. In fact, there will be a shortage of laughs all round, but the Rooster admires and respects his loyalty. Male Dog and Lady Rooster might make it to a silver wedding, even further. There isn't much about the Monkey that wins the lady Rooster's respect – certainly not his guile – a poor match.

A Cat enjoys home life, but Roosters can't bear fastidiousness. A high moral sense is one thing, but small-mindedness is another. The Cat's tidy ways will drive a Rooster batty. 'Make up your mind,' says the Rooster, 'right or wrong.' A very good match, however, is the Buffalo and Rooster. Both love gardens and a comfortable if not too fashionable home. Both enjoy high spirits and there will be little chance of extra-marital relationships coming between them. But the Rooster lady will sometimes yearn for a greater demonstration of the Buffalo's love.

Alas, the Goat has none of these qualities and does not stand up for what he believes. Poor old Goat, no match for the Rooster's high moral stance. The Chinese say that two Roosters under the same roof means unhappiness for everyone. Enough said.

HOW YOU WILL BE INFLUENCED IN THE YEAR OF THE ROOSTER

A YEAR FOR HONEST ENDEAVOUR

For the Rooster, champions of hard work and lovers of Truth, the year of the Rooster is a godsend. Not surprisingly, those who live by their sharp wits and trickery won't find much in the way of bonuses and windfalls. Even worse affected are those who are set in their ways, unable to break self-imposed methods, and those who are prone to long periods of inactivity. The wise and meditative Snake will have a disastrous year, both in commerce and love. She'll be busy enough, but the rewards are so slight for all the effort. The Cat, sensitive and methodical, conducts his life at a snail's pace compared to a Rooster working in her lowest gear. For all the Cat will achieve, he might as well stay at home and sleep in front of what remains of the fire. There's no joy for the artful Monkey, who'll get his tail pecked with every small deceit. Small though the beak of a Rooster may very well be, it is extremely sharp. And the capricious Goat, so fond of idling away her day in self-comforting dreams, will also feel

Rat	🂠🂠🂠🂠
Buffalo	🂠🂠🂠🂠
Tiger	🂠🂠🂠
Cat	☐
Dragon	🂠🂠🂠🂠🂠
Snake	☐
Horse	🂠🂠🂠🂠🂠
Goat	🂠
Monkey	🂠
Rooster	🂠🂠🂠🂠🂠
Dog	🂠🂠
Pig	🂠🂠🂠🂠🂠

the peck of the Rooster's beak. And the Goat will be criticised mercilessly for each and every indiscretion. But the Goat's year will not be a complete washout.

The Rat will find his charm not without reward and his good nature and warm wit will find him riding unusually high in a year filled with so much moralising. The Buffalo will prosper without fail. Conservative and stolid, his attitudes reflect the Rooster's in every respect. It is a good year for Buffaloes to experiment, and if they are preparing to mount a takeover or oust the boss, this is the time to do it. The solid Pig will also benefit from the emphasis on keeping busy and find no shortage of money or romance. It is a perfect year for a Pig to marry. The practical Horse will most certainly find the meadow a fine place to be, and the grass will never have seemed so rich and plentiful. A Horse might well change his job in the Rooster year, and if he does he will not regret it. The Tiger might also fancy a change of environment. He is a rebel at heart and this is not a bad year for anyone planning a military coup. But what happens if it doesn't work out? The Dog's idealism will not find a home under the Rooster's reactionary influence, but the Dog's loyalty will be his saving grace.

The glittering, brash Dragon will never have had such a splendid year. It might be a little short of the extra romantic interlude, but his level of appreciation will never have been higher. As for the Rooster, she'll make the most of her year and there will be pennies in the piggy bank at the end of the day. But her success will not come without a struggle.

FAMOUS ROOSTERS

Arts
Claudio Abbado
Francesca Annis
Maria Aitken
Francis Bacon
Janet Baker
Sidney Bechet
Julian Bream
Delius
Michael Frayn
Benny Goodman
Patricia Hayes
Elia Kazan
Otto Klemperer
David Lynch
Jelly Roll Morton

Samuel Pepys
Roman Polanski
Peter Ustinov
Verdi
Wagner

Sports
Franz Beckenbauer
Matt Busby
Robin Cousins
Steve Davis
Nick Faldo
Steffi Graf
Bruce Grobbelaar
Duncan Goodhew
David Gower

Glenn Hoddle
Pat Jennings
John Motson
Bobby Robson
Paul Shockemohle
Jane Torvill
Virginia Wade

Industry/Politics
Hardy Amies
Nicholas Fairbairn
James Goldsmith
Michael Heseltine
Peter Imbert
Tom King
Ken Livingstone
Stavros Niarchos
Mary Quant
Nancy Reagan
Robert Runcie

Royals
Prince Philip
Zara Phillips

Show Biz
Mary Archer

Joan Bakewell
Michael Bentine
Dirk Bogarde
Richard Briers
Michael Caine
Jasper Carrott
Christopher Cazenove
Joan Collins
Tommy Cooper
Les Dawson
Stephen Fry
Diane Keaton
Bill Kenwright
Barry Norman
Nicola Pagett
Jenny Seagrove

Pop
Elkie Brooks
Eric Clapton
Bryan Ferry
Jools Holland
Lieber and Stoller
Yoko Ono
Donny Osmond
Dolly Parton
Pete Townshend

THE DOG

1910	February 10th to January 29th	1911
1922	January 28th to February 15th	1923
1934	February 14th to February 3rd	1935
1946	February 2nd to January 21st	1947
1958	February 18th to February 7th	1959
1970	February 6th to January 26th	1971
1982	January 25th to February 12th	1983
1994	February 10th to January 30th	1995

Dog, dog – I like a good dog –
Towser or Bowser or Star –
Clean sort of pleasure –
A four-footed treasure –
And faithful as few humans are!
F Scott Fitzgerald & Edmund Wilson

THE YEAR OF THE DOG

The year of the Dog means a big shake up for anyone who thinks he can get by on his wits. And if the world's great injustices have seemed to have gone on too long unchecked, take heart. Under the influence of the Dog there will be more than one hand to lift the sword of righteous indignation, more than one foot to crush self-interest and indifference. The Dog's year will see the emergence of a more compassionate society, one in which the trend will be to take up lost causes and to fight for a better deal for the weak and under-privileged. In 1910, Labour Exchanges were established in Britain and in July 1970, after a long legal battle, damages were awarded to the victims of thalidomide.

The Dog's year will restore balance everywhere. It will be a time to cut down on personal excesses, to slim and get fit; no more second helpings, no more boozy nights. It is a year to put the true values of life before the possession of life's valuables. The mood everywhere will be one of serious discussion and moral issues will be the main topic. A caring philosophy will gradually replace the each-man-for-himself attitude, and few will be taken in by the empty promises of self-seeking politicians. In 1946, the General Assembly of the United Nations opened in New York, Italy voted for a Republic, and in 1958, the foundations were laid for the Common Market. 1958 was also the year that Lord Russell launched the Campaign for Nuclear Disarmament. There is no mistaking that the theme of a Dog's year will be towards unity, egalitarianism, and an honest common purpose. For loyalists, it's a time to pin your colours firmly to the mast. But remember that the nature of who demands our loyalty differs from county to country. In Germany, in 1934, Adolf Hitler became Dictator, while across the other side of the world in 1970, Dr Salvador Allende was freely elected the Marxist Socialist President of Chile.

There will be some time, amidst all the idealism, for pleasure. But don't count on anything too extravagant. Most of our energies will be spent on putting the world to rights, not entertaining it. And if it's a poor year for despots, it's worse for depositors. Dogs care nothing for wealth; rich or poor, they carry on with their reformations impervious to the size of their bank balance. Investors everywhere will have to tighten their belts, and some businessmen will become so slim they'll waste away completely. Both Laker Airways and John De Lorean's car firm went bust early in 1982. Should the left-wing Dog take over in your neck of the woods, be prepared to start shelling out. Again in 1982, the Labour controlled GLC doubled London Transport's fares. But in spite of much upheaval, and a great many anxieties over trivialities – what a fuss there was over Mark Thatcher's disappearance during the Paris-Dakar car rally in 1982 – the year will pass relatively peacefully. Wars that begin in the year of the Dog do not drag on – the Falklands War was in 1982 – and victory invariably falls to those defending freedom. There might not be much profit in the year of the Dog, but there will be no shortage of justice.

THE DOG PERSONALITY

'Sleep soundly in your beds. Enter the watchful idealist. Enter the Dog.'

From our very beginnings, no animal has served Mankind more conscientiously or shared his lot more intimately than the ever loyal and trustworthy Dog. No matter what shape or size he comes in, and there would seem to be an endless variety, the Dog's honesty and good intentions prevail come what may. Whether he be the flea-bitten mongrel who wanders loveless through the dark alleyways of our towns and cities, or Cruft's champion of champions, the Dog's eyes tell the same touching story of absolute and unconditional devotion. And while on the subject of the diversity of Dogs, it was summed up beautifully by the 16th century parish priest, the Reverend Edward Topsell. He wrote: 'There be some dogs which bark and do not bite, dogs which bark and bite, and some which bite bitterly before they bark.'

Philosopher, moralist and champion of the underdog, those born under the sign of the Dog will never be content to sit on the sidelines. And they will not simply sit and advocate change, but actively seek out injustice and fight it with an unparalleled sense of purpose. The Dog will very often give more than his fair share of energy to singling out and attempting to reform those areas of our religious, political and social life that he considers corrupt. With a plain, yet often somewhat unsympathetic voice, the straightforward dog will demand his views are given the right to be aired. And if he is denied the conventional platform, he'll build his own, and no power on earth will prevent him from preaching his gospel of freedom, justice and equality for all.

If you were born in the year of the Dog, you will share your birth sign with some very great champions of human rights. The world's only living saint, Mother Teresa of Calcutta is a Dog, so too is Brigitte Bardot, whose personal campaign for animal rights is now universally acknowledged as a major force. The mother of modern Israel, Golda Meir was a Dog, as was war hero Douglas Bader, Ilie Nastase, Pierre Cardin, Barry Manilow, David Bowie, Dr Christiaan Barnard, and would you believe, Barbara Woodhouse!

Given his long and close association with Man, it's not surprising to find that the Dog has become not only an integral part of our daily lives, but an indispensible feature of our language. In addition to leading the blind and bringing casks of brandy to those lost on mountaintops, the Dog has enriched the way we describe all manner of actions and events. When we stick to our tasks stubbornly we call ourselves 'dogged'; should we get into someone's bad books, we are in the 'doghouse'; long, inactive periods are called 'dog days'; soldiers of fortune are 'dogs of war'; and we have 'dog tired', 'dog eared', 'dogs in mangers', 'dog fights', 'hot dogs', 'hair of the dog', and so on.

But for all his immense courage and forthright desire to take on and limit suffering, the Dog very often needs to be led. Left on their own, Dogs who fail to come to a decision on which cause to take up frequently become anxious, and at times a little confused. There are after all, so many causes, which one should the idealistic Dog support? Save the Children? Amnesty International? Oxfam? Christian Aid? So many to choose from, and each and every one so worthy. That is why perhaps, a Dog needs the choice to be so overwhelmingly obvious that it ceases, in effect, to become a choice at all. The classic case of a cause choosing the Dog is to be found in the story of Britain's greatest ever war lord, Sir Winston Churchill. Before assuming the responsibility of Prime Minister *and* Minister of Defence at the beginning of the Second World War, Churchill had led a somewhat undistinguished career, changing parties when it suited him and once describing Mahatma Gandhi as a 'seditious half-naked fakir'. But Hitler's avowed determination to overthrow democracy transformed Churchill into a statesman and defender of human liberty without equal in modern times. 'I have nothing to offer but toil, blood, tears and sweat,' he said, on assuming office. Few doubted him. And I'm sure that few heavyweight boxers doubted the grit and determination of the fiercely patriotic Henry Cooper. Our 'Enry is another to have been born in the year of the Dog.

Once the orders are given and the objective defined, the Dog will move mountains to carry out his task, however menial. And once you have earned a Dog's loyalty – for it will not be given like some cheap trinket, you will never find it wanting. The history books are full of tales of canine devotion, many of which are not only extraordinary for the courage and fortitude displayed, but deeply moving. But one must treat the Dog's loyalty with care, because once he feels deserted, a Dog will re-direct it to the first outstretched hand. Abuse his trust and he will never forgive or forget. Dog people do not respond to cheap offers of friendship, and when there has been a serious breakdown in a relationship, no amount of bones and pats on the head will restore it. And it will have been your fault the trust has been broken; Dogs simply do not act dishonestly in that way. Their attitude quite simply is that they are prepared to lay their life on the line for you, so why can't you reciprocate? And if you have had a relationship with a Dog which has been soured through a breach of trust, do not be surprised if your best friend becomes your sworn enemy.

Once rejected, those born under the sign of the Dog become a serious threat to their own and the safety of those around them. Dogs will take a great deal in the way of

THE DOG PERSONALITY

unwarranted punishment, and even cruelty, but there comes a point when even our most reliable and trusted friend will say 'enough is enough'! As we have heard of those many stories that sing the praises of the Dog's great courage and loyalty, so we read of the darker side. There are also many tragic tales of Dogs who have turned against their masters and savaged them, but such stories seldom tell of the lack of love and terrible neglect these Dogs often have had to endure before they have committed their acts of savagery. And it must be admitted that there are times when Dog people behave in such a vicious manner that it truly defies all powers of human comprehension. Dr Crippen, Charles Manson, Peter Sutcliffe and Dennis Nilsen all murdered without pity. All were born in the year of the Dog.

Stubborn, watchful and sometimes defensive without cause, the Dog is quick to criticise our slowness to appreciate the world's injustices. Yet, at other times, he is the last to appreciate what is actually being done. He frequently speaks out of turn, and his remarks may often strike us as blasé, even cynical. It must be remembered that the Dog has a very simple ambition: to please. Fear of not being thought of as doing his best will tend to make the Dog over-anxious; make him speak without thinking, hoping that his sudden bark will be enough to assure you he is paying attention. The Dog's anxiety also stresses his lack of self-esteem which directly underlies his chronic pessimism. Those born in the Dog year will be those who consistently expect the worst. They are the first to point out the terrible weather we've been having, reminding us of the number of the world's starving and drawing our attention to any number of floods, famines and other disasters.

In the face of uncertainty, Dogs frequently become pre-occupied with insignificant and trivial details. Small problems get blown up out of all proportion. Even Churchill spoke of the 'Black Dog' that sat on his shoulder during his long and often deep depressions. And once the trivial has been magnified, it then becomes an obsession, as it is when a Dog licks his wound. Instead of helping it to heal, the wound gets worse.

However, once you assure a Dog of your trust he will become a most cherished ally. When you need help or consolation, no one will rush to your side quicker than a Dog. At the news of a death in the family, it will be the Dog's letter of sympathy, the Dog's flowers, the Dog's visit, that will start the ball rolling, but there is a strong chance that he might just go a little over the top. Of course, he'll be the first to realise it, and then he will regret it, and start worrying ...

Born under the sign of idealism, the Dog nevertheless has a great love of gossip. He may have a plain voice when debating public issues, but his after-dinner conversation simply sparkles. I was once privileged to write a film script for David Niven. He asked my writing colleague at that time, John Wells (born in the year of the Rat), and me to do something with what he called 'a germ of an idea'. Over the most enjoyable lunch of my life, it transpired that David Niven's germ was a fully-blown concept. He outlined the plot and embellished each character with voices from his wonderful range of accents. With the film business out of the way, the brandies and out of season strawberries arrived and David Niven gave us half an hour of his tales from Hollywood that had tears rolling down our cheeks. No one I have ever met entertained with more affection, style and wit. And as a friend, I can say that no one displayed more courage during the last fatal years. In David Niven I witnessed the kind of noble qualities that are perhaps only found in such abundance in those born under the sign of the Dog.

Although not concerned with money (David Niven always seemed to be working to stay one step ahead of the tax man), it happens that Dogs invariably make a tidy pile. Some, indeed, become incredibly wealthy. It's as if their contempt for wealth somehow works in reverse, and increases their chances of obtaining riches. At one stage, Elvis Presley must have been one of the richest men in the world, yet he lived the declining years of his life on ten cent hamburgers and the kind of junk food that even a hungry hound would pass over.

Another aspect of a Dog's character is that he is deeply affected by his own very critical voice in affairs of the heart. Because he is a fault finder, both in himself and those around him, the Dog is unhappy when asked to expose himself to great acts of faith. Real love, the kind in fact that Dogs are only interested in, seldom comes without a giant step into one's personal unknown. Yuri Gagarin, the first man in space, was a Dog, and amply illustrates the Dog's bravery when facing an external unknown, but the mysteries of the heart can often pose a much greater threat than outer space. Dogs may have a good head for figures, they may well inspire confidences and are certainly capable of facing physical hardships, but they remain wide-eyed and naive when it comes to falling in love. Once married, Dogs quickly become critical of a partner who cannot match their high ideals. The result, unhappily, is all too often a broken marriage. Try as he might, the Dog is not able to loosen his strong feelings of support for those less well off than his or herself, and marriage partners who actually attempt to place themselves above such firm principles will only succeed in ending up in a divorce court. Ava Gardner and Zsa-Zsa Gabor are Dogs. I tried working out how many times Miss Gabor had been married but my pocket calculator didn't run to it.

Whether they live on their own, divorced or single, the Dog's home – particularly the lady Dog's – will be impeccably furnished. Dog ladies prefer furniture with simple and elegant lines and very often pick out wonderful pieces from jumble sales which they renovate. Antiques feature in a Dog lady's home, providing they're not too fussy. They love paintings, prints and old photographs. Their taste in clothes reflects their taste in decor. They wear simple clothes but made with pure, natural fabric – wool, cotton, denim; why wear man-made fibres when the Dog has such a lovely natural coat? Their daytime outfits will have a well-worn look about them, but bump into a lady Dog when she's dressed to kill and you'll hardly recognise her with the low-cut gown and string of real pearls decorating her soft, slender neck. Eye shadow, lipstick, and hair down to her shoulders – is that really her?

Because of their loyalty, Dogs are good to their parents and never desert them. In fact, they will visit all their relatives regularly, and when they are ill, the Dog will do everything possible to make them comfortable. Dogs are very good with both the young and old members of society and make excellent nurses. When it comes to choosing a profession, they need to look no further than the many that demand a rigid sense of duty and idealism. Whatever he chooses, the Dog's strong fidelity to his ideals will provide its own reward.

All phases of a Dog's life will be tinged, and in some cases marred, by his anxiety. A Dog child will act dutifully and stay close to home. He will, however, be argumentative and will strike out against authority, especially when he feels it is misused. As a man, the Dog tends to place people in categories, himself included. This lack of flexibility will constantly put him at odds with all but his closest friends and relatives. Old age will be no easier, and the Dog may well find himself sitting alone regretting what might have been. The Chinese say that a Dog born in the day will have a more peaceful life than a Dog born during the night. But the message is clear: if you are a Dog, sing the songs while you can, fight your causes while you have the strength, and love when it is offered. Tomorrow is too late.

DOG AS PARENT

The Dog will only find it in himself to give openly to children who are prepared to share his high regard for justice and loyalty. This does not augur at all well for a Goat daughter in a Dog's home, especially if the parent Dog happens to be the

COMPATIBILITY OF DOG PARENT AND CHILD

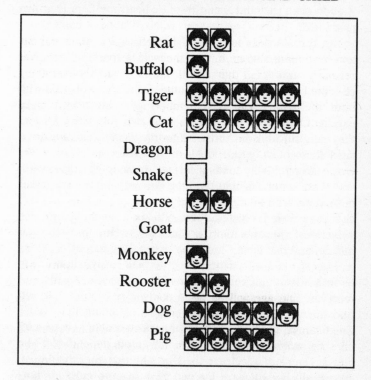

father. She will stamp her foot and demand she does what she pleases, but he'll have none of it. She'll laugh at his lectures on right and wrong and it will be a constant battle until the Goat flees. The child Snake will also suffer under a Dog. A peaceful child, her interests are in beauty and wisdom, interests that her Dog parent can only share when part of a cause. And the Dog will demand a more practical attitude than the Snake child can show. Not a happy relationship. The Dog has even less time for his Dragon son. Conceited and boastful of his skills, the Dragon adolescent will alienate his Dog parent to a point where communication will break down completely.

However, a Dog father will certainly find time for his Buffalo son's thoughtful and resolute headway. The Dog will plan for the Buffalo son, but this will be a bone of contention, as the Buffalo does not like to have his mind made up for him. As parent and child, they are worlds apart. By contrast, the baby pig will fall right in with whatever daddy Dog maps out. Public school or comprehensive, the Pig will make the most of his lot, and keep his own little life very private indeed. There will be no fun for the infant Rat with a Dog as a parent, but he will choose his moments carefully and trick himself into the good books more than once. The artful young Monkey will need all his wits to keep out of trouble, and must remember that the Dog dad won't spare the rod if he's caught with his finger in the jam pot. Child Roosters will also have their problems; there's no room in the kennel for swagger or bravado. Only commonsense. But Roosters are honest, and that goes a long way with a Dog parent.

The pert and witty Horse daughter will easily win her Dog father's affection. She'll take what's going, smile sweetly and push off just as soon as she's ready. The young Cat will benefit from the Dog's strong notions about loyalty. Under his guidance, the Kitten will feel he is better able to cope with life's big problems, and will be socially more dependable. The young Tiger will also leave the Dog's home richer than most. Above all, he will have learned both how to curb his hot-headedness, and moulded his rebelliousness into a useful tool. The puppy Dog will be better treated than any other, and will receive all the love and guidance imaginable. Dogs, young and old, stick together, and the more there are the merrier they become. Lucky Dogs.

DOG IN BUSINESS

To draw an analogy, the Dog's chances of growing filthy rich are about as slim as the home wine buff producing a vintage claret from a do-it-yourself kit. The Dog is the champion of (whoops) the underdog, not a debt collector or property speculator. But if the Dog insists on going into business, he'd better do it with the hard working and honest Pig. That way the Dog will see a return for his investment, and to the Pig's credit, he will put up with the Dog's pessimistic outlook.

The Dog should particularly avoid the Monkey in business, as he will think nothing of taking the poor old hound to the cleaners. Dogs should also avoid the Rooster, but not through any financial consideration, Roosters in business like to make a show of their success and Dogs do not. The bright and adventurous Tiger might happily tolerate the Dog's defensive stance in other walks of life, but he will want a more positive approach when it comes to finance. The Dog's pessimism also casts a blight on the success of a Dragon forming a business partnership. The Dragon relies a great deal on his self-belief to keep things moving, and won't be too happy with an associate who is always pointing out the pitfalls of a venture. The less than active Snake needs much more oomph from his partner, and like the Dragon will be worn down by the Dog's 'should we, shouldn't we?' attitude. And the fickle Goat can be a bit of a gloom monger when the chips are down. Much worse, she has no head for figures and it is difficult to imagine what the left-wing Dog and the socially inclined Goat could do together – open a Marxist wine bar?

The Buffalo can handle business, any amount of it, but the business has to be his own. He won't share any of it with a Dog, they do not see eye to eye. In fact, the Buffalo wouldn't even notice the Dog sitting at the next desk. But the Dog would know all about the Rat's desk, and the question he'd be

COMPATIBILITY OF DOG IN BUSINESS RELATIONSHIPS

Rat	💰
Buffalo	☐
Tiger	☐
Cat	💰 💰 💰
Dragon	☐
Snake	💰
Horse	💰 💰 💰
Goat	☐
Monkey	☐
Rooster	☐
Dog	💰 💰
Pig	💰 💰 💰 💰

asking is, 'Why is it empty?' Of course, the Rat can easily explain; he was out getting orders. Charming Rat gets away with it again. But there will be no tall stories between the Cat and the Dog. The Cat sniffs out a bargain a mile away, and the Dog will be watchful and supportive as the Cat pulls off the deal. But they will make no great fortunes; a modest but comfortable hotel in Eastbourne will be about their mark.

The noble and hard-working Horse is Man's other great companion and aid, and like the Dog, always willing. Dog and Horse share much in common and will do well together so long as they keep busy and let each other have their head.

A stud farm or long distance haulage contractors would do them nicely. Two Dogs, however, have only one option open to them: Bassett & Doberman, Night Security Ltd.

DOG IN LOVE

The faithful and loyal Dog finds he expresses himself much more fluently in affairs of the heart than he does in the somewhat false world of commerce. The male Dragon will be taken by a lady Dog's beauty, and her 'lost' look. But he will tire of her forever questioning their relationship, and has no like of her direct criticism, especially when he is the object. Dogs and Dragons are to be avoided.

The lady Dog will be bowled over by the charm of the Rat, and the affair will more or less take off, but the Dog lady must remember that the Rat is very physical in his expression of love. The same is true of the vigorous Tiger, but the Dog's request for fidelity might reach unsympathetic ears. The lady Pig, however, will inspire the Dog, and of all the relationships he might form, this is by far the most rewarding. What is more, the lady Pig will never tease the Dog for his petty anxieties. Instead she will pride herself on diverting him to other things – like her splendid cooking and comfy bed. Equally well matched are the Dog and lady Horse. She's so witty and charming, and will tease the Dog mercilessly, but in this case he won't mind a bit – lady Horses tease with such style, and she *is* so beautiful!

The Cat is sensuous and refined, and her demands might sometimes overstretch the Dog, but he'll do his best to act romantically to please the Cat, whom he finds most attractive. However, he'll have to try very hard to make an impression.

The Dog lady might easily fall for a Buffalo: he is so

COMPATIBILITY OF DOG IN LOVE

Rat	♥♥♥
Buffalo	♥♥♥
Tiger	♥♥
Cat	♥♥
Dragon	☐
Snake	♥♥
Horse	♥♥♥♥♥
Goat	☐
Monkey	♥♥♥
Rooster	♥
Dog	♥♥♥
Pig	♥♥♥♥♥

strong and resolute, and appears to her as one who *understands*. The Buffalo does understand, but as the lady Dog finds out, he doesn't actually *care*.

There will be no great displays of passion when the Dog meets the strait-laced Rooster. What on earth does the Dog think he's doing rolling on his back and wagging his tail? Goodness gracious! The Monkey, like the Dragon, will find the Dog lady very beautiful, as indeed they are. But he'll put up with more of the lady Dog's long talks and self-analysis than the Dragon. He might even find them amusing. But the Dog must tread carefully when he falls for the bewitching Snake. Her love of passionate romance, and his faithful outlook might clash. And if the Snake tightens her grip, the Dog will have little chance of escaping. And the Dog should steer well clear of a romantic encounter with the Goat, however brief. She will demand he flatters her, and the Dog is not the poet. There is nothing to stop two Dogs from becoming romantically linked, but they must remember to leave their worries and idealism somewhere else when they get together.

DOG IN MARRIAGE

In order for a Dog to make the most from marriage, he or she needs someone who will happily tolerate his pessimism and self-doubt, while at the same time be strong enough to share the Dog's idealism. The buoyant Tiger will make a perfect match, and deal with all sides of the Dog's difficult nature. The Tiger will encourage the Dog when he's low, and join in any fight the Dog puts his weight behind. The honest and jovial Pig will partner a Dog through life's rich pageant. Although the Pig might not share the Dog's concern for the suffering, the lady Pig will always ensure there's plenty of alternatives to keep the Dog's mind occupied – like nice big steak and kidney puddings.

The easy-going Horse will calm the Dog's more anxious moments by her wit and charm, and she might even teach him self-confidence. Similarly, the gracious Cat will reduce the anxiety level and the Dog will relax happily in front of the fire more than he might have expected before the nuptials. A happy domestic partnership here. But no happiness with the dour Buffalo. The Dog will find herself left alone to cope, and there will not be a shred of warmth or comfort during the black periods, just a kind of unvoiced blame. The passionate Rat will excite the Dog initially, but the Rat is quick to

253

COMPATIBILITY OF DOG IN MARRIAGE

grumble when things go wrong, and in the Dog's life that might be rather often. And a problematic creature like the Dog will not be an attractive proposition for the wayward lady Goat. She's no nursemaid, thank you very much! The Rooster might handle the Dog's dark side without too much difficulty, and admire his honesty, but will he never cheer up?

The Dog will happily throw himself at the lady Monkey, and do everything he can to please her, but is it right the Dog should jump at her every small command? I think not. The Snake lady will find the Dog's loyalty and honesty good grounds for a marriage, but it is a case of the attraction of opposites, and they will end up going their separate ways.

254

The essentially self-effacing Dog has nothing in common with the boastful Dragon, whose worst excesses will be magnified in the Dog's honest eyes.

The marriage of Mr and Mrs Dog has a very good chance of success, especially when they have children to keep their minds off their worries. They will make a strong team when there's work to be done and battles to find, but they must try not to criticise each other out of turn.

HOW YOU WILL BE INFLUENCED IN THE YEAR OF THE DOG

A YEAR FOR LOST CAUSES

A howling good year for the faithful and loyal Dog. At last nature's greatest worrier can hold his head high, and if the world is not exactly his oyster, it is at least paying attention to what he is saying. And it will be a rewarding year for the charitable Pig, who will find his honest approach pays dividends in unexpected ways. Never short of a bob or two, the Pig will do especially well commercially. The resourceful Dragon will also be well rewarded. His good intentions and big heart will see him through the more tricky moments, but he will have to work harder than usual, and watch his flirting. The enterprising Rat will not go short either, and will blow with the wind to make sure he gets his share of the harvest, but it will be a bad year for a Rat in love, who will be wise not to make rash promises.

A very poor year for the Goat, who will find her capricious ways out of favour with so much talk of just causes. Roosters too, must be on their guard not to interfere

---

with the Dog's plans. Roosters have a very different view on the way the world should be run, and it seldom coincides with the Dog's. This is the time for all good men and true to rally, not dress up and make high-minded speeches. On the other hand, the vigorous and rebellious Tiger will have much to say and do, but he must remember to keep to the Dog's tempo and not push too hard for quick results. After all, it is the Dog's revolution. But there'll be no revolutionary aid from the conservative Buffalo. If the world is starving, it's the world's fault. Buffaloes have a habit of blaming others when things go wrong.

The Monkey will kid himself he can easily outsmart revolutionaries, and he'll look like getting the upper hand at first, but he'll find the pack turns against him and he'll be best advised to keep to the high branches. The cautious Cat, like the Buffalo, is not a champion of lost causes, but she does admire those who are, and she will muddle through without too many upsets. The industrious Horse will also find life not too unbearable, and will enjoy the sense of equality. But the Horse must guard against his vanity. Dog years don't give much scope for show-offs.

The Snake has her wits and beauty to see her through; alas neither cut much ice. Her only saving grace is that she is a pacifist. A slow year for the Snake, but a sensational year for the Dog. He will not only have His Day, but 365 of them, filled to the brim with all his loyal heart's desires.

FAMOUS DOGS

Arts
Kingsley Amis
Pietro Annigoni
Louis Armstrong
Alan Bennett
Sir Hugh Casson
Cezanne
Judy Dench
Debussy
Philip Larkin
Rene Magritte
Jonathan Miller
Charlie Mingus
Peter Peers
Paul Robeson
Arnold Schoenberg
Artie Shaw

Sports
George Best
Jean Borotra
Terry Butcher
Henry Cooper
Christopher Dean
Jim Laker
Ilie Nastase
Kenny Samson
Kirk Stevens
Daley Thompson
Bill Webenuik

Industry/Politics
Kenneth Baker
Nigel Broackes
Pierre Cardin

Edwina Currie
Winston Churchill
Robin Cook
Freddie Laker
Golda Meir
Francis Pym
Alan Sugar
William Waldegrave

Royals
Prince William

Show Biz
Eamonn Andrews
Jane Asher
Brigitte Bardot
Alan Bates
Lewis Collins
Wendy Craig
Charles Dance
Joyce Grenfell
Tony Hancock
Russell Harty
Lenny Henry
Frankie Howerd
Barry Humphries

Felicity Kendal
Sue Lawley
Shirley MacLaine
Debbie Moore
David Niven
Anneka Rice
Sylvester Stallone
Janet Street Porter
Shelley Winters

Pop
Pat Boone
David Bowie
Kate Bush
Cher
Brian Epstein
Marianne Faithfull
Debbie Harry
Michael Jackson
Al Jolson
Simon Le Bon
Barry Manilow
Elvis Presley
Linda Ronstadt

Saint
Mother Teresa

THE PIG

猪

1911	January 30th to February 17th	**1912**
1923	February 16th to February 4th	**1924**
1935	February 4th to January 23rd	**1936**
1947	January 22nd to February 9th	**1948**
1959	February 8th to January 27th	**1960**
1971	January 27th to February 15th	**1972**
1983	February 13th to February 1st	**1984**
1995	January 31st to February 18th	**1996**

Pigs grow fat where lambs starve.

German Proverb

THE YEAR OF THE PIG

Whereas the preceding year was, under the influence of the Dog, one which strengthened our moral fibre, the year of the Pig will give muscle to our bank accounts. This is the year to indulge in personal vanities, to pamper ourselves and make sure we lose no opportunity to leave the table with a full stomach. The year of the Pig is a time to spend money on the home, invest in a new house or make changes to the one you have. Buy a washing machine, a deep freeze, a new car. An even better plan is to get married or start a family. And if you have already been married once and it didn't work out, try again. In 1971 the Divorce Reform Act came into being. In the Pig's year you will enjoy uncomplicated romance, make piles of money and without even noticing it work harder than you have in a very long time. Wealth is in evidence everywhere, and so is the freedom to express one's opinions openly. In 1971 a twenty-one-year-old trade embargo with China was lifted, and the telephone link between Britain and China was re-established. In the year of the Pig we learn that hard work is the means to a finer and richer life. In 1959 the Litter Act was passed, making it an offence to drop litter, the school leaving age was raised to sixteen and the St Lawrence Seaway was formally opened by the Queen and President Eisenhower.

But there is a very real danger that with so much growth and expansion, both on the commercial and domestic fronts, that we might grow fat and not be able to see the banana skin beneath our feet. The year of the Pig will not be so kind to those who do not look after what they have earned carefully, and there will be many an honest soul who will find themselves duped. Not everything goes smoothly. In 1959 General Batista underestimated the mood of his country and was overthrown by the young Cuban revolutionary, Fidel Castro; and amid much consternation by those who enjoyed the mixed pleasures of city night life, the Street Offences Act came into being.

By and large, though, the Pig's year is not one for great political upheavals – new dishes by the chef of the Ritz, perhaps, but no major changes on the World Stage. Confrontations will be kept to a minimum, with profits and pleasure to the maximum: in 1911 British MPs were paid for the first time. As far as the Pig is concerned, fun and hard work go hand in hand, and this year they will both be given full throttle. As long as prudence is exercised, you can start counting your chickens long before they're hatched.

THE PIG PERSONALITY

'Work hard, play hard.
Meet the honest and jovial Pig.'

For most of us who have grown up in the West, our child-hood has probably been closely associated with the hard working and goodnatured Pig. There was, 'This Little Piggy', the nursery game played with our toes, Piggy-in-the-middle, and who of us at one time or another didn't save in a Piggy bank? Unfortunately, less attractive links were made with the Pig as we grew older. We were told not to 'eat like a pig', or to stop being a 'lazy pig'. There are those who call the police 'pigs', and I imagine most men have been labelled a 'male chauvanist pig' at least once. But whatever verbal associations we in the West have forged with the pig, the truth is that most of them are entirely false. In other words, the Pig is not the way we see him at all.

For the people of China, the inclusion of a Pig in the family is considered a great blessing. No other animal, they believe, is more honest, more prepared to go out of his way to please, or makes more of his every waking moment. In short, the Pig is the best possible companion in the best of all worlds. Popular, well-informed and gregarious, the Pig shines in company and his presence in any relationship will enhance it one hundredfold. As the Chinese proverb quite rightly points out, 'A teacher should never abandon his books, nor a poor man his Pig'.

If you were born in the year of the Pig, you are in illustrious company. Humphrey Bogart, Ernest Hemingway, Noel Coward and Alfred Hitchcock were pigs. So are Elton John, Jerry Lee Lewis, Johnny Mathis, Julie Andrews, Woody Allen and David Essex. But if it appears that Pig's have got the entertainment business sewn up, it is worth mentioning that there are one or two statesmen: Henry Kissinger for example. And if you want a perfect cross between entertainer and statesman you can add the name of Ronald Reagan to the list.

The Pig is essentially a masculine sign, and it's clear from the short list of celebrities that the lady Pig is not a career woman in the grand league. And it's true that the lady Pig rates rather low in terms of achievement on the international scale – with, of course, one or two exceptions such as Maria Callas and Jean Harlow. One of the reasons why Pig ladies are comparatively rare in public life is because they attach a greater importance to family life. They place an enormously high premium on their homes, and consider the welfare of their children before anything else. The domestic life is well suited to the many talents of the lady Pig, who will ensure her home is clean, orderly and comfortable. And you will not find a Pig mother sitting staring helplessly into space with a trio of unhappy kids clinging to her apron strings. Every child in Pig's home will be well fed and well occupied. A Pig mother will choose her children's schools, their clothes, their pastimes and everything else related to their upbringing. And all her choices will be made without the slightest hint that her decisions are anything less than perfect. Pigs of both sexes have a very high opinion of their opinions.

The female Pig, in addition to her skills as mother and housewife, is an honest, open and well-organised woman who is not given to great personal analysis, or tormented by the World's problems. What difficulties she experiences will not get her down, and by her simple recipe of determination and durability will almost certainly overcome life's more thorny moments. The female Pig has great charm and will often use it to fool people into getting her own way. And they can also be more than a mite jealous, especially when they fall in love. A jealous Pig, in fact, is perhaps a Pig to be avoided. Although she has an uncomplicated heart, a lady Pig loves with a single-minded passion. She doesn't have a high moral sense, but she does believe that what's hers is her own.

If there *is* tension in the bedroom , there'll be none in the kitchen, where the Pig lady reigns supreme. Whether it's a simple meal for a few friends or a full blown dinner party, the food will be chosen with the utmost care, cooked with skill and imagination, and presented in such a way as to produce the collective 'Ahhh!' that we normally associate with a firework display. And what is more, there'll be no self-effacement. Lady Pigs know their worth, and she'll not sit around fishing for compliments either. In fact, the lady Pig is seldom bothered with winning praise – she doesn't operate in that way. Pretty and plump, or thin and exotically beautiful. Pig ladies are fond of themselves in spite of their faults or their virtues. They have a capacity to organise their lives just the way they want, and love both their work and leisure. That is all they know, and wish to know. For most lady Pigs, their home will be seen as a palace and treated like one. But there is a strange streak running through some female Pigs which is truly slovenly, and in such cases the house will look as if a bomb has hit it – all the time. It is one thing or another with a lady Pig. No shades of grey.

Male or female, there can be no doubting the Pig's ability to, as it were, bring home the bacon. No one puts more hours into a day. I have a very dear and close friend who is a perfect example of a Pig burning the candle at both ends – and looking good on it. By day he is the senior fiction editor at one of our leading publishing houses and when he returns home after a long day, it is not to put his feet up, but to put on his fencing togs. Not just any old amateur, my friend Richard Cohen has reached the highest rank possible in British sabre fencing. Four times selected to represent Britain in the Olympic Games, three times British Open, one time French, one time Commonwealth champion, Cohen's record is pretty impressive. It's even more so when you realise that every time he catches a plane and flies off to fence, he has his sabre in one bag and a half-finished manuscript in the other. When he's not editing or fencing, he plays bridge better than anyone I know. And to top it all he has now added fatherhood to his list of accomplishments. Where are the cries of 'lazy Pig' now?

In America they call him a 'regular guy', in France, '*un bon viveur*' and in England, a 'really nice chap', but whatever the phrase, when it comes to a night out with no expense spared there's no better companion than a Pig. He is the life and soul of the party – anytime, anywhere. And if there's a hint of glamour about your soirée, so much the better. For the truth is that the Pig is just a little star-struck. He's more often than not the stage door Johnny, waiting patiently with the bunch of roses, or the fan who floods his screen heroine with endless fan mail.

In fact, the Pig in love poses something of a problem, both to himself and the object of his affection. Pigs fall in love just a little too easily and fall much too hard. In most cases, a Pig hit by one of Cupid's arrows will wear his (or her) heart firmly stitched to his sleeve. The chap sitting starry-eyed at his desk, gazing at an in-tray stacked up to the ceiling is a Pig in love; no question about it.

When rejected, the Pig in love has very little inner reserve to deal with a broken heart. More often than not he'll throw himself into a frenzy of work, or sit in the pub and get sozzled every night. Either way, the rejected Pig will be a sorry sight, more than likely beyond any hope of consolation. However, if he seduces you, the Pig will not have done so by dint of his high-powered technique. The fact is the Pig has no line in sweet talk, but there is something utterly beguiling about his openness, and touching about his innocence that is as effective as any well-rehearsed, well-oiled chat. And once a Pig has won your love, do not expect him to stand humbly by and get trodden on. Quite the reverse is more often the case. You will find him talking about his love affair, boasting about it possibly, and in a most insensitive manner. The reason for the Pig's conceit in love might be found after a close examination of King Henry the Eighth, and his attitude towards his six wives. Incidentally, the wife who outlived that infamous monarch born in the year of the Pig was a Monkey, Catherine Parr.

Although he has ability to make money, works and plays hard; in spite of his great intelligence, honesty and likeable personality, the Pig has his flaws. In themselves, they do not seem to be very serious, just a series of small inconsistencies, but when added together they do become something less than trivial. For example, the Pig is no great planner, and might often decide on a course of action when it is clear to everyone else that the moment to act has long passed. Either he acts too early or too late. The right moment is one the Pig finds almost impossible to choose.

No matter what the argument, a Pig will always get straight to the point. Normally he'll tend to remain in the background on first acquaintance in order to gauge his position. But once certain of the competition, as it were, the Pig will step forward and put his argument with great force and conviction. And there will be many who accept his direct views without question. But the Pig is prone to get his facts wrong, and when pushed hard, his arguments often appear to wear a little thin.

As well as his love for good conversation, the Pig is not beyond a little gossip now and then. It might even be that the Pig was the originator of the question, 'Did you hear about old so-and-so?' But when approached, the Pig will tend to laugh it off, and outwardly appear to be relaxed. Inside it will be a very different story. Deep down, Pigs have an exceptionally obstinate streak, and can be wilful under stress. Yet contrary to most good talkers, the Pig is also an excellent listener. Tell him your troubles and you won't find a more sympathetic ear. And you won't find a quicker way for the world to know about them, either – your troubles will hardly be recognisable once the Pig has finished with them! Your operation for a hernia will have changed into having at least one limb removed, and heaven knows what else.

However, if you hurt a Pig, unless it's very serious, he won't bear you a grudge. To do so would force him into the one position he fears more than any other; that of personal confrontation. The Pig loathes disputes of any kind – at work, at home, on the sports field. And when forced into a dispute, the Pig will make matters worse by first stating his case too bluntly, and then retreating. The problem is related to the Pig's central notion that when all things are considered, he is a rather splendid fellow, and has much to support this view. Yet in spite of his self-esteem, a Pig probably won't care at all about his reputation. His attitude, more often than not is simply, 'What others think about me is up to them'. And make no mistake, the Pig knows his own value right down to the last percentage point.

As a result of his high opinion of himself, the over-confident, self-regarding Pig is a sucker for every con man that comes into sight. Kid the Pig along with tales of how clever he is and you'll dupe him as easy as winking. But once taken for a ride, the credulous Pig becomes over-suspicious, a trait that does not marry up well with his normally free and generous nature. Ultra-cautious, highly defensive and almost obsessively self-protective, the Pig once bitten will turn his gullibility into a commercial shrewdness few will match. Robert Maxwell was born in the year of the Pig.

In personal matters, no one is more prepared to take up a cause on your behalf than a Pig, doing so to a point that might even endanger his own position. The Pig will be quick to recognise your best qualities, and do everything he can to make them blossom. Having done so he'll be only too happy to see you working in top gear. Moreover, if there's a rift between you, the Pig will not sit back and let it get bigger, but make every effort to heal it. The Pig, it must be emphasised, is never negative.

When a Pig invites you to his home and says 'help yourself', he really means it. He'll give you the front door key and tell you to treat the place as your own. Pigs are very generous. But the one drawback is that the Pig will fully expect the same treatment when he's ensconced at your place. With his feet up and a glass of your best malt whisky in his hand, he'll be the very devil to shift.

Pigs of both sexes love clothes, and male Pigs in particular love to dress up, as opposed to just getting dressed. They adore the latest fashions and go for a flamboyant cut. Pigs wear shirts with loud stripes, expensive shoes and three-piece suits from Savile Row. And if you meet a gentleman sporting a bow-tie tied neatly around his well scrubbed neck, you might well find that he was born in the year of the Pig. On the other hand, bearing in mind that some Pig ladies live in homes that are no better than ... (sorry) pigsties, it is equally possible to find our Pig friend wandering around in a crumpled corduroy suit with the buttons missing, and holes in the elbows. But the truth is, both sorts of Pigs dress exactly the way they want. Woe betide those who try and get the Crumpled Suit Pig into a smart jacket and slacks, or the Bow-Tie Pig into a T-shirt.

Pigs themselves are born under the sign of honesty, and

when choosing a profession they should avoid any job that forces them into double-dealing. Because all Pigs love the sound of applause, the worlds of the theatre, film and television provide a perfect platform for their talents. And the long hours that most people in the 'profession' work will help rather than hinder the Pig's progress. What is more, the bright lights spell a fat bank balance; a point the Pig has not overlooked. But if he chooses a life on the boards, he'll be wise to find a partner. However intelligent, the Pig is not a great originator and does his best work when forming part of a team. Curiously, the greatest dance team ever to have come out of Hollywood were a pair of Pigs; Fred Astaire and Ginger Rogers. And who can forget Donald Swann's contribution to Flanders and Swann, or Dudley Moore's role in the famous Pete and Dud TV series. Royce, of Rolls Royce, was a Pig, as is Jerry Lewis whose partnership with Dean Martin was so successful in the Fifties.

The three phases of a Pig's life will not be dramatically varied. The first phase will find a young Pig enjoying an extremely contented and well-balanced childhood, although not all a Piglet's romantic dreams will be fulfilled. The middle period will be marred only by problems of the Pig's own making. Provided that he can keep a balance between his own achievements, and of those not so able, the second period will present few if any serious setbacks. The Pig was the last of the animals to have attended the Buddha's New Year party, and was not, I suspect, an accident. He waited first to see if it was worth his while, and that air of caution might be the key to a Pig's success. Old age holds no fears for a Pig who will spend his eventide happily reflecting on his busy and full life, and will to some extent re-live the contentment of his youth.

PIG AS PARENT

When it comes to parenthood, the Pig is immediately noted for the natural ease in which both father and mother deal with their offspring. They express their devotion and care without frills, but there is never a moment when their deep love is not absolutely central. Pigs provide their children with love by the bucket. Obviously, those children who do not wilt from the sometimes overwhelming affection of a Pig parent will benefit most. Of all the possible combinations, the Goat daughter and Pig mother have the happiest of relationships in which there will exist great understanding.

The Snake daughter has a quite different temperament to the Goat, but a Pig father will be enchanted by her beauty. He will also be touched by her concern for a peaceful and pleasurable life, and appreciates her highly developed sense of beauty. The young Monkey will also flourish in the spotlight created for him by his Pig parent. His tricks will be encored for once, not dismissed with a groan. The Dragon son doesn't exactly play tricks, although you can be sure there's always something up his sleeve to amuse his Pig parents. A Pig mother might not always find her Dragon daughter agreeing with her, but there'll be no lack of love. The Pig father will respect his Rooster daughter, and admire her honest method, and he'll tickle her funny bone at the first sign of high-mindedness. Roosters leaving a Pig's home will be well-balanced and well-prepared for life. The young Dog is an ever anxious creature, always on the defensive. He needs great stability to grow up a happy child, and he is lucky should either his mother or father be a Pig. Stability is very high on his list of home making qualities. The young Buffalo can be a very lonely child, but the Pig mother will provide him with much to occupy his independent mind. But the Buffalo adolescent must be careful he doesn't become

271

COMPATIBILITY OF PIG PARENT AND CHILD

Rat	☺ ☺ ☺ ☺
Buffalo	☺ ☺ ☺
Tiger	☺ ☺ ☺
Cat	☺ ☺ ☺ ☺
Dragon	☺ ☺ ☺ ☺
Snake	☺ ☺ ☺ ☺
Horse	☺ ☺
Goat	☺ ☺ ☺ ☺ ☺
Monkey	☺ ☺ ☺ ☺ ☺
Rooster	☺ ☺ ☺ ☺
Dog	☺ ☺ ☺ ☺
Pig	☺ ☺ ☺ ☺

scornful of his parent's indulgences; Pigs know all about discipline when the occasion demands.

The baby Rat will have everything his own way, and love the warmth and affection that seems never ending. But he mustn't become too greedy, for his own sake. The Cat daughter will just adore the smells from her Pig mother's kitchen, and will watch attentively as she puts the finishing touches to her latest culinary invention. There will be no restrictions on the tiny Tiger under a Pig's roof, but the Tiger might find his rebellious nature needs more to brace itself against. In this respect, the young Horse fares even less well. And if remaining true to his individualistic nature, he will leave the snug home of the Pig for a more rugged life elsewhere. Pig children, as one might expect, get the full treatment. But they mustn't get too comfortable. When the big Sow rolls over, they'd better make sure they're not asleep underneath. Ouch!!!

PIG IN BUSINESS

Not a lot can go wrong with the industrious and reliable Pig as a business partner, unless that is, you happen to be a Horse. Here the problems is in the conflict of approach. The Horse works best when given a totally free hand, and the Pig when he keeps in close touch with his partner. Two Pigs on the other hand are a splendid foundation for any kind of commercial enterprise; a chain of meat suppliers perhaps? But when he gets down to business, the Pig does not have a lot of time either for the philosophical Snake. There's far too much to be done, and sitting and thinking doesn't get anyone very far. And Pigs aren't crazy about the Rooster's big boasts, even if the Rooster does pull off the deal. However, both Snakes and Pigs have a flamboyant streak which might become pronounced when the two get together. In that case a show biz partnership might fit the bill. But Roosters should keep clear of the Pig, and vice versa. The Tiger is so full of schemes he hardly has time to think them all through. The Pig will help settle the Tiger, but there is a danger the Pig will get confused and his confusion will irritate the Tiger.

The go-getting Rat will ride happily on the back of the industrious Pig, and the Pig will benefit from having such a charmer to keep the sales reps happy. But the Rat mustn't belittle the Pig's honest toil. The clever Monkey knows exactly how to play the Pig along, he is careful with money and makes the Pig an excellent partner. Something in popular

COMPATIBILITY OF PIG IN BUSINESS
RELATIONSHIPS

Rat	🪙🪙🪙
Buffalo	🪙🪙🪙🪙
Tiger	🪙🪙🪙
Cat	🪙🪙🪙🪙
Dragon	🪙🪙🪙🪙🪙
Snake	🪙
Horse	☐
Goat	🪙🪙🪙🪙
Monkey	🪙🪙🪙🪙🪙
Rooster	🪙
Dog	🪙🪙🪙🪙
Pig	🪙🪙🪙🪙

entertainment would suit them, with lots of good times after hours. The Dragon is a perfectionist and the Pig knows how perfection can be assisted by sheer effort. This is a perfect partnership with maximum profit for each, and never an atom of self-esteem lost by either party on the way to the top. Too much mutual praise can be their only stumbling block to success.

The well-meaning Dog, although lacking the Dragon's lustre, has a good head for figures. Pigs and Dogs work extremely well together, and there'll be no nonsense when it comes to getting down to work. The Pig, however, *would* like just a little lightness in the boardroom, and the odd long lunch hour. There'll also be no nonsense in a partnership between the Pig and the toiling Buffalo, but there will be much more originality with a Buffalo in the team. And there'll be no shortage of quality should they decide to go in for manufacturing. Though the Pig will not be entirely happy with the Buffalo's tendency to sit in the driving seat too often. It's a partnership, remember?

The artistic Goat is not normally at his best in a commercial situation, but will do better than he might expect when tethering his talents to the Pig's hard line on work. The Goat *must* let the Pig make the financial decisions. With his sure and methodical approach, the Cat will find the Pig an understanding partner. Their's will be a slow, but steadily expanding outfit. Gown manufacturers? Interior decorators? Property speculators? Whatever they choose, Cats & Pigs Ltd will not act foolishly with their brass.

PIG IN LOVE

The Pig throws himself into a love affair with his heart and soul exposed to the universe, and a Pig smitten will do everything in his power to please the object of his desire. Two Pigs are a perfect match and cannot fail to reach perfect harmony of understanding. What fun they'll have! And there'll be good times for the Pig and Dog in love. The Pig's good nature brings out the best from the anxious Dog, who really begins to believe in himself. A male Pig and lady Dog's relationship is particularly auspicious.

The Pig lady will fall far too easily for the seductive Dragon, but the carnival king is not keen on too much domesticity and will lose interest before his Pig lady lover has finished baking him her special Lancashire hot pot. The Pig

COMPATIBILITY OF PIG IN LOVE

Rat	♥♥♥
Buffalo	♥♥♥♥
Tiger	♥♥♥
Cat	♥♥♥
Dragon	♥♥
Snake	♥♥♥
Horse	☐
Goat	♥♥
Monkey	♥♥♥♥
Rooster	♥♥♥
Dog	♥♥♥♥♥
Pig	♥♥♥♥♥

will find the fickle Goat no better, and like the Dragon, their affair will quickly fade.

There will be a few good times with the amorous Rat before it fizzles out; the lady Pig really does enjoy his charm and lady Pig and male Rat might well make a go of things. But don't have money on it. The female Rooster will be seduced by the Pig's honest *bonhomie*, and will enjoy his company – at arm's length. But when the lady Monkey walks into a Pig's life, the boot is on the other foot. The gallant Pig falls head over heels in love and the Monkey will have him in her palm. It will be good while it lasts, but will end up with poor old Porky nursing a broken heart.

The lady Pig will attract the male Tiger initially (who can resist her?), but Tigers are such restless creatures and Pigs are animals of habit – more or less. Pigs will also be easily taken in by the refined Cat, and they will share a night dining by candlelight. But the Pig in love wears his heart on his sleeve, and Cats have been known to get embarrassed by open displays of emotion. The Pig lady will, however, put the romantically inarticulate Buffalo at his ease, and she'll listen happily to his stories about work in the fields. She might even put up with him falling asleep while she clears away the dishes.

The sensuous Snake, like the Monkey, will quickly captivate the Pig's heart. She'll find the Pig interesting and enjoy his carefree style. But the Pig must remember the Snake has a grip that no one but a Dragon can free himself from. The Horse can be very weak in matters of romance, and will find no comfort in what she sees as the bland invitations of the male Pig. Pigs and Horses of either sex should stay as far as possible from each other in matters of the heart.

PIG IN MARRIAGE

Although the elegant and beautiful Horse lady has no time for a Pig's advances in terms of a casual relationship, they get on well once the banns have been read. The male Horse has much to offer a Pig lady when setting up home and she returns his practical help with much warmth. And the lady Pig will do a great deal to provide the Rat with the kind of home he will be happy coming home to. To his surprise, the opportunist Rat won't mind directing his nervous energy into domestic life one little bit.

The Goat sees the Pig as a first-class prospect in the marriage stakes. Once married the Pig will adore his Goat

COMPATIBILITY OF PIG IN MARRIAGE

Rat	🐷🐷🐷🐷
Buffalo	🐷🐷
Tiger	🐷🐷🐷🐷
Cat	🐷🐷🐷
Dragon	🐷🐷
Snake	🐷🐷🐷🐷
Horse	🐷🐷🐷
Goat	🐷🐷🐷🐷
Monkey	🐷🐷🐷🐷🐷
Rooster	🐷🐷
Dog	🐷🐷🐷🐷🐷
Pig	🐷🐷🐷🐷🐷

wife's sense of social occasion. But will he enjoy an empty bank account? 'But, darling, the money for my new dress had to come from somewhere.'

The Pig is captivated by the lady Monkey, and once married he'll go to every length to make her happy. And the Monkey lady will not be unappreciative. A very auspicious marriage, especially for the Monkey. A Buffalo could do worse than marry a Pig. He'll never miss a meal and his slippers will always be where he can find them. But the Buffalo must not leave his Pig bride too long on her own. She likes a bit of fun between cooking his supper and waving him off in the mornings.

The only way a Rooster and Pig could live happily under the same roof is if they agree not to mock each other's high self-esteem. Both can be extremely obstinate over trivial matters, and so an attachment to the same religion (one that preaches plenty of self-effacement and forgiveness) would be a great help. The Dog is also a fairly stubborn chap at times, but once under the wing of the lady Pig will find he undergoes a total transformation. The once-anxious Dog becomes well fed and contented, and as his confidence grows so does his ability to express his inner feelings. There can be little wrong with the marriage of a Pig and Dog – all honesty, hard work and good intentions. There will be changes, too, for the unpredictable Tiger when he marries a Pig. She is so dependable that the Tiger will almost be blackmailed into settling down. The possessive Snake will find a match with the Pig, providing her with both comfort and well-informed conversation. And they will have truly beautiful children.

There is nothing to stop the Pig from marrying the social and refined Cat. He loves her sensuousness and enjoys her peaceful ways, but the Pig's twenty-four hour day might unsettle the Cat. The Pig's lifestyle won't bother the lady Dragon, she'll even encourage it, but the male Dragon won't be over-fond of the female Pig's great domestic plans. Kids and crème brûlées are OK in their place ...

A Pig's ideal partner is another Pig. No other combination is guaranteed to provide such a long lasting, happy-go-lucky marriage. Pigs in wedlock are Pigs in clover – the perfect match.

HOW YOU WILL BE INFLUENCED IN THE YEAR OF THE PIG

A YEAR FOR JOVIALITY

Great times ahead for the Pig, but no one loses out in this the most prosperous of all years. Wealth and good living are the hallmarks of a Pig year, but there will be few artists or athletes who will find cause for complaint. Although the Pig himself never enjoys a more splendid year (he's never known a really bad one), the opportunist Rat will discover the barns groaning with sacks of grain. The Tiger, ever full of new ideas will be overflowing, and find he greets a large and receptive audience when selling his latest brilliant enterprise. And there will be no shortage of warm soft cushions for the sensuous Cat, and no shortage of Cat lovers to share them with.

The powerful and lusty Dragon will make money and new conquests. Cats and Dragons are never short of money, but in the year of the Pig, their respective bank managers will grasp their hands even more warmly. And the normally conservative Rooster will find herself swept along by the atmosphere of joviality. What's this, another glass of wine? The often defensive Dog will not wish to be seen as a damp blanket, and after a tentative start the good humoured side of his nature will be much in evidence. The dutiful Buffalo will also let his hair down and find it easier to deal with strangers, but the fun and games are not his scene, and by the end of the year he'll be back in his field, ploughing his furrows alone. The Goat, on the other hand, was made for pleasure and will take whatever the Pig's year has to offer. Her only problem will be how to squeeze into all those new clothes.

There's no fear of being overweight for the Snake, not

Rat

Buffalo

Tiger

Cat

Dragon

Snake

Horse

Goat

Monkey

Rooster

Dog

Pig

unless she really lets herself go. However, it's cash and not calories that interests a Snake. There'll be lots coming the Snake's way this year, though there might be just the thinnest of strings attached. The clever Monkey is the life and soul of every fun gathering, but he must be on his guard not to upstage his host too often.

The hard-working and practical Horse will discover a more stable relationship enter his life, and his easily impressed heart will be strengthend. And of course, the Horse will make money. Like the Pig, he'll make pots of it.

FAMOUS PIGS

Arts
Maria Callas
Ernest Hemingway
Roy Lichtenstein
Marcel Marceau
Luciano Pavarotti
Ravel
Terence Rattigan
Salman Rushdie
Willy Russell
Albert Schweitzer
Donald Swann
C J Jung
Tennessee Williams

Sports
Jack Charlton
Brian Clough
Gareth Edwards
Terry Griffiths
Emlyn Hughes
Rocky Marciano
John McEnroe
Lester Piggot
Cliff Thorburn

Industry/Politics
Oliver Cromwell
Robin Day
William Randolph Hearst
Henry Kissinger
Robert Maxwell
Aristotle Onassis
Kim Philby
Ronald Reagan
Ernest Saunders

Royals
Henry VIII
Prince Rainier
Duchess of York

Show Biz
Woody Allen
Julie Andrews
Fred Astaire
Richard Attenborough
Humphrey Bogart
James Cagney
Robert Carrier
Julian Clarey
Noel Coward
Ben Elton
Jean Harlow
Alfred Hitchcock
Dudley Moore
Patrick Moore
Michael Parkinson
Ginger Rogers
Stephen Spielberg
Terry Thomas
Tracy Ullman
Michael Winner

Pop
Alice Cooper
Kiki Dee
David Essex
Barry Gibb

Elton John
Jerry Lee Lewis
Johnny Mathis
Sonny

FAMOUS PAIRS, COUPLES AND GROUPS

Harold Wilson (Dragon) and Marcia Williams (Monkey)
John Alderton and Pauline Collins (Dragon & Dragon)
Charles Rolls (Buffalo) and Henry Royce (Pig)
Prince Rainier (Pig) and Princess Grace (Snake)
Rogers and Hart (Tiger & Goat)
Rogers and Hammerstein (Tiger & Tiger)
Dean Martin and Jerry Lewis (Snake & Pig)
Arthur Miller and Marilyn Monroe (Cat & Tiger)
Everley Bros – Don (Rat) and Phil (Tiger)
Simon (Horse) and Garfunkel (Snake)
Goffin (Tiger) and King (Horse)
Sonny and Cher (Pig & Dog)
Jerry Leiber and Mike Stoller (Rooster & Rooster)
John Lennon and Yoko Ono (Dragon & Rooster)
Frank Muir (Goat) and Denis Norden (Dog)
Lucille Ball (Pig) and Dezi Arnez (Cat)
Lauren Bacall (Rat) and Humphrey Bogart (Pig)
John F Kennedy (Snake) and Jackie Kennedy (Snake)
Jackie Kennedy (Snake) and Aristotle Onassis (Pig)
Maria Callas (Pig) and Aristotle Onassis (Pig)
Eric Morecambe (Tiger) and Ernie Wise (Buffalo)
The Queen (Tiger) and Prince Philip (Rooster)
Richard Burton (Buffalo) and Liz Taylor (Monkey)
Prince Michael of Kent (Horse) and Princess M (Monkey)
Ross and Norris McWhirter (Buffalo & Buffalo)
Margot Fonteyn (Goat) and Nureyev (Tiger)
Sophia Loren (Dog) and Carlo Ponti (Buffalo)
Winston Churchill (Dog) and Clementine (Rooster)
Twiggy (Buffalo) and Justin de Villeneuve (Cat)

Katherine Hepburn (Rooster) and Spencer Tracey (Rat)
Bonnie (Dog) and Clyde (Rooster)
Duke of Windsor (Horse) and Mrs Simpson (Monkey)
Princess Margaret (Horse) and Lord Snowdon (Horse)
Laurence Olivier (Goat) and Vivien Leigh (Buffalo)
Michael Denison (Cat) and Dulcie Gray (Monkey)
Tim Rice (Monkey) and Andrew Lloyd Webber (Rat)
Jane Torvill (Rooster) and Christopher Dean (Dog)
Margaret Thatcher (Buffalo) and Denis (Cat)

Tennis Doubles
John Newcombe (Monkey) and Tony Roche (Rooster)
Peter Fleming (Horse) and John McEnroe (Pig)
Rosie Casals (Rat) and Billie Jean King (Goat)
Shirley Fry (Cat) and Doris Hart (Buffalo)
Victor Seixas (Pig) and Doris Hart (Buffalo)
Owen Davidson (Goat) and Billie Jean King (Goat)

ROLLING STONES	Jagger	(Goat)
	Richards	(Goat)
	Jones	(Horse)
	Wyman	(Rat)
	Watts	(Snake)
ABBA	Benny	(Dog)
	Agnetha	(Tiger)
	Ann Frida	(Rooster)
	Bjorn	(Rooster)
BEATLES	George	(Goat)
	John	(Dragon)
	Paul	(Horse)
	Ringo	(Dragon)
	Brian Epstein	(Dog)
GOONS	Sellers	(Buffalo)
	Secombe	(Rooster)
	Milligan	(Horse)

MARX BROS	Groucho	(Goat)
	Harpo	(Rat)
	Chico	(Pig)
	Zeppo	(Buffalo)
SUPREMES	Diana Ross	(Monkey)
	Florence Ballard	(Goat)
	Mary Wilson	(Monkey)

THE MODIFYING AGENTS AND HOURS

If I were living in China and casting horoscopes professionally, I would need a lot more information about the subject's birth details than most of us in the West have access to. As well as the yearly sign, the Chinese assign animal influences to a wide range of periods, which include days, months and hours. In addition, each animal has its own agent, such as earth or fire, which plays a large part in modifying a person's character. With these additional sets of modifying influences, we can learn a great deal more about the complexities of the Chinese Horoscope. We can also move a lot closer to answering the most common question asked about this fascinating science; 'How can everyone born in the same year behave the same?'

As all those who have studied Chinese Horoscopes, even on a casual basis, will know only too well, the animal sign is by and large the dominant factor. But we are also aware that there are slight but noticeable differences among those of the same sign. These are explained mainly by the influence of the hour signs and the five agents. Indeed, there are some Chinese authorities who write on the subject who say that the five agents are as important as the twelve signs. Some say even more so, although I cannot fully agree.

THE FIVE AGENTS

In some books on the subject, the five agents are called the five elements. But this is not strictly accurate as an agent in this context has to do with a quality that *alters* a personality,

287

rather than an element, which wrongly suggests a fundamental change. The five agents are essential to a greater understanding of the way in which a basic animal sign's influence is modified. Not only do the agents of wood, fire, earth, metal and water help or hinder the influence of an individual's animal sign, they play a significant part in refining their influencing animal's compatibility with other signs.

The five agents are wood, fire, earth, metal and water. Each of the twelve animal signs has a fixed agent and one which occurs every 60 years. For example, a Rat born in 1900, has Water as their fixed agent, but metal as their moving agent. Put simply, this makes the Rat in question a Metal Rat with a fixed Water base. The moving agent is the stronger of the two.

As well has having both fixed and moving agents in our personal make up, it is also important to discover those of our partners. Ideally we should be composed of compatible agents ourselves and find partners who offer similar compatibility. Clearly, metal is melted by fire, and should be avoided; water is carried by metal [such as containers] and is a relationship to be encouraged. As we can detect much of our animal influence by studying the real animal in question, it is equally possible to learn much from the agent's natural form. It follows that the Fire agent tends to cause people to burn brightly, and sometimes fade suddenly; water flows freely and reaches its own level.

Like all things Chinese, there is a wonderful simplicity to the five agents. Once grasped, they add enormously to our understanding of the subtle changes they make to our influencing animal.

CORRECTIVE AND CONTROLLING AGENTS

The Chinese Horoscopes view the five agents as two parts of the whole, like sides of a coin. These parts are known as the controlling and the corrective. And it is worth noting that the world is entirely made up of the five agents, which gives some idea as to the importance placed by the influence of wood, fire, earth, metal and water on our animal sign. But it must be emphasized that no agent is stronger or more important than another. All have their equally important part to play, both in the universe as a whole and within the scope of our personal Chinese Horoscope.

CORRECTIVE

Water is corrected by Earth.

The shores prevent water from invading the land and we use variants of earth in many ways, such as pipes, pots, irrigation ditches and canals.

Earth is corrected by Wood.

Wooden fences are placed around fields and gardeners keep earth in wooden tubs. Trees set their roots in soil and are responsible for its nourishment. Earth without trees becomes sand.

Wood is corrected by Metal.

Saws cut through the largest plank and axes can fell the biggest tree. Nails keep wood together and chisels can fashion wood to any shape.

Metal is corrected by Fire.

Gold is melted by flames and the hardest metals can be turned to liquid by intense heat. But it is worth noting that fire can't destroy metal; it can only make it change its form, and then, only temporarily.

Fire is corrected by Water.

The most obvious of all the corrective relationships. Water extinguishes fire, and does so to the point that fire no longer exists.

CONTROLLING

Water controls Wood.

Without rain trees cannot grow. Obviously, wood and trees are seen here as one and the same.

Wood controls Fire.

In this sense, wood is seen as the provider of fire. Boy scouts learn to make fire by rubbing two pieces of wood together and in primitive environments fire cannot exist unless there is wood to burn.

Fire controls Earth.

It could be said that the earth is made of the ashes of wood. Once burned, everything becomes carbon and part of the earth.

Earth controls Metal.

Most, if not all metals are dug from the earth. Even the rocks that contain some metals are in essence, hardened earth.

Metal controls Water.

Metal may be used to carry water, but there is another way of looking at this combination. Metal becomes liquid, that is to say water, when heated.

THE FIXED AGENTS

Water; Rat, Buffalo, Pig.
Wood; Tiger, Cat, Dragon.
Fire; Snake, Horse, Goat.
Metal; Monkey, Rooster, Dog.

You will notice there is no earth agent in the fixed years. This is because it is thought that earth is to be found in some way or another in all the other agents. Earth is the sea bed, it is the ashes of wood and so on.

THE MOVABLE AGENTS

RAT

1900 Metal, 1912 Water, 1924 Wood, 1936 Fire, 1948 Earth, 1960 Metal, 1972 Water, 1980 Wood.

BUFFALO

1901 Metal, 1913 Water, 1925 Wood, 1937 Fire, 1949 Earth, 1961 Metal, 1973 Water, 1981 Wood.

TIGER

1902 Water, 1914 Wood, 1926 Fire, 1938 Earth, 1950 Metal, 1962 Water, 1974 Wood, 1986 Fire.

CAT

1903 Water, 1915 Wood, 1927 Fire, 1939 Earth, 1951 Metal, 1963 Water, 1975 Wood, 1987 Fire.

DRAGON

1904 Wood, 1916 Fire, 1928 Earth, 1940 Metal, 1952 Water, 1964 Wood, 1976 Fire, 1988 Earth.

SNAKE

1905 Wood, 1917 Fire, 1929 Earth, 1941 Metal, 1953 Water, 1965 Wood, 1977 Fire, 1989 Earth.

HORSE

1906 Fire, 1918 Earth, 1930 Metal, 1942 Water, 1954 Wood, 1966 Fire, 1978 Earth, 1990 Metal.

GOAT

1907 Fire, 1919 Earth, 1931 Metal, 1943 Water, 1955 Wood, 1967 Fire, 1979 Earth, 1991 Metal.

MONKEY

1908 Earth, 1920 Metal, 1932 Water, 1944 Wood, 1956 Fire, 1968 Earth, 1980 Metal, 1992 Water.

ROOSTER

1909 Earth, 1921 Metal, 1933 Water, 1945 Wood, 1957 Fire, 1969 Earth, 1981 Metal, 1993 Water.

DOG

1910 Metal, 1922 Water, 1934 Wood, 1946 Fire, 1958 Earth, 1970 Metal, 1982 Water, 1994 Wood.

PIG

1911 Metal, 1923 Water, 1935 Wood, 1947 Fire, 1959 Earth, 1971 Metal, 1983 Water, 1995 Wood.

THE WATER AGENT

The positive side of those born with water as an agent is that they will employ a great calmness and serenity in their approach to life. In normal conditions water is placid. If there are unseen cracks in the bank or pipe, water will quickly find a way through. This means that water can travel great distances, and if the source is great, not weaken in the process. It can carry anything compatible and reflect light. Water helps the mind to flow gently.

Water can carry others willing to float, but it can drown

those who do not learn its ways. Water is sometimes needed where there is no source and must itself be carried. There is danger here, for in the wrong receptacle, water might be spilled. Water needs to choose its carrier carefully. When facing an obstacle, water will wear it down by patiently brushing against it. In love, water takes time to boil and once boiled, if left unattended will turn to steam. Water seduces rather than forces change.

The negative side of those born with water as an agent is that when aroused by a storm they will lose control and crash against any barrier with a terrible force. But once water returns to its normal, placid state, it is not altered. Sometimes it is good to learn from our experiences.

THE WOOD AGENT

The positive side of those born in a wood year is that they grow slowly but surely. They plant their roots firmly before moving. They do not rush ahead of themselves or overstretch. Wood inches forward with care and deliberation, learning thoroughly as they go. In love, wood is cautious. Wood can be used to meet many different needs and can be fashioned to both artistic and practical ends when under the appropriate tool. Wood is resolute, and the great provider. Supple in youth and powerful in maturity, wood is respected by all.

No other agent has so many uses in the chain of nature and it is not surprising that trees have always been seen in mythological terms as the mother of life. They offer shade, fruit, building material, leaves for compost and shelter for birds. Wood inspires confidence and finds few, if any, difficulties working alongside others. In partnerships it is advisable to choose an agent that holds wood together. There are varying degrees of hardness and some types of wood are more easily damaged than others. The seeds of trees may be carried far.

The negative side of those with a wood agent is that they

can be blown down in extreme conditions. When a tree is uprooted it is useless trying to replant it; once the fragile tap root has snapped, nothing can be done.

THE FIRE AGENT

The positive side of those born with a fire agent is one of vitality. Fire is the centre of focus, even in daylight. Fire warms and inspires. Fire has huge appetites and devours everything in its path. Never shrinking from danger, fire has the wonderful ability to draw those with less courage to its flame. Quick to learn and quick to love, fire provides the energy to survive, for without it, we would certainly die. Fire cannot stay in one place and is constantly on the move, seeking new horizons and challenges.

Few can live with fire. Loners and individualists, those born with the fire agent will never find life lacking interest. Too often, fire is seen as a threat, especially by those who are consumed by it. But when contained, such as in a grate or an oven, fire enhances life and provides the centre of any group. Fire lights the darkness. Fireworks celebrate.

The negative side of those born with the fire agent is that they are not self sufficient. Fire needs feeding and without help, it will quickly die out. Of all the agents, fire is without question the most destructive in the negative state, there is no escape from its flame and everything on earth is a potential victim.

THE EARTH AGENT

The positive side to those born with the earth agent is that they are reliable and dependable. Earth is the substance on which all creatures walk and from which all plants grow. It is not easily moved and providing the conditions are suitable, earth will act as the foundation for all life. Although it provides much, earth in itself has a limited use. It needs skill and effort to turn it into something else. When dealing with those who are born with the earth agent, it is wise to remember that they are deeply conservative at heart. They do not travel easily and have seasons for their feelings. This can sometimes mean that love must wait its turn.

The earth is both rich and poor, depending on the location and the fortunes of those with earth as their sign will find their finances may alter with the company they keep. When they influence others, earth people will not attempt to face the opposition head on. Their plan is always to wait until the conditions are right, preferring to let natural causes and events take their own retribution. Slow to judge and slow to anger, earth is enterprising yet sometimes blunt in its dealings.

The negative side of those born with earth as their agent is that earth can be too lumpen at times. There is a slowness about the earth and a lack of originality. Often the lack of rain dries earth out and too much might turn earth into mud.

THE METAL AGENT

The positive side of those born with the metal agent is that they are unbending in their ambition. Almost totally without exception, metal is resolute and hard. It may be shaped as a result of exposure to heat, and even turned from its original form as a solid into liquid. But the substance of metal does not change or vary its quality. Metal in its many forms is both worshipped and admired, fought over and hoarded. It decorates and forms the basis for practically all man-made inventions. Nothing lasts longer than metal and no other agent will inspire the hearts of men to ambition. Metal has become our reward and the object of our desire. As such, metal can influence all men.

In love, metal people will always seek to be loved first and they will not love deeply unless loved for themselves alone.

Metal is carried everywhere. But undiscovered metal, metal that is unrefined, may lay hidden but never for long. Someone will always seek metal out.

The negative side of those born with the metal agent is that they are inflexible and find it difficult to let go of things they love. Metal makes chains and too frequently metal becomes trapped by its own links. Those who reject metal will find themselves rejected.

THE AGENTS AND THEIR USES

There are two main uses for the five modifying agents, although they can be used in countless numbers of ways in our daily lives. Primarily, they help compatibility and act as a guide to which kind of work you should do. It is said that a person with a complete set of agents, one which includes metal, water, wood and fire is rare indeed. In China, most authorities say the earth agent is present when the other four are together. Some differ but I side with the majority. If you already have earth, all well and good. If you haven't, then I'd accept the wisdom of the majority.

In China, a great deal of effort goes into trying to get as many of the modifying agents as possible. A person might have fire, wood and water in their make up, but lack metal. They may attain this by working with metal, or putting metal objects close at hand; wearing a metal bracelet might be a solution. If they lack water, they might even go so far as to add the word, or the character as it is in Chinese, to their name. Translated into Western terms, John Smith could add a middle name of Brook, or a word that is derived from or associated with water. John Kingfisher Smith, is such a possibility.

Unfortunately, the method of discovering our individual set of agents frequently breaks down in the West. This is due to the common problem of not always having the precise details of the hour of birth. The system of divining all five agents is highly complex and would need a book at least twice the length of this one to explain. But even with the few agents we might find we have, our sign's attitude to work and compatibility can be greatly enhanced. For those who have such information, or would like to know the principle, the way to discover how many agents you have is as follows. First find the agent of your year of birth. Next find the agent of your animal sign. Thirdly, find the agent of the animal of your hour of birth. And finally, find the agent of the animal sign of your month of birth. In China, the Western system corresponds exactly with the twelve Chinese calender months, which are known as the lunar agricultural almanac. They are as follows:

Aquarius	Jan 21 to Feb 19	Tiger	Fixed agent; wood.
Pisces	Feb 20 to Mar 20	Cat	Fixed agent; wood.
Aries	Mar 21 to Apr 19	Dragon	Fixed agent; wood.
Taurus	Apr 20 to May 20	Snake	Fixed agent; fire.
Gemini	May 21 to Jun 21	Horse	Fixed agent; fire.
Cancer	Jun 21 to Jul 21	Goat	Fixed agent; fire.
Leo	Jul 22 to Aug 21	Monkey	Fixed agent; metal.
Virgo	Aug 22 to Sep 22	Rooster	Fixed agent; metal.
Libra	Sep 23 to Oct 22	Dog	Fixed agent; metal.
Scorpio	Oct 23 to Nov 21	Pig	Fixed agent; water.
Sagittarius	Nov 22 to Dec 21	Rat	Fixed agent; water.
Capricorn	Dec 22 to Jan 20	Buffalo	Fixed agent; water.

It does not take much common sense to work out what is missing in our make up, and rectify it by a simple remedy. Taking a personal example, I lack the fire agent and attribute my longing to be near the sun, the hotter the better, as the reason. But having metal as my dominant agent, I also need water close to hand. So when I go on holiday abroad, I never choose an inland spot unless there is a pool.

To help familiarize ourselves with the method of finding the agents, let's look at a particular case.

The subject is a female, born on April 21st, at 2.40 pm.

Her animal sign is the Tiger and her hour sign is the Goat. The Tiger's fixed agent is wood and the moving agent is fire. The Goat's fixed agent is fire, as is that of her month.

The result is not auspicious. The hour sign, the Goat, has no compatibility with the Tiger, which dominates. The principal agent, that of the year of birth, is fire and it is dramatically heightened by the fire agent of the month and hour signs. The fixed agent, wood, is also in conflict with the three overpowering fire agents. There is no water to control the fire, or metal to help the wood. For compatibility and balance the Goat will turn to a Horse and the Tiger to Dogs. But there are no Horse or Dog signs, although a keen interest in either or both would be most helpful in creating a greater inner harmony. Although her Tiger sign is the most dominant feature, and one which usually makes its mark, all her modifying signs and agents are in conflict. This is likely to leave the subject to be deeply divided and totally ineffectual. As a matter of interest, the subject is Her Majesty Queen Elizabeth II.

THE AGENTS AND WORK

As a rule of thumb, we should always try to find occupations which are sympathetic to our agent. For example, someone born with a dominant fire agent would be foolish to get involved with water, the two agents working against each other. A dominant wood agent, on the other hand, would be highly compatible with water. And the agents are not only a useful guide to work and relationships. They can also help with almost all our everyday needs. Our homes are just one of the many places the agents can enhance. A person with a lack of wood might plant a tree, or buy wooden furniture instead of plastic or metal. Always remember, when working out our missing agents, it is the agent of the year of our birth which dominates and is always the most influential.

THE METAL AGENT

Those with a dominant metal agent should look for an occupation which is involved with wood, or is metal related. Wood works best with metal and any job which uses tools with these two elements is highly recommended. Silversmiths use such tools, and little or no fire, a danger. Carpentry is another occupation for those with the metal agent. Metal is a conductor of electricity, which means any electrically based work is a good choice. Choose anything from computers to electric guitars. Metal is controlled by water, which may suggest that work in the ship building industry – either in the design or manufacture could prove auspicious. Fire controls metal, which suggests keeping clear of a job in the fire service.

THE WATER AGENT

Those with a dominant water agent should look for an occupation which is involved with either wood or related to water. Wood controls water and any work near wood will be a good choice. Sailing wooden ships or traditional wine making, using wooden casks might do the trick. It is thought that since the human body is mainly water, those with a water agent also will be fulfilled when dealing with any area of human contact. Doctors and those professions closely linked to healing are useful for those born with a dominant water agent. Water controls fire, which means a blacksmith's job is OK. But water conflicts with earth, so stay away from digging reservoirs.

THE WOOD AGENT

Those with a dominant wood agent should look for an occupation which is involved with earth or related to water.

Best of all would be work involving paper of any kind. A job in agriculture, especially forestry would be beneficial, as would employment that included building wooden structures on earth. For example, the design of traditional wooden holiday chalets by the sea is ideally suited to the wood agent's influence. Wood is corrected by metal, which means any work which brings these agents together could prove less than successful. Cutting down trees could be positively lethal. Fire is another agent which clearly poses threats to a wood agent.

THE FIRE AGENT

Those with a dominant fire agent should seek a profession which has strong contact with metal, and to a lesser extent, wood. Metal is melted by fire and although it is never actually destroyed by fire, metal can be altered to almost any shape. Playing a metal saxophone may prove an ideal occupation, or trumpet, or, indeed any brass instrument. If you work with wood, it is better not to get too close to paper. It is more auspicious to choose a job where wood is found in its natural state. Water should be avoided at all costs as it will at the least dampen, or at worse, wash away even the strongest ideas. Earth is another agent which will slow down the chances of advancement.

THE EARTH AGENT

Those with a dominant earth agent have an advantage in the job prospect market, especially where caution and careful thought is a requirement. This agent is the most steady of all five and it is believed will help those who work in agriculture [not forestry] and geology. Earth performs well with water and metal, with water being the strongest; hydrogeologists might have the perfect job. But any occupation that is involved with regulated growth is worth considering. But earth does not work well with either water or metal. Earth is washed away by water, no matter what the circumstances. This would suggest no job close to the sea or rivers. And even related jobs, like reading water meters would be thought to be inauspicious.

THE TWELVE HOURS

THE ANIMAL SIGNS AND THEIR HOURS

In China, traditional hours were twice as long as those in the west. The first hour was from 11 am to 1 pm. Each 'two hour' period is named after an animal and follows the same order as the year signs. The animal influence is the same as the year sign. The hours are as follows;

11 pm to 1 am; The hour of the Rat
1 am to 3 am; The hour of the Buffalo
3 am to 5 am; The hour of the Cat
5 am to 7 am; The hour of the Tiger
7 am to 9 am; The hour of the Dragon
9 am to 11 am; The hour of the Snake
11 am to 1 pm; The hour of the Horse
1 pm to 3 pm; The hour of the Goat
3 pm to 5 pm; The hour of the Monkey
5 pm to 7 pm; The hour of the Rooster
7 pm to 9 pm; The hour of the Dog
9 pm to 11 pm; The hour of the Pig

There is also debate about when these hour signs come into effect. Some authorities say that it should be based on Peking time. I do not share that view. My argument, which is shared by many, is that we can only be influenced by lunar activity when it is directly active in our sphere. To argue the opposite point would be like saying you can get a suntan in Birmingham during the winter just because the sun is shining in Miami.

301

COMPATIBILITY OF AGENTS

The Chinese view the relationship between the agents with almost as much seriousness as they do the compatibility of animal signs. In China it is common to find hundreds of books on the subject of compatibility between the agents, most of which are written in an easy to understand style and obviously aimed at a popular market. But for all that, it is essential to grasp the agent's compatibility in order to fully understand the whole system of Chinese Horoscopes (remembering it is the compatibility of animal signs which govern ninety per cent of what makes a couple compatible). The following is a typical example of what you might read in a Chinese book about the agents. Obviously, for Westerners, the tone might appear a little direct. But for the peoples of the East, the world offers a cut and dried view of destiny. The free will we prize so much is centred on making a sensible choice with what is available, not having an endless selection to choose from.

MALE WOOD–FEMALE WOOD

A storm will uproot the trees and the couple will not be able to withstand the high winds. Children will add to the burden and there will be little, if any, understanding.

MALE WOOD–FEMALE FIRE

Wood leads to fire. Sudden flare-ups are common and more

302

so if the couple do not set their minds to avoiding contentious issues. Long life, though, is expected. Good relations can emerge and children are destined to be prosperous and honorable.

MALE WOOD–FEMALE EARTH

Wood is dominant, and from the soil grow the riches. A good relationship, helped by a small family. Prosperity abounds, so for balance it is advisable to live the simple life and act with charity.

MALE WOOD–FEMALE METAL

The axe chops wood. There is much danger for this couple, and the husband is not expected to be faithful. But if the boundaries are agreed in advance, there could be limited understanding. Several children.

MALE WOOD–FEMALE WATER

Water carries wood and this couple will need to work long and hard to make the relationship develop beyond the romantic phase. A career in agriculture is advised. A large family with many girls.

MALE FIRE–FEMALE WOOD

The agents flow against each other. If wood brings fire, it is also consumed by fire. When the woman is stronger, the husband will lose his self respect. Mutual understanding is essential. Many children.

MALE FIRE–FEMALE FIRE

Disaster lurks in every corner. Unless it can be agreed who does what, and no criticism is levelled at the one who fails, there can be no happiness in the home. Openness will help stop violence. Children will be bright.

MALE FIRE–FEMALE EARTH

Fire brings earth, which makes for one of the most auspicious of all relationships. A fine garden is the centre of the home and long life is expected. Prosperity is there for the taking. Many healthy offspring.

MALE FIRE–FEMALE METAL

Fire will always melt metal, which makes this an inauspicious relationship. The wife must learn to bend a little if anything is to be salvaged. Finance will be a problem and sons must marry strong women.

MALE FIRE–FEMALE WATER

Water puts out the flame. An auspicious relationship which is almost impossible to control. Exciting in the romantic stage, they become jealous of each other and the husband will behave cowardly. Weak children.

MALE EARTH–FEMALE WOOD

Earth produces wood but male earth is barren. This is an inauspicious relationship. There is little chance of wealth and although there might be many children, they will grow up badly and be ungiving.

304

MALE EARTH–FEMALE FIRE

The agents flow against each other. Not entirely auspicious, there will be much gentle understanding and love. If they give as well as receive they will live a modest but unassuming life. Children will get on well together.

MALE EARTH–FEMALE EARTH

An auspicious beginning which can easily decline in later years. Good understanding of feelings and much harmony in love. Illness can strike unless they give as much as they receive. Children will break away.

MALE EARTH–FEMALE METAL

Earth produces metal and when the metal is precious, there can be no limit as to what this couple might achieve. Moments of misunderstanding will be short and few. A large, loving and prosperous family.

MALE EARTH–FEMALE WATER

Highly inauspicious, especially if the wife is not strong minded. A promising start will fade into misunderstanding. Only genuine concern for others will keep this couple together. Children will lack affection.

MALE METAL–FEMALE WOOD

Metal may hurt wood, but if the right circumstances prevail, they can join to fight others. A difficult start leads to better understanding. Worries about health for the husband, and over the health of children.

MALE METAL–FEMALE FIRE

One of the worst of all relationships and nothing this couple do will ever be in harmony. Domestic and health problems will continually dog them. Their offspring will not make progress and only great piety will save them.

MALE METAL–FEMALE EARTH

The agents work against each other and the wife will completely dominate the husband, who she might grow to hate. Finance will be a constant worry, and there will never be enough. The children, though, will prosper.

MALE METAL–FEMAL METAL

Highly volatile with a promising start, so full of passion, quickly collapsing into animosity and even hatred. The wife might grow sick and self-centred. Three children are expected.

MALE METAL–FEMALE WATER

Metal carries water and a highly auspicious relationship is predicted. Prosperity in business and a long life for both are forecast. In many cases, a large family will include three boys.

MALE WATER–FEMALE WOOD

Water helps wood, and here finances are blessed. They flow with great ease. But too much wealth will lead to a life empty of spiritual values and depravity could follow. Much attention must be given to truth.

MALE WATER–FEMALE FIRE

Water puts out fire and there will be nothing but hardship and misunderstanding between this couple. Each will destroy the other and the husband will grow sick. A large family with two girls.

MALE WATER–FEMALE EARTH

Not at all auspicious. There is always a problem with sickness and there is never enough money. No understanding between this couple, but with effort, some headway can be made. Children will not help.

MALE WATER–FEMALE METAL

Highly auspicious and flowing. Gold is collected with the help of water. Many friends will surround this couple and there will always be prosperity to share. They trust others and are trusted. Large family.

MALE WATER–FEMALE WATER

Too much water floods understanding and leads to uncertainty. Hard work will not always bring fruit and disagreements are common. Children will not respect the parents and leave home early.

RATS AND THEIR AGENTS

THE METAL RAT
1900, 1960

Metal Rats tend to cover their true feelings. They are often the most charming and as a result are the best loved of all Rats. But in nearly all cases there is another, less inviting story. They are open to sudden bursts of anger and envy, and Metal Rats might easily carry a grudge to the grave. They can be extremely selfish at times, but metal Rats are also often given to spontaneous bursts of great generosity.

The sharpest of critics, a Metal Rat has the most pronounced streak of opportunism. They tend to rise quickly to the top and tenaciously fight off any attempt to remove them. Metal Rats find any form of denial difficult and they adore partying, pomp and ceremony. Curiously, though, they are often surprisingly traditional in their tastes but like to mix with influential people.

Given their bright and quick intelligence, Metal Rats have all that is necessary to make the very most of life's opportunities.

FAMOUS METAL RATS

The Queen Mother, Ivan Lendl, Gary Lineker.

THE WATER RAT
1912, 1972

Water Rats are firm in their views and often express them with great assurance. On the whole, they are less tenacious

308

and more adaptable to the moods of others. Water Rats have a thirst for knowledge and never stop learning. They argue with facts not ideas and few will get them to turn the tide of their thought. They are skilled thinkers and shrewd in their business dealings.

Water Rats will go anywhere and do anything for self advancement and not be proud when accepting gifts. In love they are less demonstrative, but their feelings run deep. They express their thoughts most effectively with the written word and have a wide range of interests, which are often physical.

Water, combined with the Rat's great tenacity means that whenever forced into a corner, the Water Rat will fight relentlessly to escape. It might not be an honourable exit, but a gradual gnawing away at the barriers.

FAMOUS WATER RATS

Richard Nixon, Earl Louis Mountbatten, Enoch Powell.

THE WOOD RAT
1924, 1984

Whatever talents fall to Rats born with the wood agent, they will make the most of them. Ambitious, Wood Rats will move with caution and be less trusting of their instinct. At the same time they will be far more able to hold their aggressive streak in check.

As lovers, they will tend to be more secretive about their feelings but will often be the parent of a large and warm family. They are thoughtful and protective, and will fight tenaciously to support any member of their close circle who find themselves in trouble. But they tend to be fretful in their help, and a sudden change in events might blow them over.

Wood Rats hold high principles and place a high priority on routine. Protective and generous, the Wood Rat can often feel suddenly insecure. This causes them to plan earnestly for the future and sometimes to do so at the expense of the present.

Over confident at times, Wood Rats may sell themselves short. They frequently mistake flattery for respect and are left slightly more vulnerable than Rats of other agents.

FAMOUS WOOD RATS

Marlon Brando, Sir Clement Freud, Gerald Durrell.

THE FIRE RAT
1936, 1996

Fire excites a Fire Rat's normally aggressive streak and this, the least attractive aspect of the Rat's personality is usually more pronounced than in any other. Aggression is a key feature of Fire Rat's temperament. Poor diplomats, they lack discipline and often let their fiery passions rule their head. But most Fire Rats are bright enough to channel their aggression into positive areas.

Often gifted, Fire Rats must fight an inclination to be too rash to succeed. Few enjoy the great passion of the Fire Rat and this combination, when linked with an artistic skill, can produce work of a startlingly original nature. Fire Rats have great energy and love travelling, often packing their bags with no more than the basics and taking off at a minute's notice. Fire Rats will dangerously and frequently take risks, both in love and business. They are extremely generous and usually enjoy open relationships with all those they love.

A Fire Rat might easily dress to impress, and will usually succeed.

FAMOUS FIRE RATS

Yves St Laurent, Glenda Jackson, Buddy Holly.

THE EARTH RAT
1948, 2008

There is a tendency for Earth Rats to hold back their natural exuberance and zest for life. The eagerness which Rats display in living life to the full is less evident and there may be resentment when comparing their own achievements with those of others.

Always fighting to let their deeper and more positive, fun attitude to living free, Earth Rats advance slower in their chosen field than most. It is also common for Earth Rats to give up something they crave for, it could be a bar of chocolate or a lover, in an effort to prove themselves more moral. The least original of all the Rat types, Earth Rats are great at developing other people's ideas and like a good soil, produce goods in great quantity, if not quality.

Earth Rats tend to hold on to their jobs, staying in one place for long periods and they avoid taking risks. Their lunar sign's influence might lead the Earth Rat to a sudden change of mood. But a secure home will stabilize matters.

FAMOUS EARTH RATS

Prince Charles, Andrew Lloyd Webber, Lulu.

THE RAT AND THEIR HOURS

The hour of the Rat
[11 pm to 1 am]

A double dose of Rat influence. For the rare group of introverted Rats, life is spent planning every detail to the very last. For the extrovert, too much food and wine but plenty of bright conversation.

311

The hour of the Buffalo
[1 am to 3 am]

The Buffalo and Rat are not ideally suited. The strong differences of character lead Rats born in this hour to develop really aggressive stances, but they will always show individuality in creative areas.

The hour of the Tiger
[3 am to 5 am]

A big-hearted Rat. But the Tiger's unpredictability can cause problems and there will be a more aggressive streak, even if it is only on a short term basis. Reckless and impatient in love and combat.

The hour of the Cat
[5 am to 7 am]

The least happy of combinations but not without some benefits. A less aggressive Rat will have a pronounced set of diplomatic skills. More sensitive than passionate.

The hour of the Dragon
[7 am to 9 am]

An excellent combination with the Dragon's influence helping to keep in check the Rat's more willful excesses. Introvert Rats find the going more difficult, trying as they do, to put life into rigid boxes.

The hour of the Snake
[9 am to 11 am]

One of the most sexually active of all Rats. Even the introvert Rat will find release through their emotions. But there will be moments when no decision is forthcoming, and periods of inactivity that feel foreign.

The hour of the Horse
[11 am to 1 pm]

The Rat and Horse have little understanding and will create

problems for both introvert and extrovert Rat. Hard working and dominant, there will be difficulties in any romantic encounter. Strong personality.

The hour of the Goat
[1 pm to 3 pm]

A highly social Rat. These signs are compatible, but mainly in the non-working areas. The capricious element in all Goats causes some indecision but stokes a warm heart.

The hour of the Monkey
[3 pm to 5 pm]

Good combination, especially in any commercial field. More mischievous, spiteful and with a great sense of opportunism. But the passion is cooler and there is a lack of notable originality. No shortage of humour.

The hour of the Rooster
[5 pm to 7 pm]

Poor understanding between these two contrasting signs means problems, especially in terms of finance. Roosters tend not to save, nor does the Rat. Moral differences are huge. But there is much common sense.

The hour of the Dog
[7 pm to 9 pm]

Dogs do not normally have much in common with Rats, but they can evolve an understanding. The Rat will develop an unusual sense of idealism and work harder for others. Better at self restraint.

The hour of the Pig
[9 pm to 11 pm]

A well adjusted and easy going Rat. The two signs have huge areas in common and a rich social life. Not good at restraint but no great sense of guilt either. Introverted Pig hour Rats are rare. Less crafty.

BUFFALOES AND THEIR AGENTS

THE METAL BUFFALO
1901, 1961

Few come off best in confrontation with a Metal Buffalo. They automatically assume authority and exert enormous power, often by their physical presence alone. Not great talkers, metal Buffaloes like to get the job done without fuss and bother. They have tremendous energy and few others will match them for endeavour and tenacity. But although many may admire, even worship the Metal Buffalo, they might find true friendships hard to come by. Not stable emotionally, they are subject to sudden bouts of melancholy, or they might fall blindly in love.

In all relationships, the Metal Buffalo will attempt to dominate, and in love, they always fix the emotional timetable.

No matter what path they choose, the Metal Buffalo will exert enormous influence. In some cases their success will be as a result of their huge originality, and for others it will be down to nothing more than their massive personal magnetism.

FAMOUS METAL BUFFALOES

Princess Diana, Walt Disney, Frank Bruno.

THE WATER BUFFALO
1913, 1973

Water Buffaloes are more flexible than most and they have an

314

open approach to difficult problems. This presents them with a greater chance of achieving their goal without treading too heavily on others. Water Buffaloes make friends more easily but do not like to be taken for granted. They place a high premium on security at home and work steadily to improve their standard of living. There is much idealism in the Water Buffalo and whereas some Buffaloes might rush headlong at the opposition, they will invariably maintain a marked degree of patience in reaching their goal.

Emotionally they are more stable than most but a complex romance might easily flood out of control. In such cases, the great emotional reservoir that resides in the heart of all Water Buffaloes will burst, like water through the walls of a damn. Few have a greater influence, one which, like a warm sea, draws us in.

FAMOUS WATER BUFFALOES

Vincent Van Gogh, Vivien Leigh, Burt Lancaster.

THE WOOD BUFFALO
1925, 1985

When allowed to grow deep, the roots of the Wood Buffalo will make them the least flexible of all the types of Buffaloes. They are possessed by a powerful ambition which, when realized, is certain to exert a strong influence. Often blind to the thoughts of others, the Wood Buffalo nevertheless arouses deep admiration. Those who support them are in turn sheltered by their great strength of character, which seldom, if ever, wavers.

Wood Buffaloes offer lasting protection to their family and hold rigid views on ethics and morality. At home in the country and garden, the Wood Buffalo is less happy in modern urban surroundings. Poor team members, they only really flourish when in total control.

Once on top, Wood Buffaloes are in constant danger of being toppled by a sudden change of circumstances.

Their problem is one of inflexibility. Once they reach maturity they find it almost impossible to alter course. Like old trees, they are prone to strong winds.

FAMOUS WOOD BUFFALOES

Margaret Thatcher, Peter Sellers, Richard Burton.

THE FIRE BUFFALO
1937, 1997

Fire Buffaloes often have a brilliant imagination which they might not always be able to control. They possess all their sign's conservative values, but these are off-set by a powerful, original mind which frequently runs in stark contrast. This creates a personality in constant conflict, from which springs the most remarkable thoughts. Never conventional and at the same time seldom entirely ruled by their deep rooted conservatism, Fire Buffaloes enjoy the best of both worlds without ever fully committing themselves to either.

Fire Buffaloes are impossible to match in a confrontation and they frequently enjoy creating systems from a base of eccentric personal beliefs. The long hours of toil commonly associated with the Buffalo sign are not found in such large quantities in Fire Buffaloes, but they are nevertheless relentless in achieving their goal.

Prone to sudden failure, Fire Buffaloes find romance quite impossible to cope with. The Chinese say Fire Buffaloes will marry many times, but never find the right partner. They seek shelter in family life.

FAMOUS FIRE BUFFALOES

Peter Cook, Laura Ashley, Arthur Scargill.

THE EARTH BUFFALO
1949, 2009

Earth Buffaloes are sure footed and solid, and are practical in the extreme. They offer help willingly and are highly appreciative when assisted themselves. Quick to repay loyalty, often generously, Earth Buffaloes are equally nippy in repaying those who act treacherously. An Earth Buffalo's enemies can expect harsh, sometimes quite brutal treatment and absolutely no forgiveness.

Because they endure setbacks and suffering with a noble spirit, Earth Buffaloes are often thought insensitive. This could not be further from the truth. They just disguise it well.

Less demanding in love, the Earth Buffalo's passions run very deep. But they need a great deal of nourishment to bring their emotions to maturity. This is also true of other aspects of their life and it leaves them more vulnerable since the overriding Buffalo influence is one of self sufficiency.

Should the earth dry up through lack of water, it cracks. This may well happen to Earth Buffaloes who face severe problems alone, when it is obvious that others hold the answer.

FAMOUS EARTH BUFFALOES

Adolf Hitler, Twiggy, Peter Shilton.

THE BUFFALO AND THEIR HOURS

The hour of the Rat
[11 pm to 1 am]

Not an easy pairing with a constant conflict, especially over moral attitudes. Love is made less complex and personal relations are easier. Stubbornness combines with aggression. Brilliant minds.

317

The hour of the Buffalo
[1 am to 3 am]

A double Buffalo leads to an ultra conservative who is incapable of sharing any form of power. Either terribly destructive or highly creative. There is no in between.

The hour of the Cat
[3 am to 5 am]

More refinement and a greater sense of dress and public grace. There will be less show of power and more understanding of other's problems. Very routine minded. Sexually less complicated but secretive.

The hour of the Tiger
[5 am to 7 am]

Not compatible and a divided Buffalo emerges. The need to rebel is in constant conflict with the need to retain traditional values. Helpless in romance and totally unpredictable.

The hour of the Dragon
[7 am to 9 am]

Heavy on leadership with a confusion about the method. A Buffalo who is hot headed and impulsive. Unable to keep out of the limelight, the need to win others over to their way of thinking is relentless. More open lovers.

The hour of the Snake
[9 am to 11 am]

A more sensuous Buffalo who combines a greater wisdom with an imposingly original view of life. Less likely to forgive a wrong and tight with money. A charismatic leader who could be dangerous.

The hour of the Horse
[11 am to 1 pm]

Extremely hard working but not happy in sudden romantic encounters, where there will be much misunderstanding. A strong personality with a highly political mind. Practical and individual when creating.

The hour of the Goat
[1 pm to 3 pm]

Not two signs who live happily together and there is much confusion. The normal compulsion to lead is dragged down by the Goat. But sexually there is a brighter outlook, where the complex interior is less so.

The hour of the Monkey
[3 pm to 5 pm]

The Monkey acts as a break on the traditionally minded Buffalo who will be more flexible in his work attitudes. A cool response to sexual encounters, there is nevertheless, greater opportunity.

The hour of the Rooster
[5 pm to 7 pm]

Highly moral and extremely conservative. The love of natural order is intensified and there is virtually no room for double standards. Rules are there to be kept and woe betide those who break them.

The hour of the Dog
[7 pm to 9 pm]

Loyalty is a major factor, both demanded and, under the Dog hour, returned. Double doses of stubbornness and a touch of anxiety creeping into important decisions. Romance is not a problem, but not important either.

319

The hour of the Pig
[9 am to 11 pm]

An open and warmer type of Buffalo. More aware of the social whirl, they are often keen on food and wine, and dressing up. They tend to boast about sexual matters and are not easily bothered by gossip.

TIGERS AND THEIR AGENTS

THE METAL TIGER
1950, 2010

The metal agent is a powerful aid. The norm is for Tigers to run out of steam over long distances or to cave in when their reserve of self belief runs dry. But the metal agent is quick to reinforce the Tiger's flagging spirit. Metal enables them to get back into the race and quickly regain lost ground.

Often self obsessed, a Metal Tiger can at times go to extraordinary lengths to get people to notice them, and they can be terrible bullies. Not a good judge of others, they are even worse at judging the value of the task in hand. They either overburden themselves with preparation or take it for granted that they will succeed.

Only when they hit a balance, usually as a result of outside circumstances will they fully reach their true potential. But even if they fall short, Metal Tigers are guaranteed to leave an indelible mark on society. What is their near miss for a Metal Tiger will often be head and shoulders above the closest rival.

It is in their demanding results too soon that Metal Tigers often come a cropper. But they are true originals and no other Tiger type enjoys more breaking down the barriers of orthodoxy.

FAMOUS METAL TIGERS

Beethoven, Richard Branson, Karen Carpenter.

THE WATER TIGER
1902, 1962

Normally hot headed, the Tiger's rebellious instincts are heavily muted by the water agent. Obviously, moments of recklessness will break through the calmer surface, but as a rule, Water Tigers can pace themselves to do the job. An alert and open mind is a key characteristic, and the Water Tiger is at times alarmingly honest, achieving his aims by truthful means. But beware of a Water Tiger in a storm. They can be treacherous. Water Tigers are unusually extremely compassionate and sympathetic to the plight of others. The watery influence will curb the Tiger's natural ambition. And success, should it come, will come only after a constant struggle against a tide which seems determined to flow in the wrong direction.

In romantic encounters, Water Tigers are passionate but seldom reckless. In matters of finance, it is possible for Water Tigers to lose everything through failure to make investments watertight.

FAMOUS WATER TIGERS

Jimmy White, John Steinbeck, Hana Mandlikova.

THE WOOD TIGER
1914, 1974

Less impetuous than other Tigers, the wood agent offers this Tiger a more even balanced view of life. Wood Tigers will mix happily with a wide range of friends and display more refined social graces than Tigers of other agents. But they can be tough as oak.

Wood Tigers are splendid hosts, given to great generosity. And because they have a genuine interest in others, Wood Tigers also attract a large following of admirers. These will be

322

used to build their support, which will be given openly. But the Tiger's influence is one that chops and changes, and if the roots are not given time to settle the Wood Tiger will tend to fall at the most important hurdle.

If you break off relationships with a Wood Tiger, don't expect them to beg you to come back. A solid friendship is promised and providing you do not attempt to dominate, it will be generously given.

If a Wood Tiger does manage to find a home that suits there is every chance he will settle down or retire, allowing his vitality only the rarest of opportunities to emerge.

FAMOUS WOOD TIGERS

Alec Guinness, John Arlott, Joe Louis.

THE FIRE TIGER
1926, 1986

The mixture of the fire agent with a sign which is by nature fiery produces a brilliant if unstable Tiger. Constantly in search of new ways of self expression, the Fire Tiger has a mercurial temperament which is forever under threat.

Rich in imagination, the problem facing the Fire Tiger is that the sign's tendency to be fast over short distances is amplified. This means Fire Tigers burn out even more rapidly than Tigers of other agents. The Tiger's fixed agent is wood, one which burns only too easily when attached to fire. The plus is that Fire Tigers really have great innovative skills and they are most definitely one-offs. When you meet a Fire Tiger you are left in no doubt that they are natural leaders who demand our attention.

Naturally optimistic, the Fire Tiger seldom sees the pit falls until too late. Then the depression is like a bottomless pit. But everything, even the depression is acted out with maximum feeling, energy and originality.

FAMOUS FIRE TIGERS

Marilyn Monroe, Miles Davis, Dylan Thomas.

THE EARTH TIGER
1938, 1998

Earth is the one agent which has the ability to reduce the speed at which a Tiger moves and offers a more sure-footed path. Earth Tigers will therefore appear clear headed and balanced in their judgements, but it should be remembered that such clarity will only be skin deep. There is a conflict with the earth agent and the Tiger's lunar influence. Earth Tigers who manage to reconcile these two important and contradictory influences often become strong leaders and more stable than Tigers with other agents. They will be able to lead large groups with determination, seldom giving up, even when all looks lost. Earth Tigers may find it difficult to then take on board the needs of those around them. And if they sink, their followers will join them. Relationships are seen for their usefulness, which may act against long term success. As a result, Earth Tigers tend to have as many friends as enemies.

FAMOUS EARTH TIGERS

David Steel, David Owen, Terry Wogan.

THE TIGER AND THEIR HOURS

The hour of the Rat
[11 pm to 1 am]

The Tiger's rebellious instincts curtailed and replaced by a greater sense of self gratification. Not so easily pushed off course and a deeper sense of personal awareness. Passionate and reckless.

The hour of the Buffalo
[1 am to 3 am]

Not an easy pairing, one that leaves a conflict in areas of work and romance. A constant need to dominate is offset by a shortage of endurance. Great in very short bursts. Highly creative where tradition versus the new.

The hour of the Tiger
[3 am to 5 am]

The double Tiger spells an even greater need to rush headlong into life. In love they are totally without caution and are incapable of any kind of power sharing. Ultra generous but given to long periods of depression.

The hour of the Cat
[5 am to 7 am]

Cautious and less likely to rush at a problem. A greater sense of diplomacy, there will still be a good deal of fire. A neater, more tidy Tiger who moves with grace but not much courage.

The hour of the Dragon
[7 am to 9 am]

An impetuous hot head and hopelessly unpredictable. Less likely to suffer from self doubts, there is great generosity coupled with a more boastful nature. Rebellious and passionate in the extreme.

The hour of the Snake
[9 am to 11 am]

The periodical lack of self belief is less painful and frequently replaced by sudden glimpses of self awareness. Less generous but wiser, there tends to be fewer acts of a rebellious nature. Sensuous and refined.

325

The hour of the Horse
[11 am to 1 pm]

Greater endurance but weaker in love. A heightened need to lead with the accent on personality. More easily bored, they are given to change their jobs and partners with surprising ease.

The hour of the Goat
[1 pm to 3 pm]

Not an easy coupling with the Goat adding little but dead weight to the need to take control. Things improve hugely in the world of art where high performance matches original thought.

The hour of the Monkey
[3 pm to 5 pm]

Too much Monkey business means less rebellion and a greater emphasis on cunning. A cooler attitude to most things and fewer romantic encounters that end in heartbreak. More adaptable and less reckless.

The hour of the Rooster
[5 pm to 7 pm]

Less rebellious and hot headed, there is still plenty of candour. Not two signs that live easily together, they might come together more happily in a military setting. A bit priggish but seldom lacking self belief.

The hour of the Dog
[7 pm to 9 pm]

A fine coupling with the need to lead small groups paramount. Both loyal and fiery, a strong will adds to an uncompromising adversary. A bit touchy with a generous nature. Short on romance.

The hour of the Pig
[9 pm to 11 pm]

More at one with themselves and less likely to rush headlong into danger. A sociable Tiger with robust energy and healthy appetites. Often strong in a physical sense, love leads to a weak if not reckless heart.

CATS AND THEIR AGENTS

THE METAL CAT
1951, 2011

The Metal Cat is sturdier and less prone to sudden collapse than Cats of other agents. Unlike those Cats who either shy away from leadership, or misuse it, Metal Cats display a sense of ambition which usually ends up with them heading a group. But there is a drawback. The group must themselves share the Cat's beliefs and goals.

Open opposition will awaken the Metal Cat's more fearful lunar influence, causing the metal agent to bend or melt.

The arts are a perfect area for a Metal Cat to perform in, although the metal agent will give a sporting Cat more than a sporting chance. Quick to put on an amiable front, there are depths to Metal Cats which often leave them dispirited, at which point they are apt to lash out.

Metal Cats are the most romantic lovers but might easily find they have bitten off more than they can chew.

FAMOUS METAL CATS

Kenny Dalglish, Selina Scott, Bob Geldof.

THE WATER CAT
1903, 1963

Water Cats are often too sensitive for their own good. The water agent acts like a tide on the Cat's lunar influence, causing them to all too often sink back into the past. This they may do with either pleasure or, more commonly regret. And there is a touch of the Water Cat seeking safety from too many pressures by their trips backwards.

The Chinese say there is something almost mystical about the Water Cat's reflective imagination, which offers them an interesting role in society.

Historians or visionaries, the Water Cat has pronounced artistic qualities which when protected, can be used to great effect. But when the emotional side of the Water Cat's nature is disrupted, their normally gentle and sophisticated personality, few will escape their sarcasm.

Quick to tune into the thoughts and feelings of those around them, Water Cats are not great at dealing with pressure and gravitate towards polite society and well mannered company.

FAMOUS WATER CATS

John Barnes, George Orwell, Bob Hope.

THE WOOD CAT
1915, 1975

The wood agent provides a powerful base from which Wood Cats are able to explore any number of directions. But the problem is that the feeling of security is so strong, Wood Cats might frequently find themselves reluctant to wander out from the comfort and safety of their well organized routines.

Wood Cats are in a sense victims of their own carefulness. They often reject the chance of leadership, a common attribute of the wood agent, opting for a less responsible position. Groups are appealing to a Wood Cat as they provide the kind of anonymity they sometimes crave.

Not so easily hurt as some other types of Cat, the Wood Cat nevertheless has an artistic nature which might easily be bruised by thoughtless criticism.

They are reserved lovers and prefer evenly balanced relationships. But being defenceless, a bad relationship might easily provoke bitter retaliation.

FAMOUS WOOD CATS

Stanley Matthews, Ingrid Bergman, Frank Sinatra.

THE FIRE CAT
1927, 1987

Cats normally cave in under pressure, but the fire agent will provide a substantial tool to overcome difficulties. Personal suffering will always floor the Cat, no matter what the influencing agent, but with fire added, the Cat can act swiftly to save a situation. It will also create a more aggressive Cat, one who might easily lash out with open claws for no apparent reason.

Fire will also provide the opportunity to advance the Cat into a more forward position. But they will find themselves more isolated than Cats of other agents. They also require constant approval for their actions. The Cat's great gift is diplomacy and in order to lead effectively, the Fire Cats will find themselves short of their normally calming tone.

Fire Cats are the warmest emotionally and as lovers, the most likely to run off the rails.

FAMOUS FIRE CATS

Fidel Castro, Ken Dodd, Sheila Scott.

THE EARTH CAT
1939, 1999

Earth Cats are in a way less ambitious than Cats of other agents. Always cool and collected, except when under severe pressure, Earth Cats are more so. But because their earth agent creates such an even balance, they often find themselves promoted into positions of influence.

Their unruffled appearance marks them out as reliable and steadfast. Yet when leaned on too heavily, the Earth Cat becomes increasingly uncomfortable.

There is something about the constant demands of leadership which runs against the grain of a Cat's more gentle lunar influence.

Extremely capable at dealing with finance, the Earth Cat may be highly acquisitive. Realizing their weaknesses is a salient feature of the Earth Cat, as is working hard to strengthen themselves. This they do with a great deal of sharp humour, and not a little snobbery.

Relationships are often less passionate than in Cats of other agents, but usually longer lasting. And the right appearance is absolutely essential to Earth Cats, as is to be seen in the right places with the right people.

FAMOUS EARTH CATS

John Cleese, David Frost, Dusty Springfield.

THE CAT AND THEIR HOURS

The hour of the Rat
[11 pm to 1 am]

A more tenacious Cat. Less frightened by external danger and extremely cutting in their humour. Routine minded, there is a tendency to become somewhat obsessive about planning.

331

The hour of the Buffalo
[1 am to 3 am]

A stronger more stubborn Cat with quite definite views on political issues. Less happy in romance and generally not inclined to wander. Original and hard working. Not so easy to push around.

The hour of the Tiger
[3 am to 5 am]

Quite pushy with little sense of routine or planning. The need to lead is more in evidence but the courage often required to perform as front man might produce great strain. Generous but quick to cave in.

The hour of the Cat
[5 am to 7 am]

The double Cat influence produces a hypersensitive personality. This might mean more routines and plans, or more artistic creativity. In love they are extremely diligent and their humour can be quite biting.

The hour of the Dragon
[7 am to 9 am]

Diplomacy is overturned by the Dragon's impulsive and often downright rudeness. Wonderfully sensuous and artistic, and more inclined to consider the outward appearance. But leadership qualities are blunted.

The hour of the Snake
[9 am to 11 am]

Wisdom is added to the Cat and their sensuous skills in romance are greatly heightened. A well balanced and slow moving Cat, who tends to take plenty of time making up his mind. Good with finances.

The hour of the Horse
[11 am to 1 pm]

Much elegance is in evidence, but fewer of the daily routines that often highlight the Cat personality. Less capable in a romance, there is a tendency to get bored and wander off. Very independent.

The hour of the Goat
[1 pm to 3 pm]

Strong on social graces and extremely gifted in the world of art. But the diplomacy for which Cats are noted is generally lacking to the point of non-existence. Moody lovers and poor planners, they are very trendy.

The hour of the Monkey
[3 pm to 5 pm]

A tricky Cat who's brain works overtime to get life to work the way they want it. A bit sly at times and slippery in the face of truth, there's great linguistic skills and a very clever financial operator.

The hour of the Rooster
[5 pm to 7 pm]

A combination which produces diplomacy flavoured with a strong dose of candour. Highly organized but lacking the spark of initiative. A much braver Cat but less romantic. Proud, courageous and generous.

The hour of the Dog
[7 pm to 9 pm]

A good combination which adds a dimension of idealism to the Cat's sensitivity. A noble Cat who will be more likely to put the comfort of others before their own. Less romantic lovers, but more faithful.

333

The hour of the Pig
[9 pm to 11 pm]

Immaculate dressers with both eyes on the fashion world. Hard working there is always a chance to make money and hang on to it. An open hearted Cat who is less secretive but more of a gossip.

DRAGONS AND THEIR AGENTS

THE METAL DRAGON
1940, 2000

Metal Dragons never stop to think as they rush at the world, imposing on all and sundry their headstrong views. They have virtually no powers of diplomacy coupled with a relentless need to poke their nose into other people's business.

Their moving agent, metal, when added to wood, their fixed agent, provides a powerful weapon. In a Dragon's hands the wood and metal frequently becomes an instrument of combat, an axe or a hammer. This they use to chop others down to size, or grind down to their way of thinking. But the Metal Dragon is seldom cruel, and those on the receiving end of their self-appointed justice are usually bullies, law breakers and those who exploit the weak.

Whatever enters their mind, they believe is right and their tendency to cut off all those who disagree with them means they have few if any real friends. But they are admired for their passion and those who are loved by the metal Dragon will be protected for life. And no other Dragon is capable of leaving a more lasting mark or casting their influence more widely.

FAMOUS METAL DRAGONS

John Lennon, Jeffrey Archer, Esther Rantzen.

THE WATER DRAGON
1952, 2012

The normally hot headed Dragon temperament is brought dramatically to heel under the calming water influence. It is thought that some Dragons lived in caves under the sea, which suggests they are at home with the water agent.

Not all Dragons feel easy with their natural inclination to rush headlong into things curtailed. But the Water Dragon does enjoy a great many advantages.

As well as being tactful and diplomatic, an almost unheard of quality in other Dragons, Water Dragons are better equipped to face defeat. And whereas Dragons of other agents are blessed, or in some cases cursed, by an overpowering sense of ambition. Water Dragons tend to move more thoughtfully towards their goal. But because they think long and hard before they act, planning more than other Dragons, some might miss their chance.

When subjected to unfair decisions, or opposed to injustice, Water Dragons will simply swamp the opposition in a deluge of heated argument. And if there are no facts, be prepared for a flood of quite irrational abuse.

FAMOUS WATER DRAGONS

Jimmy Connors, Mel Smith, Elaine Paige.

THE WOOD DRAGON
1904, 1964

Often lacking direction early on, once a Wood Dragon finds their roots, they will quickly develop into solid and dependable citizens. Wood Dragons have a broad vision as a rule, but they also have a tendency to argue trivial personal issues as if they were of world shattering importance. This can often lead to a Wood Dragon acting a touch condescending.

In the sense that wood needs roots and the tops of trees have no limit, in theory that is, Wood Dragons are either extremely conservative or revolutionary. But whichever type, Wood Dragons will be less impetuous in style than those of the other elements.

The wood element is an advantage to Dragons whose work is by nature thoughtful or reflective, adding a logical arm and the ability to analyse. Wood Dragons are fearless when pushed into a corner, and will be quick to support a worthwhile course and will enlist the help of others.

The Chinese say Wood Dragons may live for a very long time and that they will become extremely wise. They are also expected to remain active, creative and influential. Senior Wood Dragons, it seems, should be treated as venerable old oaks.

FAMOUS WOOD DRAGONS

Barbara Cartland, Grahame Greene, Lady Helen Windsor.

THE FIRE DRAGON
1916, 1976

The Fire Dragon, in keeping with those Dragons who traditionally breathed fire, tends to affect absolutely everyone they come into contact with. High on personality, they inspire and frustrate, sometimes seeing the world with astonishing clarity and at other times, missing the point completely. They seldom sit still or stop talking.

The Fire Dragon is one to mature early and very often, fizzle out long before they have reached their four score and ten. They are super perfectionists who have an extraordinary power to attract massive bands of followers. Few other signs, and certainly no other Dragon type, has such leadership potential. But this may work against them.

The problem is that with so much hero worship, their

considerable skills are lost behind the adulation. Fire Dragons may find that relationships are less than stable, and their need for perfection in all things is a positive hindrance to understanding partners who are more accepting.

Some Dragons are happy to let fate take its course, but not the Fire Dragon, who demands they take control. And no other Dragon has such a hot head, and that's saying something.

FAMOUS FIRE DRAGONS

Yehudi Menhuin, Roald Dahl, Jennifer Capriati.

THE EARTH DRAGON
1928, 1988

Earth on the Dragon forces a dampening down of their natural tendency to rush at problems and to demand quick solutions. This Dragon is a supplier, a creator of opportunities for others and altogether less imperious. They enjoy a much more even temperament than Dragons of other agents, and when crossed are slower to anger and less likely to hold grudges for long periods.

A good listener, the Earth Dragon gives sound advice. However, the Chinese say that they at times seem detached, which some might find disconcerting. Also, their temper will be terrible should they lose their considerable self control. Fortunately, this doesn't happen often and the Earth Dragon guides with a cool head.

Earth Dragons are quite comfortable about their ability to lead and feel less threatened by those they have appointed to work with, or chosen to live close to. Unless the Earth Dragon has an active goal, they will become dangerously lethargic.

FAMOUS EARTH DRAGONS

Martin Luther King, Shirley Temple, Sir Alastair Burnett.

THE DRAGON AND THEIR HOURS

The hour of the Rat
[11 pm to 1 am]

Tenacious and passionate, these Dragons are less likely to grumble. But the aggression level could be very high and difficult to control at times. Better awareness of their limitations.

The hour of the Buffalo
[1 am to 3 am]

Bone headed and even more dominating. Power orientated, the heart is a little more complex but the need to be free of all restrictions is less of a force. Romantically complex but hugely original in the arts.

The hour of the Tiger
[3 am to 5 am]

Hot headed and reckless. Totally unpredictable, especially in romance. The need to rebel is high on the list and a pushy intolerant Dragon emerges. Tough and inflexible but short paced.

The hour of the Cat
[5 am to 7 am]

Sensuous and more methodical. The need for a smoother life puts the break on the Dragon's hot headed influence. Love is a more gentle affair and business becomes less of a bind. More subtle than most.

The hour of the Dragon
[7 am to 9 am]

The double Dragon is believed to be even more lucky and blessed. But the impetuous nature grows along with the good fortune. Over confident at times and never short of push, these Dragons are hard to beat.

The hour of the Snake
[9 am to 11 am]

Wiser and more mature in the areas of science and religion. In love there is a greater depth and the need to possess is more pronounced. A slower mover in most things, they can be treacherous when crossed.

The hour of the Horse
[11 am to 1 pm]

The practical side of the Dragon, such as it is, is greatly enhanced. So is the fear of restriction and the need to be free to express inner feelings, whatever they are, is paramount. Emotionally very weak.

The hour of the Goat
[1 pm to 3 pm]

More fickle and less positive about important decisions. Love is a problem in that they have a tendency to fight shy of long term commitments. Feeble business sense coupled with high artistic skills.

The hour of the Monkey
[3 pm to 5 pm]

Tricky and quick witted. The trait of this Dragon is always a need to gain control of others, using whatever method is available. A cooler response to romance is balanced by a powerful business sense.

The hour of the Rooster
[5 pm to 7 pm]

A less devious Dragon. There is a candid morality here and at the same time a greater need for personal secrecy. Self confidence is at a high, with little or no time for casual romance. Thrifty and well organized.

The hour of the Dog
[7 pm to 9 pm]

There could easily be a bit of a split. There is one side of the personality which wishes to change the world and the other half wanting to lead it, no matter where. Honest in love but terribly easily fooled.

The hour of the Pig
[9 pm to 11 pm]

Extremely hard working, the wardrobe and its contents exercise a great influence. Emotionally a little suspect, and falling too easily for the wrong type is typical. Good with finance, when advised.

SNAKES AND THEIR AGENTS

THE METAL SNAKE
1941, 2001

The deep intuitive power that drives a Snake is amplified by the metal agent, which acts as a kind of conductor to the mystic energy which dominates all Snakes. This means that both the negative and positive are open to greater exploration. If Snakes bend metal, it is usually into a form of chain, to secure that which they possess.

Metal Snakes are often highly secretive and unless they offer you the key to their inner sanctum, you will never know what they really think. And some Metal Snakes don't even know what they think themselves.

As a rule, Metal Snakes prefer their own company, although both sexes can be highly social should the opportunity present itself.

Metal Snakes can use their gifts to the full potential and attract money. No other Snake has such a huge reservoir of talent, or the skill to make the most of it. A powerful and pronounced sexuality might easily dominate their life.

FAMOUS METAL SNAKES

Picasso, Mohammed Ali, Bob Dylan.

THE WATER SNAKE
1953, 2013

The water agent creates a strong sense of materialism. The

Snake's lunar influence, to cling to things they love, when combined with the water agent, frequently leads to thrift.

Water Snakes have powerful memories and are able to concentrate for long periods. If there are obstacles they will take their time removing them, but they will eventually succeed.

Quick to find other's weaknesses, Water Snakes might be slow realizing their own ambition, although once they register a personal goal, no other type of Snake will be more dedicated in achieving it. Cultured and broad based artistically, Water Snakes are not natural leaders and tend to work better within a partnership.

More than any other agent, water finds its own level, which means Water Snakes usually know their worth. Since water is the natural home of many Snakes, those born with it as an agent might be said to have a head start.

FAMOUS WATER SNAKES

Victoria Wood, J Paul Getty, Graham Gooch.

THE WOOD SNAKE
1905, 1965

Wood Snakes build firmly and use a wide variety of skills to make a success of themselves. Snakes are deeply intuitive and wood, in its form as a tree, grows safest with deep roots. This combination points to Wood Snakes developing a dependable nature, the type who will give their time patiently for others.

Conscious about their appearance and attracted to large numbers, Wood Snakes are often vain and unaware of the actual effect they have on those whose admiration they win.

Without roots, Wood Snakes may easily get blown over and in the event, take some time to recover. Indeed, there are those who never get back to normal and end up clinging to

343

their bad luck. For these Snakes, life becomes a long hibernation. And there is no guarantee that the Wood Snake will eventually emerge with a new skin. The chances are that they will find life has changed around them but they themselves will remain the same.

FAMOUS WOOD SNAKES

Greta Garbo, Stefan Edberg, Howard Hughs.

THE FIRE SNAKE
[1917, 1977]

Of all the agents, fire has the most profound influence on the Snake. The Snake's immense power to bewitch, when aligned with fire, creates an almost impossible to resist personality. This can be seen most clearly when a Fire Snake takes up a position in public life.

Snake politicians exercise amazing charisma, as do performers in the arts or light entertainment. They almost burn with personality and quickly seduce others to their ways. But the brilliance of a Snake governed by the fire agent has a negative side, and one which may not always be reversed.

Fire Snakes have a strong need to secure their position with wealth and possessions, but these tend only to create barriers and prevent the all important escape route.

Fire Snakes do not enjoy a wide circle of friends and tend to expect too much from those few people close to them. No Snake, however, is more jealous or passionate. And if their flame is too quickly extinguished, no one will forget it.

FAMOUS FIRE SNAKES

John F Kennedy, Nat King Cole, Ferdinand Marcos.

THE EARTH SNAKE
1929, 1989

Earth Snakes are the most able to make quick decisions. They have great skills in those areas which require careful thought and can tackle complex problems with ease. It is as if the earth, so close to the reptile snake, naturally supports and responds to their more subtle movements.

Earth Snakes are not easily pushed off course. They are loyal to their friends and lead, when they have to, with authority and charm.

In financial matters, Earth Snakes will show an aptitude for saving and the Chinese expression that Snakes are more free with their time than their money, might fit them more than the other types.

Earth Snakes are patient as they are resourceful and they know the measure of their own abilities. Good at communication, Earth Snakes listen well and reply sensibly.

They are the most honest of Snakes and the most difficult to dislodge once they have made up their mind.

FAMOUS EARTH SNAKES

Jackie Onassis, André Previn, Magnus Magnusson.

THE SNAKE AND THEIR HOURS

The hour of the Rat
[11 pm to 1 am]

A more restless type and not always in total control of their emotions. A tendency to put themselves first is not helped by a marked aggression. Sensual and passionate in romance. Mixed financial skills.

The hour of the Buffalo
[1 am to 3 am]

There's a side which acts in a positive way, but does not necessarily always bring results. Loyalty is preferred to love and the need to dominate others is more pronounced, and a problem.

The hour of the Tiger
[3 am to 5 am]

A Snake is prone to sudden ups and downs. Not reliable when under emotional stress and sometimes too domineering. But ideas which fight to emerge are often brilliant and original.

The hour of the Cat
[5 am to 7 am]

High degree of compatibility leads to a deeply sensuous and artistic personality. Careful in financial dealings there will always be a safe routine to cope with life's tricky moments.

The hour of the Dragon
[7 am to 9 am]

Perfect harmony of influences with a strong self belief to back up the wise interior. Less slow to respond, there are massive reserves of vital energy which can be used in any direction. Sexually complete.

The hour of the Snake
[9 am to 11 am]

An even more possessive and at times, uncertain Snake. The wisdom is there, but to drag it up from the hidden interior requires huge effort. At times extremely bewitching. Mean with money.

The hour of the Horse
[11 am to 1 pm]

A good balance of signs. The practical side is highly deve-

346

loped. But when pure logic is applied to instinctive wisdom there may be conflicting results. In romance there's the chance of great instability.

The hour of the Goat
[1 pm to 3 pm]

There will be times when a need to be loved and understood, come what may, will override everything. The family should play a strong role and any artistic endeavour will have the greatest chance of success.

The hour of the Monkey
[3 pm to 5 pm]

Tricks in abundance, and no end of wit and self confidence. Highly skilled in dealing with people, there is a tendency to take others for granted. Love blows hot and cold.

The hour of the Rooster
[5 pm to 7 pm]

A division of objectives might sometimes mean that not all goals are reached easily. Candid at times, occasionally too much so. But the ability to organize brilliantly holds many rewards. Love is never smooth.

The hour of the Dog
[7 pm to 9 pm]

Honesty prevails and there is less tendency to recoil from ugliness, in whatever shape or form. A more idealistic streak brings many friends and fewer heartaches.

The hour of the Pig
[9 pm to 11 pm]

Highly social, hard working and less time spent hibernating. More robust in dealing with others, the romantic side might pose problems. The heart could be given too quickly.

HORSES AND THEIR AGENTS

THE METAL HORSE
1930, 1990

Metal Horses suffer more than other types of Horse from ardour, one of their twin lunar signs (the other being elegance). Not only are Metal Horses curiously less resilient in matters of romance, falling terribly easily, but they also tend to have a fatal attraction to the opposite sex. They have massive personalities, to which large numbers find themselves irresistibly drawn. No other Horse has such a magnetic personality, and once they move to the head of the pack, a Metal Horse will impose their considerable will on any who follow them.

Metal Horses rely a lot on intuition, which is rare for Horses. This makes for an original thinker but one, uncharacteristically, prone to long periods of self doubt. Fortunately, Metal Horses have strong constitutions and quickly recover.

They should steer clear, though, of any job with routine and long term relationships tend to be elusive.

FAMOUS METAL HORSES

Princess Margaret, James Dean, Clint Eastwood.

THE WATER HORSE
1942, 2002

The water agent adds patience to the Horse's existing combination of practicality and logic, and creates the basis for wealth and good humour. Water Horses will enjoy a powerful business sense with the necessary practical skills to turn it into something more than just a gift.

The Water Horse tends to dress with style and will often lead others to follow their example. Because water moves only when driven by a tide or the wind, a Horse's influence over water means sudden flurries of brilliance.

Water Horses have a broad range of opinions, which they are eager to share, but they do not always have an entirely original mind. They quickly absorb information and recycle it.

Preoccupied at times with their own health, Water Horses tend to think carefully about their diet and exercise. They also become more easily bored than other Horse types, and might change jobs many times before settling on something long term.

FAMOUS WATER HORSES

Paul McCartney, Barbra Streisand, Neil Kinnock.

THE WOOD HORSE
1954, 2014

Most Horses are at ease in company and make wonderful hosts and hostesses. They provide amusing and witty conversation in any group, and no other Horse does all this with more élan than the Wood Horse. Always eager to try out a new idea, and quick to spot the usefulness of newly designed gadgets, Wood Horses are a perfect social barometer.

They think in clean straight lines, and what they think is usually right up to date. Less vain than other types of Horse, the Wood Horse is accommodating and listens with greater attention to detail.

You might easily think of the wooden Horse of Troy as typical. It had space inside for others and while on the surface, looked totally innocent, inside there were many undisclosed secrets.

In the turmoil of love, Wood Horses really do find life intolerable and frequently go completely off the rails. They suffer from not being able to reconcile their heart with their head, and when smitten, nothing can be done but to wait until the storm blows over.

FAMOUS WOOD HORSES

Duke of Windsor, Chrissie Evert, Rowan Atkinson.

THE FIRE HORSE
1906, 1966

The Fire Horse is the most complex of Chinese signs. Fire is the Horse's fixed agent and when fire meets fire in the shape of a Horse, all hell or all heaven is let loose. No other agent produces such a bright intellect and imagination, or the will power to get ideas turned into reality.

The Chinese believe that Fire Horses will be either exceptionally gifted or bring bad luck by the ton. They will be gifted with genius on one hand, and dogged by the worst misfortune on the other.

There are those who are simply frightened by the very idea of a Fire Horse, the image, perhaps representing something of the apocalypse. Fire Horse people love to explore and find sitting still for long periods almost impossible.

Fire Horses are forever on the brink of an exciting or dreadful event, or seem as if they are. Their personality has great flexibility and they'll move homes and change jobs many times in their rich and varied lives. They are hopeless in love, falling time and again for the wrong type. Above all, Fire Horses don't like to be thought of as part of a pack and are never comfortable when forced to play a part in a team. In other words, they must lead from the front or not at all.

FAMOUS FIRE HORSES

Mike Tyson, Zola Budd, Rembrandt.

THE EARTH HORSE
1918, 1978

More dependable and solid than other types of Horses, the Earth Horse can build up massive reserves of energy and work tirelessly when called on. Thoughtful and less prone to dismiss ideas that are not entirely logical, Earth Horses like to think things through before acting. But once settled on a plan of action, they will move with considerable weight to see it succeed.

Not as vain as some Horses, and far less judgemental, Earth Horses nevertheless make full use of their carefully tuned personality. As leaders, they present their case with clear words and no frills. In many ways, the Earth Horse is a 'nuts and bolts' person. Happy to work in partnerships, the Earth Horse in love also has fewer problems.

FAMOUS EARTH HORSES

Billy Graham, Leonard Bernstein, Spike Milligan.

HORSES AND THEIR HOURS

The hour of the Rat
[11 pm to 1 am]

Little dress sense and less appetite for long hours at toil. The tendency is to live more off the back of others, and let them take the blame when things go wrong. Passionate in love, but a bit helpless.

351

The hour of the Buffalo
[1 am to 3 am]

Leadership counts for a great deal, and hard though a Horse may work, this one will work the hardest. The need for independence will be even greater, as will the complexities of the heart.

The hour of the Tiger
[3 am to 5 am]

A touch too much energy up front, on any project, means there will be little left in reserve. A short paced Horse who is best given to work on projects that do not demand endurance. Exuberant in love.

The hour of the Cat
[5 am to 7 am]

Method and routine are added to an established need for order and logic. But the tendency to lead through personality alone will not materialize. A neat dresser and sensuous lover.

The hour of the Dragon
[7 am to 9 am]

The need to direct others and take control will be paramount. Short on diplomacy, strong on attacking shirkers and bullies, there will be little time for family life. Romantic at heart.

The hour of the Snake
[9 am to 11 am]

Instinct is likely to feature more, and the practical side could take a back seat. Less active and prone to lead, the arts will be more the style, with a heightened dress awareness. In love there will always be conflict.

The hour of the Horse
[11 am to 1 pm]

The double Horse means the practical and logical side is given a huge boost and the need to lead is paramount. But the weak heart suffers and romantic relationships are extremely fraught. Highly independent.

The hour of the Goat
[1 pm to 3 pm]

A more capricious nature but one in which performance is likely to play a major part. In some senses, this is perhaps the best hour to have as a secondary sign. A somewhat thoughtless lover.

The hour of the Monkey
[3 pm to 5 pm]

Not straightforward in business, with a tendency to let others do the hard work. Clever organizer and better read, with an agile memory. Invariably controls from behind the scenes. Less demonstrative in love.

The hour of the Rooster
[5 pm to 7 pm]

A combination which adds the benefit of candour to the already existing practical nature. Open displays of rage might be more frequent, especially in the face of dishonesty. A bit standoffish in love.

The hour of the Dog
[7 pm to 9 pm]

Highly idealistic and loyal, but with a dominant streak of stubbornness. Not always good at getting a point across, there will be no shortage of good intentions and warmth. A gentle lover.

The hour of the Pig
[9 pm to 11 pm]

Robust and extremely hard working. Dress sense might be a touch over the top, but never short on style. Highly social and a terrific mixer in any group. Honest in love, if hopeless at keeping it secret.

GOATS AND THEIR AGENTS

THE METAL GOAT
1931, 1991

Metal is an agent which reinforces the positive side to a sign and in the case of a Goat means they'll be more rigid than other types and know their worth. Strong in the arts, Metal Goats strive to work for the family, home and peace generally.

Metal Goats are wonderful home builders, with a great eye for detail. But metal emphasizes the Goat's poor public relations. They express themselves badly in public, often making their point too late or too bluntly.

There is a bit of a snob lurking beneath the exterior charm of a Metal Goat, and it does not take much to get them giving all and sundry a swift kick with their powerful back legs. But no other Goat is more quick to capitalize on a good thing, even though those who work with a Metal Goat frequently wish that they were given more credit.

Metal Goats may make fortunes, but keeping them, and/or long term partners might prove a problem.

FAMOUS METAL GOATS

Mikhail Gorbachev, Terence Conran, Rupert Murdoch.

THE WATER GOAT
1943, 2003

Great socialites and hosts, Water Goats are often extremely popular, partly because they are not naturally combative, preferring the easy life and all that goes with it.

Water has a habit of finding unexpected ways out of a confined area and when asked to face up to harsh reality, the Water Goat may at times take what appears to be a devious route from often self created problems. Water Goats are quick to take on board stylistic changes.

Although not always prolific when inventing new ideas, they are wonderful interpreters. Even though interpretation is a strength, Water Goats are easily impressed by stronger characters and tend to copy them, however unwittingly.

Not over generous with money as a rule, Water Goats might easily collapse under extreme pressure.

FAMOUS WATER GOATS

Mick Jagger, John Major, Cilla Black.

THE WOOD GOAT
1955, 2015

The wood agent, like a tethering pole driven into the ground, has the useful effect of curtailing the Goat's more capricious tendencies. Once tethered, Wood Goats have the world at their feet and their destiny depends upon just how hard they are prepared to work to achieve their goal. Wood Goats have a high sense of morality, compassion and generosity. This advances them in society and opens doors otherwise closed.

The Chinese describe the Wood Goat as sentimental, clinging to those they love or need. And although they may dig their roots in deeply, Wood Goats are never keen to dig them up. If other Goats wander, Wood Goats are relatively happy to stay put.

Highly artistic and startlingly original, they tend to place themselves too readily into the care of others, and whereas their trust can be touching they might find it sadly misplaced.

No other Goat cares so much for the plight of others, or demands less limelight.

FAMOUS WOOD GOATS

King George VI, Steve Ovett, William Turner.

THE FIRE GOAT
1907, 1967

There is a pronounced side to the Fire Goat which demands luxury and refinement. The centre of a Goat's being, the home, if possible, would be a perfectly restored mansion or castle. But if home is no more than a rented bedsit, it will have as many fine trimmings as the overdraft will permit.

All Goats need to put on a performance and fire greatly enhances this ability. Fire Goats who become performers will recognize that they possess an almost unique gift.

They have tremendous energy and are more industrious than Goats of other agents. But they also have a tendency to fade more quickly. If pushed, no other Goat will have a quicker temper or less control over their tongue.

Poor with finances and capricious in love, Fire Goats do have immense charm, even if there is not much else beneath the brilliant surface.

It is common for the Goat to form strong partnerships in order to make the most of their talents. In the case of the Fire Goat, this need is less necessary. Fire gives Goats the opportunity to face life on their own terms. Whether they do so or not is up to them.

FAMOUS FIRE GOATS

Lord Olivier, Herbert Von Karajan, Paul Gascoigne.

THE EARTH GOAT
1919, 1979

Earth Goats could, in some senses, be likened to rich pastures. There is something honest and at times, not surprisingly, even earthy about Earth Goats. They often feel compelled to write things down, to put their thoughts on paper, as if by doing so they give themselves a fixed point to work from.

On the surface Earth Goats give the impression of being above worldly goods but their heart demands the good things in life.

Sure footed, Earth Goats may sometimes break out and act quite irresponsibly, especially if there is gold at the end of the rainbow. And some Earth Goats will do anything to get themselves in the picture. Good companions, Earth Goats will develop firm family connections which they might find difficult to break. Earth provides the Goat with balance, which means that whatever job they choose, the Earth Goats will be blessed with an even temper and great dedication.

When an Earth Goat goes off the rails, it will be a disaster.

FAMOUS EARTH GOATS

Sir Edmund Hillary, Billy the Kid, Iris Murdoch.

THE GOAT AND THEIR HOURS

The hour of the Rat
[11 pm to 1 am]

More inclined to grumble when things go wrong, there will be a greater sense of self awareness. A sharp wit and skill with words would be more useful with stronger self motivation. Sexually devious.

The hour of the Buffalo
[1 am to 3 am]

The need to dominate is unusually pronounced. A more solid and reliable personality could mean greater opportunities in business. But there might be insurmountable problems in romance.

The hour of the Tiger
[3 am to 5 am]

Reckless at times, the problem is matching the need to recover from a bad blow with the need to walk away from danger. Extremely dynamic in most areas and original. Love will never act as a threat.

The hour of the Cat
[5 am to 7 am]

Very well balanced with a great love of home life. The family will act as a bond, but never a bind. Smooth and uncomplicated in relationships, an enjoyment of beauty is paramount. Sex and wine are drunk deep.

The hour of the Dragon
[7 am to 9 am]

Too many influences pulling in opposite directions for the good of this Goat. But romance might benefit from a deeper passion and less fickle behaviour. Artists will really be helped.

The hour of the Snake
[9 am to 11 am]

Slow to decide and a touch too slow to act is the problem. But deeper wisdom is on offer and a great sense of beauty is there in abundance. Sexually very active, but very possessive.

The hour of the Horse
[11 am to 1 pm]

A happy combination with maximum possibilities in just

about every single department. More capable of self motivation with plenty of practical skills. But the heart might suffer, being a little too weak.

The hour of the Goat
[1 pm to 3 pm]

The double Goat provides an awkward division. Too many opportunities get squandered by a tendency to keep too many open. But performers get a great boost. Long term relationships might be rare.

The hour of the Monkey
[3 pm to 5 pm]

A highly skillful operator with the possibility to make more than usual headway in business. A better salesperson with a cooler than normal head in a crisis. A cooler lover, also.

The hour of the Rooster
[5 pm to 7 pm]

The need to act more openly will offer many great business advantages. Relationships, though, will be more difficult to maintain, with a constant conflict of candour against capriciousness.

The hour of the Dog
[7 pm to 9 pm]

A sense of idealism will prevail and the tendency in Goats to fight only for their own self interest be less so. A touch anxious, the stubborn streak will be unhappily over pronounced. A loyal lover.

The hour of the Pig
[9 pm to 11 pm]

Heavily social, robust in health and a good companion, if more so during the good times. A capricious lover, there is a tendency to leap before looking. Terrific performers and very hard working.

MONKEYS AND THEIR AGENTS

THE METAL MONKEY
1920, 1980

Most Monkeys have the ability to move quickly when trouble brews, but the Metal Monkey is one who will more than likely face the problem head on. And they shift ground only as a last resort.

The Metal Monkey is by far the most original. And no one is better than taking an old outworn idea and revitalizing it.

Not keen on sharing the limelight, Metal Monkeys can be extremely argumentative, but they have an overwhelming charm which quickly disarms any who try to take advantage. They are stimulating, both socially and in the work place.

Capable of earning large sums, they might well make fortunes and lose them. No matter what, money will always feature most prominently in their lives. The Chinese see the Metal Monkey as a trend setter, but one who may be blessed, or cursed with much arrogance and pride.

FAMOUS METAL MONKEYS

Dave Brubeck, Ronald Searle, Arthur Hailey.

THE WATER MONKEY
1932, 1992

Water moves at its own pace and finds its own level. It also overcomes resistance by patiently wearing it away. A student of human relationships, the Water Monkey's advice is often sought on how to repair those that are damaged.

Water Monkeys have a great skill in their ability to put across their ideas in a way that their audience wants to hear. No matter that their product is recycled from someone else's thoughts, or one they have devised themselves, Water Monkeys will sell it with just the right degree of insider chat and flattery.

Good with money, Water Monkeys nevertheless have a tendency to be secretive. This might lead to one or two not quite absolutely honest dealings. But they will be quick to cover any tracks.

There are times when Water Monkeys should be more positive in their approach, but it is not something that comes easily. When pressed, they rather tend to turn, like a tide, and gently disappear.

FAMOUS WATER MONKEYS

Nigel Lawson, Lady Antonia Fraser, Michael Aspel.

THE WOOD MONKEY
1944, 2004

The wood agent's influence on the Monkey leads to a less changeable personality. But in keeping with Monkeys everywhere, Wood Monkeys will always keep their options open. They tend to dig their roots in deeply, but if the roots have to be dug up, so be it. There'll be few tears.

Wood Monkeys quickly establish themselves in pretty well any situation. They have great powers of communication and will always look for a path which brings them into contact with others.

Highly credible in what they say, Wood Monkeys gravitate towards occupations that demands direct contact with others.

At the same time, Wood Monkeys suffer setbacks with less indifference than Monkeys with other agents. Although they often live in trees, Monkeys are not happy about their home being chopped down. This means a more thoughtful kind of Monkey, one who plans with greater care and attention to detail.

FAMOUS WOOD MONKEYS

Angela Rippon, Tim Rice, Diana Ross.

THE FIRE MONKEY
1956, 2016

The fire agent has a devastating effect on the Monkey personality. Although most Monkey types end up organizing life to suit themselves, they usually accommodate others in their plans. But the Fire Monkey is recognized at once for their relentless competitiveness. No other type possesses such a need to win, to come out on top, to push others down. There is always just a little spite under the surface of all Monkeys, but the fire agent has it in abundance. Confront a Fire Monkey openly and you will find the easy going charm replaced by a determined individual who has never heard the word defeat. But no one can win all the time, and when beaten, a Fire Monkey will not hang around for the wake. They'll be planning the next campaign, possibly in another field.

Fire Monkeys have it within their grasp to make fortunes, and keep what they earn.

FAMOUS FIRE MONKEYS

Bjorn Borg, Martina Navratilova, Koo Stark.

THE EARTH MONKEY
1908, 1968

Earth gives the Monkey the coolest and most calculating of all minds. No matter what the problem, an Earth Monkey will sit down and patiently work it out. They have open hearts and are more generous than Monkeys of other agents. But the Chinese point out that any charitable act will usually mean the Earth Monkey also stands to gain something. But they care a great deal for those who are deemed disadvantaged.

The Earth Monkey's public stance will invariably be even tempered. And it is the case that Earth Monkeys are capable of working under huge pressure without it putting them off their stroke.

Earth Monkeys are honest in their dealings. But they tend to sulk when things don't go their way, which, due to the growing influence of the earth agent, is not very often.

FAMOUS EARTH MONKEYS

Stephen Hendry, Kylie Minogue, Rex Harrison.

THE MONKEY AND THEIR HOURS

The hour of the Rat
[11 pm to 1 am]

No one has a greater gift for talking their way out of a tight spot. More materialistic, opportunist and the most quick witted. Passion runs deep but it comes in fits and starts.

The hour of the Buffalo
[1 am to 3 am]

Highly original with a stronger than average sense of leadership and self reliance. Difficult to push off course, a more stubborn nature might prove a problem. Romantically, too often a damp squib.

The hour of the Tiger
[3 am to 5 am]

Less staying power and lacking humour, there will be a greater need to rebel and make a personal point. Business is up and down, as is any romantic encounter. Tough to deal with when in a corner.

The hour of the Cat
[5 am to 7 am]

Very methodical and cautious, this offers all sorts of business advantages. Less adaptable, there is a greater sense of beauty and love of refinement. Fantastically good with money. Gentle lovers.

The hour of the Dragon
[7 am to 9 am]

An almost perfect combination, especially in business where the Dragon's luck is a blessing. But there might be problems distinguishing truth from fiction. Impulsive in love.

The hour of the Snake
[9 am to 11 am]

Never short of an idea, wisdom is added to the list of tools used to make the pitch. But there will be more mistakes and failures. Artistically, very original. Poor gamblers, but warm lovers.

The hour of the Horse
[11 am to 1 pm]

A sense of practicality and logic will inspire great things, especially in a business which requires manual skills as well as brains. An unsure heart will mean romance might prove a problem at times.

The hour of the Goat
[1 pm to 3 pm]

A help in the social world, where most of this Monkey's time is spent. Quick to spot new trends and adapt them is common. In love there will be promises and lies.

The hour of the Monkey
[3 pm to 5 pm]

A double Monkey provides the opportunity to steam ahead in almost any business venture. Terrific salespeople, human contact is essential to make the most of this combination. A very cool customer, romantically.

The hour of the Rooster
[5 pm to 7 pm]

Something of a divided self, with the natural ease of creating fantasy seriously curtailed by a need to be candid. Military life might be the answer. Love is a struggle.

The hour of the Dog
[7 pm to 9 pm]

Idealism is a quality which will be more readily to the fore, with a strong sense of loyalty. Not ideal for business, a combination which would suggest a job that sought reform. Open in love.

The hour of the Pig
[9 pm to 11 pm]

A big heart and open wallet. Happier to let the golden financial chance go by, especially if there's fun to be had. Less guarded and hard working when it is demanded. Rather simple in love.

ROOSTERS AND THEIR AGENTS

THE METAL ROOSTER
1921, 1981

The candour which marks all Roosters gets a huge boost under the influence of the metal agent. No other type of Rooster is as outspoken or headstrong.

Metal Roosters are never happy when forced into the shadows and fight ferociously to gain the centre of any stage. The Chinese say Metal Roosters find every opportunity to draw attention to themselves. And it must be said that on the whole, the Metal Rooster has something well worth boasting about. They have highly analytical minds and are often brilliant public speakers.

Keen on wealth, Metal Roosters are also extremely generous. They give their advice with a good heart and funds, should they be required. But it should be noted that they don't take advice easily themselves.

In spite of the bright and confident exterior, Metal Roosters are the most prudish of all.

FAMOUS METAL ROOSTERS

Prince Philip, Nancy Reagan, Peter Ustinov.

THE WATER ROOSTER
1933, 1993

Because water finds its own level, the Water Rooster is altogether a more calm type, one with less impatience. Typically, when others build castles in the air, the Water Rooster will create a castle surrounded by a moat. This will have the effect of making it accessible only by the Water Rooster's invitation.

Water Roosters have a sharp eye for detail, and no matter what their chosen field, they will check everything thoroughly before trusting it. This applies to human relationships, as well as job prospects and things in general.

Most Roosters resent the help of others, especially if they do not meet fully with their approval. The Water Rooster has less resistance to outside influences, and might easily find themselves swimming reluctantly with the tide.

FAMOUS WATER ROOSTERS

Michael Heseltine, Michael Caine, Mary Quant.

THE WOOD ROOSTER
1945, 2005

Wood, in the shape of trees, is capable of great expansion and it follows that a Wood Rooster will continually build. They often are driven to expand, but are constantly in danger.

All Roosters tend to daydream and unless the roots of a Rooster's growing concern are firm and secure, there is every chance they will come crashing down at the first real gale. But when committed to any kind of responsibility, Wood Roosters take their role very seriously. This is especially so if they are placed in a position of leadership.

No other Rooster is more generous but those who oppose them will meet with a formidable opponent. A Wood Rooster might harbour a grudge a lifetime. And wood tends to complicate a Rooster's thinking, creating indecision at vital moments. But few are more honest. The Wood Rooster is equally as happy in large groups as with their own company.

FAMOUS WOOD ROOSTERS

Mary Archer, Ken Livingstone, Eric Clapton.

THE FIRE ROOSTER
1957, 2017

The Rooster's fixed agent is metal and the combination of fire and metal means degree of conflict. The upright and moral lunar influence is constantly being melted by the fire agent, so that the Fire Rooster is usually to be found fighting a battle to overcome themselves. But any victor will prove to be exceptional.

Shining brightly one day, there is every chance that the next will find the Fire Rooster scratching around for some kind of consistency, either in their work or their relationships.

No other Rooster believes more solidly in their own ability to pick their way out of a scrape, and it is the case that few fade totally or let themselves go to pieces.

Fire Roosters do not suffer the lack of initiative of some other Rooster types, although it could be that they would achieve more by taking a little well intentioned advice from time to time. Fire also enhances a Rooster's organizing skills and routine is often a welcome friend.

FAMOUS FIRE ROOSTERS

Steve Davis, Nick Faldo, Jane Torvill.

THE EARTH ROOSTER
1909, 1969

The most dependable and self assured of all the Roosters, the Earth Rooster is a stickler for truth and honesty. Never short of a candid opinion when asked, the Earth Rooster is more reticent. They are deep thinkers who like to weigh up the facts before committing themselves.

Earth Roosters tend to be extremely secretive about what they really think, even though they might seem to express a candid opinion. And they are certainly more shy than Roosters of other agents. Yet they are never afraid to carry responsibility on their considerable shoulders, although because of their reticence, they are less likely to step forward.

Earth Roosters are the types most driven to putting ideas and thoughts on paper. No one has more files and books and systems to record events. Some plan for today. Earth Roosters plan for eternity.

FAMOUS EARTH ROOSTERS

Steffi Graf, Hardy Amies, Francis Bacon.

THE ROOSTER AND THEIR HOURS

The hour of the Rat
[11 pm to 1 am]

Less frank and more easy going, there is a tendency to use charm in larger doses. Not as well organized as some, but extremely tenacious. And there's a sharp temper on occasions. Sexually direct.

The hour of the Buffalo
[1 am to 3 am]

A perfect combination which offers success in any area where traditional values are paramount. Agriculture is ideal. Imperious and boastful, these Roosters are highly responsible. Doubly complex in love.

The hour of the Tiger
[3 am to 5 am]

Upfront and outspoken. A quick tongue and rebellious, there's a powerful need to be boss. Extremely generous in almost all things. Full of original ideas. A bit reckless in love.

The hour of the Cat
[5 am to 7 am]

An inclination to be more sensual and reserved. Brilliant at any kind of job involving routine. A greater sense of diplomacy is helped by a less imperious nature. Very private about romance.

The hour of the Dragon
[7 am to 9 am]

A combination which brings out a strong sense of justice and accelerates the need to put matters right. No nonsense and hot headed, there will be absolutely no beating about the bush. Romantically impulsive.

The hour of the Snake
[9 am to 11 am]

The normally candid and frank opinions are less in evidence. They are replaced with a quieter and wiser approach. Skillful in the world of art, especially painting and writing. A tendency to cling in romance.

The hour of the Horse
[11 am to 1 pm]

A combination which aids the Rooster, bringing a considerable level of practicality. The tendency to overspend is more in evidence, and there is less need to form partnerships.

The hour of the Goat
[1 pm to 3 pm]

A difficult and not altogether happy pairing of signs. Capricious moments will creep in and there will be less of the moral tone. But socially at ease and a much more carefree attitude to sex is likely.

The hour of the Monkey
[3 pm to 5 pm]

There is an element of the wheeler-dealer, plus less insistence on the truth. Very clever at any kind of deal, where there will be a subtle mix of originality and borrowed ideas. Cool sexually.

The hour of the Rooster
[5 pm to 7 pm]

The double Rooster brings out a strong mix of candour, bragging and brilliant organizational skills. Artists benefit, as do Roosters who wish only to build a wonderful home and garden. Very private emotionally.

The hour of the Dog
[7 pm to 9 pm]

Idealistic and very outspoken. Stubborn when put on the spot, and extremely tough when on the side of right. Not great diplomats, honesty works as a more effective alternative. Love might be functional.

The hour of the Pig
[9 pm to 11 pm]

Saving will not be easy, but making enough to live on, and more, should never pose a problem. Extremely hard working and social, there is a tendency to be taken for a ride. Open hearted in romance.

DOGS AND THEIR AGENTS

THE METAL DOG
1910, 1970

The Metal Dog is considered the most dedicated and determined, not only of the five Dog types, but of all the animal signs. Their fixed and moving agents are both metal, which produces a Dog of immense power. Tibetans call the Metal Dog the 'Iron Dog', and it is easy to see why. No matter what the task, a Metal Dog will achieve it. They are blessed above all with that precious gift of selflessness. Offer a Metal Dog a worthy cause and you may consider it done.

No one is more concerned with human rights or more committed to supporting the eternal underdog and less privileged.

But it is also true to say that a Metal Dog will show no mercy. Should you prove you are unworthy of their trust, or worse, betray it in some way, then they will never give up until they see justice has been done. And justice will always be the bench mark which the Metal Dog uses to assess his or her value.

FAMOUS METAL DOGS
Mother Teresa, David Niven, Douglas Bader.

THE WATER DOG
1922, 1982

Of all the Dog types, those born with a water agent have the least positive views and are less 'political' in their approach.

373

All Dogs are idealists at heart but the Water Dog has a more placid temperament and is less likely to be stubborn in the face of opposition. This might lead to an inconclusive nature, where the Water Dog is left acting just a little too early or too late to be truly effective. At times, Water Dogs might find themselves swimming alone.

The Chinese say that female Water Dogs are blessed with great beauty, suggesting that the water agent reflects their often surprisingly sensuous and seductively passive interior.

Water also helps those Dogs born with its agent to make a more analytical assessment of the world around them. It leads to greater diplomacy and balanced judgement. They frequently have a highly personal sense of humour and elegance.

FAMOUS WATER DOGS

Ava Gardner, Pierre Cardin, Tony Hancock.

THE WOOD DOG
1934, 1994

Wood Dogs are more inclined to enjoy the good things in life and tend to indulge themselves in comfortable surroundings and fine clothes. But Wood Dogs are not materialists. If money comes their way, all well and good. And if it goes, too bad.

There is also a point at which wood, in the shape of a tree might suddenly topple. But when faced with great adversity, a Wood Dog is likely to put up a tremendous fight and few who take on a Wood Dog in any form of combat will emerge an outright winner.

Generous and hard working, Wood Dogs may take on a number of causes to prove their worth. But they sometimes find it difficult to make important decisions without the co-operation of those they admire or love.

Wood Dogs, it is said, love to entertain large groups and in any gathering they will be quick to use their natural warmth and good humour to this end.

FAMOUS WOOD DOGS

Elvis Presley, Sir Winston Churchill, Brigitte Bardot.

THE FIRE DOG
1946, 2006

The fire agent offers Dogs great creative energy. Often quite spectacular in their achievements, fire sometimes has a negative side for Dogs. It may act like a hypnotic flame, beckoning the normally idealistic and selfless Dog towards a less constructive goal. When turned inwards, the fire agent can result in a self-destructive personality.

The fire agent may also compel a Dog to act against their better self. Although quite rare, if there is one Dog who is more likely to go off the rails, and in a sense, 'bite' without any thought of the harm they do, it is the Fire Dog.

But the fire agent, with its strong vitality, when combined with the Dog's powerful lunar influence of loyalty and idealism, will result in a Dog who may inspire everyone they meet to better things.

The Chinese say that Fire Dogs attract the opposite sex. They also are more ambitious than other Dogs, although success might be hard to handle.

FAMOUS FIRE DOGS

George Best, Peter Sutcliff, Jane Asher.

THE EARTH DOG
1958, 2018

The least anxious of all, Earth Dogs have a practical nature and take responsibility with a mixture of good humour and great dedication. They have a realistic approach to problems and when confronted with problems, tend to take a long look, rather than rush at them.

The Chinese point to the Earth Dog as being a touch secretive, but there is no doubting their generosity. As is the case of many Dogs, those with the earth agent care little or nothing about money and give freely to those in need.

Earth Dogs tend to move with caution and build their varying forms of success on a base of realism and far sightedness. But they have to be appreciated for their efforts. A pat on the head goes a long way. Although extremely confident in their own beliefs, Earth Dogs often find themselves at the mercy of the opinions of others. Here, they might well compromise. But no one will doubt the Earth Dog's dedication. They treat victory and defeat with equanimity.

FAMOUS EARTH DOGS

Madonna, Michael Jackson, Daley Thompson.

THE DOG AND THEIR HOURS

The hour of the Rat
[11 pm to 1 am]

More charming and with a greater degree of opportunism. Some of the anxiety will develop into a tendency to grumble endlessly. But there will be more charm. A lover who is passionate but not always faithful.

The hour of the Buffalo
[1 am to 3 am]

A greater need to stand centre stage and take control. A very hard worker and although they give loyalty, they will also want to see it returned. A complex love life and a bit heavy.

The hour of the Tiger
[3 am to 5 am]

A fine combination with much effort put into reshaping the lives of those less fortunate. A strong will and bustling energy provides many advantages. A well balanced sex life and strong on parenthood.

The hour of the Cat
[5 am to 7 am]

A touch more timid in the face of danger. Less able to stand up to a crisis, there is nevertheless, a greater ease when dealing with life in its more relaxed moments. More sensuous in romance.

The hour of the Dragon
[7 am to 9 am]

Something of a split personality in that the need to help others might fight with the need to put themselves first. Poor diplomat, a sharp temper is another problem. Volatile when in love.

The hour of the Snake
[9 am to 11 am]

Good intentions are helped by a stubborn refusal to let go. But decision making is a problem, especially when asked to do so in a hurry. Less anxious and often bewitching when in love.

The hour of the Horse
[11 am to 1 pm]

Both signs are compatible, most of all in the area of human

relationships. The need to support the underdog is aided by the ability to think logically. Practical in all things, a lover who falls easily.

The hour of the Goat
[1 pm to 3 pm]

More capricious and somewhat self obsessed. Much time is given to charity and any artistic performance will be wonderful. But loyalty in love is pulled by a hopelessly capricious heart.

The hour of the Monkey
[3 pm to 5 pm]

Loyalty takes a back seat, but bright ideas and the wheeler-dealer influence will help when assisting those less well off. Strong on sales but cooler in love.

The hour of the Rooster
[5 pm to 7 pm]

Candour and a sense of privacy lead to a less anxious outlook. All good intentions are given a boost, although there will be the odd occasion when what is promised fails to arrive. Frank about their feelings.

The hour of the Dog
[7 pm to 9 pm]

The double Dog means an extra dose of loyalty, idealism and stubbornness. More likely to talk out of turn, few will give more to those who are in need. Strong on the family and eager to please romantically.

The hour of the Pig
[9 pm to 11 pm]

A perfect combination with a large helping of robust energy to assist the need to support the many who cannot help themselves. Very much more relaxed socially. Romantically more of a pushover.

PIGS AND THEIR AGENTS

THE METAL PIG
1911, 1971

The Pig's fixed agent is Water. When combined with the stronger moving Metal agent, this creates a personality prone to uncertainty. Metal Pigs will woefully misread those with whom they are closely associated. They will underestimate those opposing them, and seriously overestimate their friends.

More sentimental than other Pigs, they do not hide their feelings and it is unlikely you'll find them hanging on to secrets. Metal Pigs are extremely ambitious, though, and are not known to give in without a fierce fight.

Over-fond of themselves at times, the Metal Pig may lack social graces. Metal Pigs may also put their own interests before those of others. Metal Pigs are open in their affection but when smitten by love, lack tact or self control. Metal Pigs, it is believed, work hard for a peaceful life.

FAMOUS METAL PIGS

Ronald Reagan, Ginger Rogers, Sir Michael Horden.

THE WATER PIG
1923, 1983

Water always finds its own level and when contained will leak from even the smallest gap. It is the same with Water Pigs. Usually self contained and hugely confident in their own abilities, if there is just the slightest chink in their protective shield, there is a great possibility that the worst will happen.

Once they let go of their self restraint, a Water Pig may easily become boastful and dishonest. Water Pig's have a tendency to trust too much in others and live by the idea that 'something will come along'.

But this great belief in other people is the Water Pig's redeeming feature. No other Pig strikes such a skilful bargain, even if the long term prospects tend to mean a little renegotiation. Too much self gratification, though, must be overcome if they are to succeed long term.

FAMOUS WATER PIGS

Robert Maxwell, Ernest Saunders, Maria Callas.

THE WOOD PIG
1935, 1995

Wood Pigs are great providers and no other Pig has so much ease when dealing with others. This means a Wood Pig is happiest when working in partnership, although the Chinese warn that some might well take advantage of their generosity. This is especially true when the Wood Pig makes money. And wealth may well come to a Wood Pig as they are capable of tireless effort.

The problem facing Wood Pigs is that too many others abuse their warm nature. Then a Wood Pig might easily become mean and grasping.

Wood Pigs adore entertaining and it could easily be that no other Pig is better suited to put on some kind of show; no matter whether it be on a public stage or holding the table's attention at a supper party.

A touch of a social snob, Wood Pigs love company, and do their best when finding a truly reliable and loving partner.

FAMOUS WOOD PIGS

Woody Allen, Lester Piggott, Dudley Moore.

THE FIRE PIG
1947, 2007

The expression 'pigheadedness' might easily apply to the Fire
Pig. They are the most vibrant and heroic of all Pigs and once
they set their mind on a goal, they put their head down and
charge.

The Fire Pig is optimistic, powerful and the Chinese say
they will trust their own judgement up to the hilt. No other Pig
works harder to prove their worth, but at the same time they
are well loved and give openly to all who come under their
protective wing.

Because they genuinely enjoy good company, Fire Pigs are
believed to gravitate towards jobs that give them a chance to
employ lots of people. They like to be looked up to and Fire
Pigs go out of their way to please. But it must be remembered
that the family will always come first and a Fire Pig will fight
to the bitter end to protect it.

On a downward path, Fire Pigs can sink into a state of
despair and it is then possible that they will lose all sense of
self respect.

FAMOUS FIRE PIGS

Salman Rushdie, Stephen Spielberg, Elton John.

THE EARTH PIG
1959, 2019

Of all the types, Earth Pigs are the most contented. They are
easily pleased and enjoy giving pleasure. The earth agent

provides an injection of positive thinking for the naturally robust and hard working Pig, which has many benefits. Happy to handle large sums of money, they are able to make plenty when the opportunity arises.

Earth also offers the Pig a tendency to over indulge and it takes plenty of will power to keep their voracious appetite in check.

When problems arise, the Earth Pig is apt to shrug them off, believing, often correctly, that by doing nothing even the biggest threat will eventually disappear. And certainly the Earth Pig's great fun loving optimism will go a long way to assist this process.

Over-keen on dressing up, Earth Pigs do not always know how to make the most of their passion and in trying to make an impact, and they will sometimes present themselves wearing an unhappy clash of styles. But again it won't bother them unduly. Little does!

Once they have set their heart on something, they will not give up in their effort to attain it. Sexually, they are thought to be a bit of a pushover.

FAMOUS EARTH PIGS

Duchess of York, Julian Clarey, Ben Elton.

THE EARTH PIG AND THEIR HOURS

The hour of the Rat
[11 pm to 1 am]

Highly compatible with the extra ingredient of sharpness clearly noticeable. Quick witted but dressing well will not be an important issue. Passionate in love and less easily duped.

The hour of the Buffalo
[1 am to 3 am]

Demanding and less likely to enjoy partnerships. A more solitary type who can quite easily make it without the help of others. Extremely hard working, romance will not be taken lightly.

The hour of the Tiger
[3 am to 5 am]

A tough temperament and one which cares less for authority. Not as vain as others, there is something of the rebel waiting to act. Hot headed, especially in love.

The hour of the Cat
[5 am to 7 am]

Highly dress conscious and quite brilliant at dealing with both people and finance. Diplomatic and cautious, routine will play an important part in daily life. A more sensuous attitude to romance.

The hour of the Dragon
[7 am to 9 am]

Quite irrational at times, there is a tendency to judge others too quickly. But there is no one more open and generous, even if the need to believe too much in others works against them. Loyal in love.

The hour of the Snake
[9 am to 11 am]

Normally at home with finance, a greater appreciation of the arts is more than likely. But there might be less of the big spender, although time will still be given freely. A secretive and subtle lover.

The hour of the Horse
[11 am to 1 pm]

Capable of a more practical approach to problems with the

emphasis on logic in most cases. Few can put more hours into a day, with elegance and enthusiasm much to the fore. A warm lover, if too easily smitten.

The hour of the Goat
[1 pm to 3 pm]

Social life is a major factor and there will be less certainty when handling really important issues. Not good with finances, but the greatest performer of all. Capricious in love.

The hour of the Monkey
[3 pm to 5 pm]

More tricks than normally found in the Pig sign leads to a formidable business person. Very intelligent and not one to be easily tricked. In love, a cool response. Splendid parent.

The hour of the Rooster
[5 pm to 7 pm]

A candid outlook which will not always serve the business-minded. But in areas where frankness is required there will be great opportunities. Fond of the country and a totally conventional lover.

The hour of the Dog
[7 pm to 9 pm]

An extremely auspicious combination which adds loyalty and idealism to the robust honesty. Great at lending a helping hand, there will be fewer moments of spite. Well meaning in love.

The hour of the Pig
[9 pm to 11 pm]

The double Pig offers a chance to take on the world and win. No one works with such honest endeavour or plays with more enthusiasm. Financially a wizard. In love, far too easily impressed, but big hearted.

☐	BARRY FANTONI'S CHINESE HOROSCOPES: RAT	£1.99
☐	BARRY FANTONI'S CHINESE HOROSCOPES: BUFFALO	£1.99
☐	BARRY FANTONI'S CHINESE HOROSCOPES: TIGER	£1.99
☐	BARRY FANTONI'S CHINESE HOROSCOPES: CAT	£1.99
☐	BARRY FANTONI'S CHINESE HOROSCOPES: DRAGON	£1.99
☐	BARRY FANTONI'S CHINESE HOROSCOPES: SNAKE	£1.99
☐	BARRY FANTONI'S CHINESE HOROSCOPES: HORSE	£1.99
☐	BARRY FANTONI'S CHINESE HOROSCOPES: GOAT	£1.99
☐	BARRY FANTONI'S CHINESE HOROSCOPES: MONKEY	£1.99
☐	BARRY FANTONI'S CHINESE HOROSCOPES: ROOSTER	£1.99
☐	BARRY FANTONI'S CHINESE HOROSCOPES: DOG	£1.99
☐	BARRY FANTONI'S CHINESE HOROSCOPES: PIG	£1.99
☐	BARRY FANTONI'S CHINESE HOROSCOPES: A GUIDE TO LOVE, MARRIAGE AND FRIENDSHIP	£4.99

Warner Books now offers an exciting range of quality titles by both established and new authors. All of the books in this series are available from:
Little, Brown and Company (UK) Limited,
P.O. Box 11,
Falmouth,
Cornwall TR10 9EN

Alternatively you may fax your order to the above address. Fax No. 0326 376423.

Payments can be made as follows: cheque, postal order (payable to Little, Brown and Company) or by credit cards, Visa/Access. Do not send cash or currency. UK customers and B.F.P.O. please allow £1.00 for postage and packing for the first book, plus 50p for the second book, plus 30p for each additional book up to a maximum charge of £3.00 (7 books plus).

Overseas customers including Ireland, please allow £2.00 for the first book plus £1.00 for the second book, plus 50p for each additional book.

NAME (Block Letters) ....

ADDRESS ....

....

☐ I enclose my remittance for _____

☐ I wish to pay by Access/Visa Card

Number ☐☐☐☐☐☐☐☐☐☐☐☐☐☐☐☐☐

Card Expiry Date ☐☐☐☐